SPORTING DOG and RETRIEVER TRAINING

THE WILDROSE WAY

RAISING A GENTLEMAN'S GUNDOG FOR HOME AND FIELD

Mike Stewart

with Paul Fersen

ORVIS
UNIVERSE

Published by Universe Publishing
A Division of Rizzoli International Publications, Inc.
300 Park Avenue South
New York, NY 10010
www.rizzoliusa.com

All photographs © Days Afield Photography, LLC, except for the following:
Courtesy of Blixt and Co.: 220, 222, 224T, 226L, 232, 235
Courtesy of Brett Henry: 9
Courtesy of Richard Adkerson: 215

Project Editor: Candice Fehrman
Book Design: Lori S. Malkin
Text: Mike Stewart and Paul Fersen
Photography: Chip Laughton / Days Afield Photography
Illustrations: James Daley

For more information about Mike Stewart and his methods,
or to order your own sporting companion or supporting DVDs, contact:
Wildrose Kennels
260 CR 425
Oxford, MS 38655
www.uklabs.com
info@uklabs.com
662-234-5788

2019 2020 2021 2022 / 10 9 8

Printed in China

ISBN-13: 978-0-7893-2446-7

Library of Congress Catalog Control Number: 2012932096

·✦ CO-AUTHOR'S NOTE ⊱·

I first heard of Wildrose Kennels through my work at The Orvis Company. I already had a Labrador I'd trained myself with what I perceived as some degree of success, but as I read more about Wildrose and Mike Stewart's methods, I determined that one day I would get a Wildrose dog. I finally met Mike at Sandanona, the Orvis hunting preserve in Millbrook, New York, a few months before I was to pick up my Wildrose puppy.

What I discovered was a remarkable approach to dog training based on thousands of years of evolutionary canine pack behavior. The best way to get a dog to do what you want it to do is to become the lead dog. Mike accomplishes with a look, simple hand gesture, or body position what many struggle to accomplish with electricity and force. He reads the dog and acts in such a way that the dog can read him and understand what is expected. He trains the dog so that natural instinct is the prime motivator.

What I also discovered was that Mike didn't have a book. He had everything else, but he didn't have a comprehensive book chronicling his more than 30 years of experience. This book is the result of that first meeting. What made this project even more fascinating was acquiring Murphy, my Wildrose puppy, and training him at the same time that we were working together on this manuscript. It was essentially a yearlong private lesson. The difference between my rudimentary success with Pickett, my older Lab, and the ongoing progress with Murphy is significant in ways that are far too numerous to mention here. Suffice it to say I learned a great deal about dog training, but perhaps the most important fact is that Mike trains people as well. A well-bred hunting dog is genetically programmed to do the right things. People are not genetically programmed to train dogs. Easily the most important part of the book is Chapter Two: Train Yourself to Train Your Dog.

The words in this book are Mike's; I simply helped to organize them. You will notice that when referring to dogs we used the masculine for the sake of expediency in the text, but this method obviously applies to the lovely female sporting companions as well. If you love hunting dogs, follow this book, dedicate yourself to its tenets, and it will add an entirely new dimension of understanding between you and your dog. Eventually, you will have the sporting companion you desire—one that not only hunts well, but is a well-mannered and full-time companion no matter where or what the circumstance. I can assure you it's a most rewarding journey.

— *PAUL FERSEN*

❖ THE ESSENTIALS ❖

❖ FIELD TRAINING ❖

TABLE OF CONTENTS

✄ FINISHING WORK ✄

Focus. Obedience. Loyalty. That's what came to mind while watching Angus, a black Lab, walk off lead at Mike Stewart's side. Angus was in lockstep with Mike, eager to catch a command. His ears were perked; his black eyes were intent on Mike's every move, just waiting for a glance or signal. Occasionally, Angus would divert his gaze to check the road ahead, but his eyes would quickly dart back to Mike. I was jealous. Who wouldn't be? Dogs like that are hard to come by—or so I thought.

That was years ago, and today I'm the proud owner of two Labrador retrievers from Wildrose Kennels—Dixie and Kate. Sometimes, I secretly enjoy seeing that same look of envy on my hunting buddies' faces when they see the focused, obedient, and loyal look in the eyes of Dixie and Kate, when their attention is all on me. More often, however, I wish that everyone who owns a retriever—whether it's a sporting dog, family companion, or both—could experience the satisfaction of having a retriever trained the Wildrose Way.

To fully understand why training the Wildrose Way works, some history is required. About 40 years ago, when most retriever training techniques revolved around electric collars and force-fetching, Mike Stewart entered the world of dog training and began laying the groundwork for a new, more positive training experience. Mike studied the science behind how dogs learn and communicate, and then applied that knowledge to his training methods. The result is a program based not on fear and force, but on communication and consistency. *Sporting Dog and Retriever Training the Wildrose Way: Raising a Gentleman's Gundog for Home and Field* teaches dog owners how to systematically build on a retriever's natural instincts through gentle, positive reinforcement, with no more fear for the dog or frustration for the owner. Training is fun and rewarding for both.

When Mike Stewart told me he was writing this book, my initial thought was, "Finally! After 40 years of training dogs, it's about time you shared your secrets with the rest of the world!" I was ruminating about how this book would revolutionize dog training as we know it when Mike asked me to write the foreword.

"Why me?" I thought.

While I am pleased and honored that he chose me, I have concluded that the answer to my question must be that I'm a great before-and-after example of how training the Wildrose Way can enrich and improve one's experience as a duck hunter, dog owner, and amateur trainer. I've known Mike Stewart for 10 years, as a customer and proud owner of two Wildrose Labs, and also through his affiliation with Ducks Unlimited (he's the owner and trainer of Drake and Deke, the official dogs of DU). As the president of Ducks Unlimited, I've had the unique opportunity to experience the Wildrose Way firsthand.

Until now, if you wanted to learn Mike Stewart's secrets to retriever training success, you had three choices: watch his instructional videos, attend his seminars, or buy a pup from Wildrose Kennels, in which case personal instruction is required before you are allowed to take the pup home. Mike calls it "training the trainer," which is often harder than training the dog. In my case,

FOREWORD

By John W. Newman, President, Ducks Unlimited, Inc.

after meeting Mike, hunting with his dogs, and seeing how effective his training program is, I did all three: bought the DVDs, attended the seminars, and eventually got Dixie and Kate.

In many respects, this book begins and progresses in much the same way as owning a dog from Wildrose. After months of eagerly awaiting your pup's homecoming, you arrive at Wildrose, take a tour of the facility, receive a briefing on the puppy's health and nutritional needs, and finally receive instruction on basic obedience training and the pack behavior of dogs. Before leaving with your bundle of joy, Mike and his wife, Cathy, reiterate (again and again) that they're always available to help. And as you leave the sprawling grounds, you—like every Wildrose customer—will put a pin on a huge map of North America to mark the pup's new home.

It was eight years ago that I brought Dixie home, and my life as a duck hunter, dog owner, and amateur trainer has been better ever since. Dixie and Kate are amazing dogs, but they're no exception among retrievers trained the Wildrose Way. I've seen, hunted, and traveled with many other dogs trained this way, and the result is always a calm, steady, obedient companion—whether hunting ducks in the marsh, pheasants in the field, or lounging with family in the living room.

My advice to anyone who owns a retriever is to read this book, follow this plan, and then enjoy the reward I know you'll receive. As a friend and customer, I know from experience that the Wildrose Way works, and I am confident that you will be an improved trainer and dog owner as a result of this book.

The Wildrose Way

▓ The Gentleman's Gundog

'Ve given hundreds of seminars across the country and my first question to a group is always: "What do you want most from your hunting dog?" Invariably, the answers relate to four basic behaviors: steadiness, control, quiet behavior and retrieving.

Rarely does a wingshooter desiring an exceptional hunting companion place his or her highest values on a game dog that can complete competition-standard multiple retrieves of birds at 200 yards with little direction or a pointer that ranges so far and fast that miles of terrain may be covered on a morning hunt. These are marvelous and achievable advanced qualities to be sure, but these skills are rarely used on the hunt and are essentially useless if the dog breaks on every shot and is uncontrollable in the blind or on a flush.

A Gentleman's Gundog is equally a calm companion and a natural game-finder. Hunters likely value the same traits in their gundogs that they value in their close friends and hunting companions. A great dog is a complement to a hunt, not a distraction. A Gentleman's Gundog behaves in the field, in the blind, in the vehicle, in the home, and in public with the same controlled and focused demeanor. The Wildrose Way is a training methodology designed to take you step-by-step from your first thoughts of acquiring a hunting dog to a dog you would be proud to take anywhere, anytime, on any hunt, and under any circumstances—a true gentleman in all circumstances.

▓ About Wildrose Kennels

Wildrose Kennels is the largest breeder, trainer, and importer of British and Irish Labradors in North and South America, specializing in its own signature brands of sporting dog—the Gentleman's Gundog and the Adventure Dog. The company has a simple mission statement:

⋅∞✦⧓⋅

Wildrose Kennels is dedicated to breeding and training the classic British and Irish Labrador retriever to become the perfect complement to a family's sporting lifestyle.

⋅∞✦⧓⋅

These are more than just hunting dogs in the traditional sense; Wildrose Labradors are game dogs of versatility and compatibility prepared for any wingshooting sport or adventure at any destination. To produce such a dog requires the proper genetics—a dog bred to have a biddable temperament, athletic ability, natural game-finding ability, and trainability. Taking these genetic traits and pairing them with a positive

By Mike Stewart

training methodology that naturally develops these inherent abilities is the Wildrose Way—field-tested and perfected for decades.

The Wildrose approach to training is applicable to most field gundogs—obviously retrievers, but also flushers, trackers, and pointers. So, what exactly is the Wildrose Way? Years ago, I was interviewed by Brian Lynn, then a writer for *Field and Stream*, as he prepared an online article featuring my training methods and was asked this very question. Initially, my simplistic answer—one I thought could be easily understood—was: "We specialize in developing hunting retriever companions, bringing out the natural ability of each dog, applying controls, and finally, training owners." Lynn was quick to point out that with the exception of the emphasis on training the owner, my description was similar to language used to describe other training methods, even those that are force-based. Right! So it is important to understand the difference as to how the Wildrose Way—versus other training programs—achieves its goal of developing a classic Gentleman's Gundog using positive methods.

■ The Wildrose Philosophy

Early on, it became apparent that there was a need for retrievers of impeccable genetics from proven hunting lineage, specifically trained as versatile hunting companions and game-finders for wingshooting enthusiasts. At the time, most training methods commonly published were force-based and more heavily weighted toward trial and competition dogs. There was a need for a comprehensive training methodology for the close-working, game-finding, companion style of hunting dog.

A new approach was needed to train this ultimate sporting companion, one that was behavior-based with easily applied methods, and one that would produce a calm, controllable gundog who would be as compatible in the home as he would be effective in the field or blind. We needed to develop this methodology, and then perfect it in fields and marshes in actual hunting situations. So began the journey at Wildrose to discover ways to apply the science of canine behavioral development to field training applications that worked the positive way: natural, progressive, low-force methods easily understood by both the dog and the handler, plus training that would be totally focused on the needs of the average wingshooter and his or her family. The outcome: a new way, a better way, the Wildrose Way.

The Wildrose Way is a hybrid training methodology. Many of its methods are proprietary, unique, and custom-designed to meet the needs of the outdoorsman. They are based in concept, if not practice, on both American and British retriever training methodologies, but the

Wildrose Way goes further to include training methods for spaniels, close-working pointers, and even hounds for tracking. In addition, Wildrose has evolved to include effective methods for scent-discriminating canines and service dogs, including shed hunters, diabetic alert dogs, search-and-rescue canines, and even accelerant detection dogs for arson.

The uniqueness of many of Wildrose's training methods and approaches to developing gundogs originated over the years in the field with our own dogs, finding ourselves in situations requiring special skill sets or discovering the shortcomings in our dogs' abilities. As we recognized these needs, we began to develop more practical training techniques.

To introduce one to the logic of the Wildrose training philosophy and to fully understand and appreciate its application, a few basic, fundamental concepts must be embraced:

POSITIVE TRAINING METHODS: Positive training methods, supported by consistent reinforcers, build stronger and more enduring behaviors than force- or avoidance-based training (which includes force-fetch, spike collars, electric collars, heeling sticks, and whips). The use of force to train a behavior in a dog, especially if misapplied, will likely have a negative effect in another area of the dog's behavior, progression, or development. Force often chases force—apply force in one area of training and you will likely find it necessary or at least tempting to do the same in another. Also, this approach only gets results when the threat of force is present. Wildrose methodology does use low-force corrections, selectively applied, to stop or eliminate undesirable behavior when other positive means prove ineffective. Force eliminates unwanted behaviors, while positive reinforcement captures and shapes desirable skills and behaviors and entrenches them for the long-term.

PACK BEHAVIOR: Wildrose subscribes to the concept of the Law of the Pack as it relates to canine behavior. Leadership and pack dynamics are an integral part of the Wildrose training philosophy.

Dogs desire to be part of a stable group with clearly established leaders, followers, and boundaries.

CONSISTENCY: The basis of the Wildrose training model is to set up the dog to be successful, capture and reward the best behaviors and performance, then repeat the action, response, or command over and over again. Nothing is learned or accomplished through failure. We want behaviors shaped through rewards to the point of an ingrained, predictable habit. These behaviors will endure throughout a lifetime. Dogs are really pleasure seekers and tend to repeat behaviors that bring them pleasure. The Wildrose Way simply capitalizes on this condition.

TRAIN THE TRAINER: The handler is a significant factor in the success or failure of a gundog's progress in training and field performance. The Wildrose system requires that an interdependent relationship exist between dog and handler. Productive communication depends on clarity, consistency, and stability. The relationship is a balance of trust and confidence first, then respect. The competency of the handler must complement the abilities of the dog.

PERSONALIZED TRAINING PROGRAM: At Wildrose, we believe in a client-based, bottom-up approach to developing gundogs, and our training methods have been developed based on this premise. We listen to the client's expectations and desires. Then, with flexibility, we tailor the training curriculum to fit the particular dog and the expectations of the client. Will the dog be used for upland, travel and adventure, waterfowl, or tracking large game? These are questions that direct the training curriculum. Our concern is driven by the individual client's expectations and not competition criteria. The entire training process, flexible as it may be, is designed to produce a compatible gundog to meet a variety of needs for each individual sporting client.

Our ultimate goal is to train a versatile gundog companion that complements the client's sporting lifestyle. Retrieving or locating game is only part of the equation. The training of such a canine requires a broad approach to include several disciplines and an animal with special characteristics:

- ✦ A calm temperament.
- ✦ Scenting ability to locate a variety of game.
- ✦ Comfortable with travel.
- ✦ Ability to handle varied terrains.
- ✦ Adaptability to work from various platforms, such as Jeeps, boats, ATVs, or horses.

In short, our training process is designed to produce dogs of intelligent thought; with flexibility and stability; having total trust and confidence in and respect for their handlers; and with a disciplined nature to handle any situation at any location.

◾ The Wildrose Result

A Gentleman's Gundog trained the Wildrose Way can adapt to any situation—duck hunting in the morning, quail hunting in the afternoon, and relaxing fireside with the family in the evening. The essential behaviors listed below are valued by sportsmen and are the objectives of the Wildrose Way. These essentials should become the guidelines for the development of a fine wing-shooter's sporting companion, the cornerstones of your training objectives.

COMPANIONSHIP: A go-anywhere destination retriever or gundog that is pleasing in nature, patient, calm, and focused. A dog that remains civil around other people and dogs. A dog that is confident despite his surroundings. A dog that is an intelligent thinker and problem solver and that is a pleasure to be around in the field or at home.

STEADINESS: A dog that honors other working dogs, does not make noise or move in the blind, and does not run in or switch to another bird while retrieving or on a flush. A dog that is steady to shot, flush, and fall. A dog that backs other dogs on point and never interferes with another dog's retrieve.

DELIVERY: A dog that delivers to hand a bird—wounded or dead—with a soft mouth. A dog that does not drop, pluck, or chew the bird.

CONTROL: A dog that is responsive to the whistle and recalls and casts easily with hand signals.

GAME-FINDER: A dog that is an enthusiastic hunter, lover of water and cover, and has great scenting abilities.

With these essential behaviors as goals, it's time to get started. This book will take you through the entire process. In these pages, we share decades of accumulated knowledge and proven methods that are the building blocks of the Wildrose Way. These selection, behavioral, and training approaches, consistently applied, will help you to develop not just a hunting dog, but a complement to a sporting lifestyle—your very own Gentleman's Gundog.

THE ESSENTIALS

THE WILDROSE WAY OF DEVELOPING a classic sporting dog companion is an organized approach to the ultimate goal. As with any long-term project of value, always begin the process with a clear vision of the end result. From selecting the prospect to your own leadership development, from fostering essential behaviors to basic training skills, the Wildrose Way is a universal method for those wanting to field a personal sporting dog—be it a retriever, flusher, or close-in working pointer. The Wildrose Way is a proven, positive approach to gundog development, but it is a method totally dependent on entrenched essential behaviors, which in the beginning are universal among the hunting breeds. With that in mind, let's begin your journey to developing a sporting companion of which you can be proud.

CHAPTER 1

Begin with the End in Mind

▩ Decision for a Decade:
Four Steps to Choosing Your Sporting Companion

Acquiring a new hunting companion is a remarkable and memorable moment in the life of a sportsman and his family, but many people make a mistake right at the start by not thinking of the event as a long-term process. Instead, they allow excitement and emotion to take over, make a snap decision to acquire a dog, find the nearest available dog of the breed they think they want, hop in their truck, and bring home a puppy. What they fail to think about is the fact that they are going to live with that dog for more than a decade, and it will become an integral part of their family life, for better or worse.

There are a number of things that can influence a person's decision to get a dog. Unfortunately, many of these things have no real bearing on what the actual expectations of the families or even the hunters will be. Advertising and television are huge influences. People see ads with yellow Labs or golden retrievers romping in the background and immediately gravitate toward those breeds or colors.

Certainly, there is nothing wrong with these dogs, but they may not be the proper fit for a sportsman's situation. The reason these particular dogs are in so many ads could be nothing more than that they photograph well.

A prime example of the media influencing decisions about dog purchases is the television show *Frasier*. The main character and his father lived with a wonderful little Jack Russell terrier in a high-rise apartment in Seattle, Washington. Viewers fell in love with the dog and the breed skyrocketed in popularity. People began buying these dogs as family pets, but they did not realize that Jack Russells are extremely energetic hunters, need space and freedom, and are not necessarily good with children. The dog on the show was professionally trained to be cute. The reality of owning one of these dogs in a city is much different than the show's portrayal, which resulted in disappointed owners who then abandoned their dogs, leading to the creation of Jack Russell rescue organizations across the country. For this reason, it is very important to do extensive research on various breeds before making a decision.

How many times have you seen people being dragged around by their dog, having no control other than the leash? They are often yelling at the dog and are unable to enjoy their outdoor experience and the company of their pet. These could be people who made a quick, emotional decision to get a dog without any thought to their ability to handle the dog, the specific breed characteristics, the dog's training, or the dog's ability to fit into their lifestyle.

At Wildrose, our specialty is producing the Gentleman's Gundog, but the process and principles of selecting the correct family dog are universal. While this book will focus on acquiring and training a sporting companion, the selection process and background training methods will work for anyone who wants to have a calm, controllable canine companion.

Once the decision has been made to bring a sporting dog into your life, undoubtedly everyone in your family will be excited. Thoughts of days in the field or a curled-up dog in front of the fire will be foremost in everyone's mind. It is important, however, to put your emotion aside for a moment. After you've gone through an organized process to determine the right dog to fit your desires and lifestyle, then you can let your excitement take over.

As with any process, there are steps to follow to make sure emotion doesn't interfere with a logical decision when acquiring a sporting dog. There needs to be a balance of research and thought relative to your expectations first, and then this information can be applied to the different breeds and categories within those breeds.

STEP ONE:
BEGIN WITH THE END IN MIND

Beginning by knowing what you want in a trained adult dog is the critical and most important first step. I can't emphasize this enough, for it will make all the difference in your relationship with this dog for the next 12 to 14 years. You must determine your expectations for the dog once it is mature. Is this dog going to hunt ducks 40 days a year in demanding conditions? Will it be a working dog for a hunting guide months on end? Or is the dog intended to be a family companion that resides in the home, but will hunt occasionally in a variety of situations? Perhaps your dog will spend more time on family adventures like canoeing or camping than hunting?

A classic Gentleman's Gundog sits fireside.

Your decision should begin with a shopping list of desired outcomes you will want to see two years from now. Sit down with your family and discuss all the things you will want to do with this dog. Once you've compiled this list, begin the second step, which is developing a plan for selection.

STEP TWO: THE PLAN

To make your vision a reality, you need a plan. The pre-selection plan should be carefully thought out before you make a decision on what breed (and what category within that breed) to bring home. The first part of the selection plan is determining who is going to train the dog—you or a professional. If you plan to use a professional, a consultation is advisable before choosing a pup. The pro's advice may play a significant role in helping you decide what type of dog to get and where to find the best prospects. If the training is going to be a personal project, there are many other considerations, including the prospect's trainability, the time you have to invest in training, and available training grounds.

Another thing to consider when planning your purchase is the pup's genetics. Genetics will be explored in greater detail later in this chapter, but the main thing to know is if you select the wrong type of genetic material to match your plan or desirable outcomes, problems may occur. By genetic material, I mean the pup's bloodline—the strengths and weaknesses of its parents and grandparents that will be passed down to the pup. Think of this selection process as art, like a beautiful painting. An artist doesn't just go out and buy paints and canvas on a whim. First, he has a vision of the outcome; then, he selects the best available materials to complement his efforts before work actually begins. The background of the dog, its lineage, and its intended use are all things you should carefully consider to better ensure that you are choosing the right dog.

The second part of the plan is to outline a day in the life of your dog (see pages 20–21 for

Early puppy socialization involves exploring new things.

more information). How will the dog be managed daily? You need to build some training time into each day. A dog left to its own devices and alone for long durations of time is rarely if ever going to become a dog of distinction. It likely won't train itself in a way you would prefer; the relationship between the two of you won't solidify; and, furthermore, it's a disservice to the dog. Bob Murphy, a very devoted hunter and lover of hunting Labs, once said, "Training a dog to its full potential is what is owed the dog, not the owner." The more daily interactions between you and the pup, the better the development of the dog will be.

The third part of the plan is determining the method you are going to use to train the dog, be it the Wildrose Way or any other. Regardless of what system you use, please recognize that consistency and progressive training are vital to the dog's development. Owners can train a good gundog in their spare time if they do three things: select a pup with the highest quality

A Day in the Life of Your Dog Journal

There are three parts to the Day in the Life of Your Dog journal. This exercise becomes an excellent daily planner for the pup's appropriate development. In column one, list at least five desirable outcomes you have for your dog at two years of age. In the second column, consider how the pup's daily routine will be managed. Think about the following: Where do you live? Are you alone or are there kids involved? Where will the dog live? Is the family onboard with the training and do they understand how to avoid the dysfunctional activities that can affect a dog? List in detail each activity the dog will encounter for the entire day, from the time he wakes up until the time he goes to sleep. In the third column, list the methods by which the pup will be taught essential behaviors and skills. Items in columns two and three should be in balance and complement each other. For example, during the exercise portion of the pup's day, you should work on leading and obedience skills rather than free running with other dogs. Ultimately, the routine and methods you use in training your pup should result in the desirable outcomes you listed in the first column.

The dog is always learning. Be careful of what is being taught.

This journal should be a living, ever-changing document that keeps track of your overall expectations and creates a stable, predictable routine for the animal, plus training exercises and lessons that directly produce the desired results.

For a counterexample, an unbalanced routine could look like this: You desire a steady dog to flush and shot. The actual daily activities while you are away at work include the kids playing chase in the backyard with the dog, repeatedly throwing a tennis ball for mindless, meaningless retrieves. The dog enthusiastically participates to the point of exhaustion without regard to patient, calm behavior. Chew toys are scattered about for the dog's enjoyment and the dog has free run of the house without limitations. By allowing this imbalance, you are setting the dog up for failure when it comes time to actually train. You and your family's consistent behavior will help to ensure the dog's consistent behavior. Train yourself and your family to train the dog. Chapter Two will explain this concept in significant detail; it is the most important aspect of the Wildrose Way.

While doing this exercise, you may discover that an older dog, rather than a puppy, may better fit your lifestyle. This planner will assist in determining whether a puppy, started, or finished dog would be the best fit. Overall, what you desire and can manage must be in alignment with the raw material you select. Remain realistic about your ability to form the prospect into your desired work of art.

A well-socialized pup is a bold, inquisitive, eager learner.

The flat-coated retriever is best trained through repetition and consistency.

genetics for the type of hunting it will eventually do, properly socialize the pup in preparation for training, and, finally, train the pup with patience and repetition to the point of habit formation. All three steps are equally important, but many people focus on the training aspect too much at the expense of the other two.

It is fairly easy to develop an excellent dog with a structured training plan and an understanding of how dogs learn. You can also accomplish this goal with little force. A properly trained gundog is an obedient companion, eager to please, and accepting of its place in the pack. Retrieving or pointing characteristics should be innate in a well-bred hunting dog, only requiring an awakening by your efforts. With the application of controls and behavioral modification, chances are you will develop a fine hunting dog.

STEP THREE: CHOOSING A BREED

A discussion of breeds could be a separate book in itself. This is a training book based on the Wildrose method, which can work with a variety of sporting breeds, including pointers, flushers, and retrievers. Regardless, the careful research of breeds remains critical to the success of the entire process. Between the Internet and a wide variety of books, more information exists on the subject of canine breeds than one will ever use, so take advantage of it. By beginning your plan with a clear understanding of the outcome you desire, selecting a breed becomes much easier as you consider lifestyle, ease of training, size of the dog, temperament, natural ability, living space, and available training grounds. When selecting a breed, consider function (the breed's inherent performance characteristics), then fashion (color, appearance, and length of coat).

First, decide what type of dog you want: a pointing dog, a flusher of game, or a retriever? As stated previously, you're going to be living with this dog for 12 to 14 years. If you make the wrong decision concerning the genetic material initially, then the likelihood of you really enjoying this dog long-term—in training, hunting, and family activities—could be compromised, perhaps severely. There is really nothing more unsatisfying than living with and trying to train a dog you don't like. As much as we all love dogs, there are some dogs that are just more challenging than others. Working with a canine you truly like is much easier and more enjoyable.

If you read the introduction to this book closely and understand the thought process behind the Wildrose Way, you will understand that there are certain breeds that are independent in nature and others that are more interdependent. For example, a big English pointer is an independent hunting dog bred specifically to work long distances, whereas a Labrador is more suited to working closely with its handler. These considerations should become the criteria driving your research of the different breeds, and help you pick the one that will best fit your lifestyle and the way you hunt. The Wildrose Way is effective with both types, but especially with dogs that are more interdependent and desire a close relationship with their owner. There are many breeds from which to choose and certainly one will best fit your needs.

Once you narrow the search based on the dog's potential ability and your desires, you can streamline even further by considering size, color,

A young pointer demonstrates instinctive ability at quite a young age.

and coat, or what we refer to as "fashion." Perhaps you live in a downtown high-rise, but love to go to Vermont to hunt grouse and woodcock. This should definitely factor into the type of breed you choose. A spaniel's size and temperament may be better suited to an urban apartment than a big rangy pointer. A springer may fit a dense urban setting better than an English setter. Both hunt grouse well, but the flusher is more handler-oriented and smaller in size. In this case, size matters. The setter has a more independent nature and would need space to exercise. If pointing is important, you might consider a Brittany spaniel in this setting. Hunting is only part of the equation. The other half is compatibility with your lifestyle.

The next consideration is matching the preferred training method to the specific breed. Ease of training is an important consideration when selecting a dog. The Wildrose training methodology is designed for the sportsman looking for the ultimate shooting dog. While we specialize in British Labradors, most breeds respond quite well to our gentle, logical approach to training. We define the Wildrose Way as bringing out the natural ability of a dog, whatever the breed, instilled from generations of selective breeding; applying controls; and training the handler. This limited discussion of breeds is to help ensure that you begin with the best prospect possible.

The adventure companion complements the family's sporting lifestyle.

The final step is selecting a category within the breed that you have chosen. Each breed may have a range of characteristics within it that vary widely, including size, color, performance, and temperament. In the selection of a sporting companion, the category within the chosen breed places emphasis on temperament, trainability, intelligence, and natural hunting instincts. Since Wildrose is most familiar with Labradors, I will use that breed as an illustration of the range of categories available within a specific breed of dogs. There are pointing Labs, show-bred Labs, trackers, flushers, and field trial competitors—all are of the Labrador breed, but each category possesses its own defining characteristics and attributes.

Let's say you want a non-hunting companion to be a family-friendly dog, accompany you wherever you go, and be exposed to a number of different situations ranging from kid's soccer games to family camping trips. A show-bred bloodline may be a good fit—the kind we all know—with square heads, thick coats, a calm temperament, and thick otter tails. These dogs are bred specifically for conformation and for quiet, calm, gentle dispositions. If your desired outcome is more competition-oriented, you'll be looking for something very different. The dog selected would need to be a wide-ranging, high-drive dog that works at amazing distances with a high threshold for endurance. Such an animal, although splendid at what it is bred to do, would not be a wise choice

The ability to respond to hand signals is a quality of any well-trained retriever.

for an urban family dog. If your goal is to own a Labrador hunting companion, you should search for a smaller Lab ideally suited for the hunting gentleman and adventure traveler, a dog of calm temperament that possesses exceptional scent discrimination abilities. You'll want a companion game-finder that is adaptable to many different hunting situations, ranging from duck hunting in Louisiana to flushing pheasant in the Dakotas. All of the aforementioned dogs are Labs, but they are different in so many ways.

These are several categories within the Labrador breed and each one is well suited to a particular goal. It's easy to see that acquiring a Lab without careful consideration of categories within the breed could be a mistake, and this will hold true for most of the breeds. Show springers and field springers differ in size, look, and function. The cocker spaniel in America is generally a show or family pet, while the English field-bred cocker is a dynamic bird-finding animal with incredible energy. There are big powerful setters that will cover ground with speed, and there are close-working setters that are perfect for the foot hunter in thick cover. You will need to narrow your search by looking within the desired breed for the specific type of dog that will fit your criteria, and that is where a knowledgeable breeder becomes invaluable.

The Breeder

The breeder is your best resource for finding the correct category or type of dog within a breed. By carefully reviewing breeders and the kinds of dogs they produce, you can work through your checklist of desirable traits to fine-tune your selection.

When someone calls Wildrose, we ask the following questions: What are you going to do with the dog? What are your expectations? Many times these questions actually stun the caller:

"Well, I want to hunt."

"Hunt what?"

"Ducks."

"What kind of ducks? Where will you be hunting? In what conditions? Will you be doing any other types of wingshooting or outdoor sports? What are you going to do with your dog when you're not hunting?"

We challenge the potential client to think about their true desires and then we help determine whether or not a Wildrose dog is a good match for their intentions. If so, we then work to select a dog that will come closest to filling the client's needs. We, as do most competent breeders, actually interview the potential buyers to help them create a checklist of desirable traits. Only then can we make a potentially correct match between a family and a dog.

When selecting a trained or started dog you have some idea of the size, temperament, nature, and ability of the dog in the field, but with a pup you're really buying genetic predictability. In other words, you're making a decision based on the probability that a pup from a proven bloodline will inherit the desirable traits from its parents and grandparents. In doing so, you have to be reasonable about expected outcomes. Variables do exist between pups and even between littermates. Think of a family with four children. All four children are not going to be the same; they will differ in size, temperament, personality, learning ability, development, and even likes and dislikes. The same variables will exist between pups within a litter. A good breeder can give you genetic predictability, but it can't give you absolutes.

There is no perfect dog—at least I have not met one—so it is reasonable to assume that there is no perfect pup. Perfection is a lofty goal, and it's highly unlikely to be accomplished with any animal. Even so, relying on chance is not always a good approach. The selection process should be viewed as a means of acquiring the correct dog right from the start, and a professional breeder can be an invaluable resource.

STEP FOUR: SELECTING THE PUPPY

By the time you arrive to visit the puppies in a selected litter, most of the work has been done. You've looked at sires, dams, and pedigrees, and you've told the breeder what you want. You've agonized over picking the correct litter, but now that you have, it's time to enjoy picking the puppy. What is most important is the picking of the litter itself, not so much the picking of a pup within the litter.

Once on-site, there are important considerations that will help your selection process. First, meet the sire and dam if you have not seen them yet. The sire may not be on the premises, which is not a problem if you have previously checked on his capabilities and health, but at the very least you should have a copy of a three-generation pedigree, a copy of the sire's registration papers, a picture, and any relevant health certifications.

Second, look at the dam. As previously stated, she is as important if not more so than the sire. The mother's body changes significantly during the gestation period, so don't expect her to be worked in any type of demonstration, but do expect to meet her. Check out her personality. Is she what you expected? Don't be concerned if she is losing hair. It's called "casting," a normal event toward the end of the weaning process. She may be quite thin, too, as she has thrown a lot of her body weight and fat into the nurturing of her pups.

Third, view the facilities where the dogs and puppies are kept, including the kennels, the water buckets, and the condition of the entire grounds. Is the facility impeccably clean? Is it indicative of a caring breeder? Look at the kennels, where the dogs are kept, the water buckets. Are the kennels clean and bright? Is the area climate-controlled? Make sure you are satisfied that the animal care is up to high standards. Consider how the pups were socialized, by what methods, and the results of the efforts.

Some breeders won't allow you to tour the puppy area due to contaminants that could be tracked in, but they will have viewing areas. See the pups in action as a group if you can, even if you have already been assigned a pup.

Last, review puppy health and registration paperwork for accuracy.

Now the fun begins. What you should look for in your pup is the following:

+ Good tail action—This indicates boldness.
+ Clear eyes—This is an indicator of good health.
+ Teeth placement—Check for overbites or underbites.
+ Expressions—Is the pup alert and active?

This is the Wildrose Super Learner Center, which conditions young pups well before their family's arrival.

Common Desirables for a Sporting Companion

Consider the following categories when talking to a breeder about a potential game dog:

SIZE: How big a dog do you need or want? Will you be doing boat work that may call for a smaller dog? Or will you be doing field work in heavy brush, where longer legs and greater lung capacity are important? Do you drive a big truck or a small Honda Civic? Size matters in these regards, so be careful to choose the correct pup.

TEMPERAMENT: Does athletic ability or a calm temperament matter most to you? Does the dog have patience in the home as well as the blind? Does it have a pleasing, people-friendly disposition? The preferred dog for a sporting gentleman has the ability to be patient and calm, but retains the drive and stamina to perform afield in tough conditions.

ATHLETIC ABILITY: How is the dog's stamina, endurance, and heart capacity? How long are its legs? Longer legs would be beneficial in a marsh, while dogs with shorter legs may be more suited to working closely with hunters and in heavy cover. High-energy dogs perform well on all-day hunts in tough terrain, but their energy level may prove difficult in the home.

COMPATIBILITY: How well do these particular dogs get along with people? Is there any aggression in the bloodline? Will the dog get along with children and other dogs? Does this line of dogs have the potential to travel well? Have previous offspring proven to be good in the home as well as in the field? Consider the dog's lineage, specifically its record of compatibility as well as performance in the field, when making your decision.

BIDDABILITY: Will the dog potentially seek the approval of the handler or is it more likely to become an independent hunter? A biddable dog is one that is willing to please, and the biddable dog responds best to positive training approaches.

EASE OF TRAINING: How much force is needed in the training of dogs from this bloodline? What natural abilities are likely to be evident? Did the pup's predecessors require the use of force techniques to achieve results? Or did they respond to a soft touch in training and display natural ability? Some bloodlines are noted for an independent, tough nature with a high pain threshold and may prove to be more difficult to manage, while other breeds develop slowly and require patience.

SCENTING ABILITY: Is the dog able to locate game in varied conditions? Some facilities breed for the use of eyes or marking ability rather than scenting ability, so be aware of this when choosing a sporting dog. Game-finders need great noses!

HEALTH AND SOUNDNESS: Have you reviewed the bloodline's hip, elbow, and eye certifications? Consider other hereditary problems relevant to the specific breed, such as ear infections or knee, skin, and coat problems. Make sure to check grandsires and granddams, too, as quality problems can skip generations.

BLOODLINES: Do the parents of the pup hunt? Do not pick litters solely based upon fancy pedigrees, as they are not always indicative of natural abilities such as game finding, temperament, or trainability. Nor will they indicate whether traits may be passed successfully to offspring. Select parents of litters based upon gundog standards and their demonstrated ability to pass along desirable traits, such as calm temperament; retrieving or pointing instinct; soft mouth; intelligence; and love of water, birds, and gunfire.

◆ **WILDROSE TIP** ◆

Select litters with strong maternal lines as well as excellent sires. Dams should be good hunting dogs demonstrating the qualities you desire in your dog, not just in the sire. The mother has the pups with her for five weeks and her influence is paramount. Good bitches are seldom mated to poor dogs, yet the opposite frequently occurs. A poor bitch is unlikely to produce good pups despite the virtues of the sire. Look closely for desirable traits and strength in the trailing bottom line of the pedigree—that is the mother, grandmother, and great-grandmother. Excellent mothers are as important as excellent sires.

✦ Feet and legs—Does the pup have good foot pads? Are its legs straight?

✦ Condition of coat and body fat—A good pup should have a healthy-looking coat that is shiny and smooth and a slight layer of fat over the ribs. (Please note a small umbilical hernia is not a long-term problem and will most likely rectify itself.)

✦ Chasing moving objects—This indicates a good prey drive.

✦ Socialization—Does the pup like people? Is it active with its mates or is it reclusive?

To get a preliminary idea of temperament, reach completely around the ribcage with both hands and pick the pup up slightly off the ground. If it squirms and wiggles and snaps, this is a bolder pup. If it's passive, remaining still, this is a mellower pup.

Cradle the pup upside down between your chest and arms; apply a slight amount of pressure with its head resting against your arm. Again, if it struggles and tries to get away, this is a bolder pup. If the pup relaxes, does it look at you? If so, this is probably a more biddable pup.

Retrieval of a thrown object is not necessarily a valid test, as the pup's eyes can't focus well at distances at seven weeks. Instead, roll something in front of the pup and see if it engages in a chase.

If the pup likes to chase objects, chase other pups, or carry something around, those are good signs. A carrier is a good indication, and if you clap your hands and the pup comes to you with the object, that's even better. Dogs develop their scenting ability first. If the pup is using its nose actively, that's a good sign. Blow a soft whistle and see if the puppy moves toward the sound or away. These are good indications of interest in you and inquisitiveness. These tests are not absolute, but they give you a general idea.

A bold versus passive personality is something to think about when choosing a pup. If

Lift the pup to determine its reaction. A calm, stable response to the intrusion indicates the acceptance of control and a passive nature. A tussle or resistance is an indication of a bolder, more assertive pup.

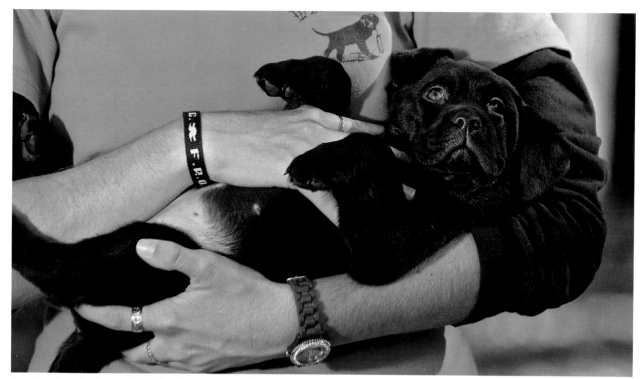

Invert and cradle the pup for a simple assessment of passive or bold tendencies.

you're a hard-core hunter that needs loads of drive, speed, and stamina in your gundog, the bold pup may be just fine. The passive pup may be more suitable as a companion or adventure

A pup experiences its first retrieve.

dog. Otherwise, the middle of the pack is always a good choice.

Exposing a pup at this age to water, gunfire, or birds is not a good idea; actually, it is a waste of time and can possibly be detrimental. These types of exposure come much, much later. A wing or a whistle is great to use, but no startling shots or noises. Common sense always prevails in the picking of a pup.

Started and Finished Dogs

What about selecting a started or finished trained dog? If you've decided a pup may not be the way to go, then you need to understand the selection process for a started or finished dog. There is quite a spectrum in what may be called a started dog. A starter could be a prospect seven to eight months old that has just begun training, or it could be a dog that is ready to hunt. Wildrose defines a started dog as proficient in all seven basic gundog skills (see Chapters Five and Six for more details about these skills). All that is needed is game exposure and hunting. Others

A finished retriever picks a green-winged teal.

may define a starter by completely different criteria. When talking to a trainer or owner about buying a started dog, make sure you understand the level of training being offered.

A finished dog needs to be defined as well. How complete is the training and how extensively has the dog been hunted? Is the dog finished in the disciplines you want and will your expectations be met? Has it been exposed to and trained in all the skills you require? If the dog is only finished in one discipline and your first hunt is different than its training, you may be disappointed. Also, remember to consider the elements of actual hunting experience, temperament, ease of handling, acclimation to people, socialization, and exposure to home and travel. Expectations should all be strictly defined when you initially talk to the trainer or owner.

Don't make the mistake of buying a started or finished dog over the phone and having it shipped to you. At Wildrose, we refuse to do this.

We will not send a started or finished dog out until the potential owner meets and experiences the dog, and learns proper handling techniques. Only when satisfied with the new owner's confidence as a handler will we turn over the dog.

When you're picking up a started or finished dog, there are some very important things to do. Not unlike picking a puppy, you want to evaluate the dog and understand its temperament. Do you see a happy expression and alert, active behavior? Is the dog good around people, carrying its tail high, or is it afraid? Does a quick move send the dog to the ground with its tail between its legs? Examine the dog's conformation—the legs, feet, nails, dental condition, coat, and weight—does it match what you're looking for? Check out the kennel grounds, just as you would if choosing a puppy. The breeder or owner should furnish everything from health records to registrations and pedigrees.

A field-bred English cocker makes an excellent quail flusher and retriever.

Observe the dog in the field. Are bumpers or birds delivered to hand without dropping or chewing? How does the dog respond to the whistle and hand signals? The dog should be steady and quiet despite distractions, even when you throw bumpers around it or when another dog runs past. Does it take force to maintain steadiness? Is the dog accustomed to gunfire, water, and birds? Test scenting ability with a feather-laced bumper. Take the dog out with other dogs and see how they interact. For pointers and flushers, check out the dog's game-finding ability.

Once the decision is made, it's up to you to learn to properly handle your new companion and know the procedures and methods relevant to the dog's level of training. The dog learns through consistency. Inconsistency will confuse even the best of dogs and will never result in the establishment of a productive relationship of trust and teamwork. Adequate handler training is imperative. Your new hunting companion needs to fit your lifestyle and expectations right from the beginning, plus a well-trained dog deserves a knowledgeable handler.

CHAPTER 2

Train Yourself to Train Your Dog

This chapter is extensive for a very good reason: your dog's success depends as much on you as it does on him or her. A good hunting dog is bred to do many things naturally. You, on the other hand, are not genetically predisposed to train a dog. You need to spend as much time learning how to be a great canine leader and communicator as you do learning to apply the principles of effective dog training. An understanding of why dogs act the way they do, how canines learn, and how they communicate is imperative if you are to train hunting dogs in a positive, natural manner. This chapter takes you through that process. Making sure you understand these concepts now will pay huge dividends throughout the relationship between you and your sporting companion. Establish trust first, then respect.

■ The Four Levels of Wildrose Training

There are four levels of training that should be followed throughout a dog's life. The levels provide the framework for a dog's continuous development despite age or level of proficiency. These levels are not to be regarded simply as steps to be completed in order; they are guidelines for a long-term approach to development and the basis of your training plan. Your dog will continue to participate in and revisit each of these categories throughout his life. For

A trainer can shape instinct at a very young age with yard work.

example, a finished gundog like Deke, one of the Ducks Unlimited mascots, still does yard work at the start of every training session to maintain obedience skills.

LEVEL ONE: YARD WORK

This is where you start training a young puppy, establishing new skills and commands, and it is also the level at which you begin each day's training session, despite the dog's age, to reinforce the basic patterns of obedience and to burn energy. Yard work includes: denials (throwing the bumper without allowing retrieves) to build steadiness, reinforcing obedience commands, heel work, remote sit, sit to the whistle while recalling, steadiness at heel as you walk among distractions, and, with the upland gundog, sitting to the flush.

LEVEL TWO: FIELD WORK

Field work is where most of the heavy lifting in training occurs. Here, the core fundamental skills are combined with structured lessons designed to teach a dog the behaviors and principles needed in the field. These include the concepts of diversions, lining, and marking—and skill sets such as hand signals, crossing water, handling on the water, and working through decoys—which pre-

A young retriever is being lined for a memory.

During transitional work, always practice as you will play.

pare a dog for all the field experiences you may encounter on the hunt. In the case of upland hunters, this is when you would concentrate on quartering, pointing, backing, and steadiness to the flush of live birds, and introduce pre-planted birds to develop pointing instinct.

LEVEL THREE: TRANSITION WORK

This is the most underused and often overlooked area of training and yet it just might be the most critical. Consider this level comparable to a scrimmage in football or war games in a military unit, a "practice as you will play" concept. You should dress and gear up to simulate as nearly as possible the conditions of a real hunt, then train while assessing your dog's abilities under these realistic conditions. In England, some of the more experienced trainers will actually purchase a

day's shooting to work their dogs in realistic situations. At Wildrose, we do the same, picking up for a tower shoot with a retriever or planted birds for a pointer. Use all the equipment that may be used on a hunt. A simulated duck hunt would have duck calls, spinners, decoys, layout blinds, hides, or anything else the dog may encounter. This exercise should be completed before the dog ever goes to the field and should precede each type of hunting situation unfamiliar to the dog. The first time your dog experiences something new on the hunt shouldn't be opening day at sunrise. Dogs don't work well in generalities; that is, transferring a skill from one area to another. A duck hunt and a dove hunt may both involve retrieving birds the dog sees fall in the cover, but the conditions are very different. You should train for each distinct experience that could be encountered in the field.

On the first hunt, ensure steadiness by securing the dog to the blind.

LEVEL FOUR: THE HUNT

Yes, the hunt itself is a training experience, particularly the first few outings. *A dog is always in training.* On the first couple of hunts, you will be there to train your dog. To work on denials, pick up some birds yourself. Focus on developing a few essential skills like handling, honoring, and retrieving to hand. The biggest mistake you can make is ignoring the dog on the hunt to concentrate on shooting while the dog begins to break or learns other dysfunctional behaviors. What's worse, the dog is often rewarded for misbehavior by getting a bird. Train the dog first and shoot second, or let others shoot. As your dog progresses, the hunt is where you will refine his skills and provide new experiences. This sacrifice is a commitment on your part to produce a hunting dog of which you can be proud.

▉ The Fundamentals of the Pack

In the wilderness, wild dogs, wolves, and coyotes learn important lessons very early from their mothers and other pack members that will endure throughout a lifetime. Wild pups learn about pack order, boundaries, essential behaviors of survival, and how to hunt beginning as early as five weeks after they emerge from the den. The mother applies the proper disciplines and encouragement, as well as rewards of affection, attention, and spoils of the hunt, all shaping the pups' behaviors that will enable them to survive. These are ingrained behaviors that become automatic reactions to a given stimulus. The canine brain is designed to absorb these lessons early and quickly, and will retain them forever.

Herein lies one of the secrets to positive dog training the Wildrose Way. In the Wildrose system, a pup or dog becomes a member of the family pack. The concept needs to be embraced by the entire family, as every pup seeks a stable social order that he clearly understands and where he feels comfortable and in balance. In order to accomplish this properly, you and your family need to understand pack mentality, how the dog thinks, and how best to interact with the dog every moment you're together. This is not an overwhelming task. It is simply a matter of learning how to communicate with consistency and establishing clear boundaries for behavior. Incorporating your dog into your family "pack" and establishing his proper place in the pack order is the foundation for your relationship with your new sporting companion.

Dogs crave stability, balance, and predictability in the group relationship. Even though there are some writings to the contrary, there's no way to escape this law of nature. Although dogs have evolved through centuries of domestication, they remain pack animals just as horses remain herd beasts. A stable pack produces a stable dog and dogs emulate their pack members. The first thing any pup will want to discover is who is in charge. Where does he fit in, what are the boundaries of the pack, and what are the rules? What actions get rewarded and what actions get disciplined? If such clarity in the relationship can't be established, then dysfunctional behaviors may occur and bad habits may develop.

Dogs learn to follow a stable trusted leader right from the start. This is not to say that a young dog won't challenge that authority and test the boundaries, but that is natural adolescent rebel-

Canines trust and follow stable leaders.

lion. This can be especially true in a more dominant dog or breed of a more independent nature.

For a companion-hunting canine, the goal is for the puppy to come to view the family, including kids and other dogs, as part of his pack. From the moment you first pick up the pup, you're training. Make sure to establish a relationship of leadership, trust, and confidence. *It bears repeating—a dog is always learning, so he is always in training.* You are establishing the order of the pack—both leaders and followers—and entrenching essential behaviors and social skills. You are laying down the appropriate conduct guidelines for all pack members, not just the pup. You are training yourself and your family to train the pup, and most importantly, to avoid unintentionally establishing any undesirable behaviors you'd like to avoid seeing two years from now. Always keep the end in mind as you train and interact with your canine companion.

Understanding and applying pack mentality makes the Wildrose training method work effectively, and realizing that a new pup is always learning directs every interaction with your dog. Each interaction is significant at this young age,

and if you reward a behavior—good or bad, intentionally or unintentionally—you may well be entrenching that behavior.

The Art of Canine Leadership

There is an art to being a great canine pack leader. If successful, you will likely develop a great sporting dog companion that both trusts and respects you. In learning to be a pack leader, you will discover a great deal about not only dogs but relationships in general.

Dog and horse trainers alike have historically used the words "dominant" and "submissive" in their descriptions of relationships with animals. Unfortunately, in recent years, the terms have taken on a negative connotation among some animal behaviorists and even the public. The labels were not necessarily meant to denote cruelty or abusiveness in training methods, but given the perception attached to these terms we will use the words "leader" and "follower" instead.

There are three parts to becoming an effective, positive leader: communication with the dog, understanding canine behavior, and becoming a problem solver. First and foremost, effective canine leaders are splendid communicators.

COMMUNICATION

Productive communication with your dog involves both trust and confidence, and requires that you clearly communicate intent, purpose, and direction during all interactions. There are several different ways to communicate with dogs through their own language, each with a very definite hierarchal ranking of influence.

BODY LANGUAGE is by far the most powerful. Your body language should be that of the canine pack leader. Watch a dog approach another dog. The posture, gait, and expression reflect intent. The leader has a very distinct, confident, bold, and upright posture and stance with direct eye contact. Leaders project authority visually. Body language can communicate friendliness. Getting down low and making yourself small with a big smile on your face will encourage a little pup to approach. The handler's facial expressions are powerful communicators. A smile welcomes the approach of a pup and indicates pleasure and satisfaction, whereas an expression of displeasure will not be inviting to the pup. Smile at your dog. Your canine pal will read your intent.

TONE is the second communicator, a tone such as a low growl in your command to denote displeasure, or a quick, high-pitched "good" to denote pleasure. A hiss can be a definite indicator of displeasure, or it may be established as a cue of a behavior like "sit." The whistle is a tone and can become a meaningful communication tool. Tones are more meaningful than words in the canine world because dogs don't talk—thank goodness—but they do interpret your tone of voice.

VERBAL is the third communicator, words like "good," "no," "sit," and "back." A spoken word may be attached to an understood behavior; still, it is the least important to the dog in the hierarchy of communication.

You can, through progressive training, make one communicator more significant than the others. At Wildrose, we want the tone of the whistle to become the most important communicator with a young hunting dog. Body language at 100 yards may well be indiscernible to the dog and no one wants to be yelling commands on the

Minimize posture with a welcoming smile and outstretched arms to encourage a prompt return.

Posture and direct eye contact are both meaningful communicators.

The Three Ts of Canine Communication:
Timing, Tempo, and Tone

TIMING of a communication is critical. Dogs live in the present, in what's occurring now. You want to time your communication—be it positive to reward a good behavior or negative to eliminate a bad behavior—the instant the behavior occurs in order to capture or eliminate it. For example, try casting a dog from sit to retrieve a bumper. The moment your student correctly goes in the direction of the bumper, capture that success with a verbal marker previously established, such as "good" or "yes." If you wait until the dog returns with the bumper to provide the reward, you are rewarding the return, not the correct cast. The various ways to reinforce behaviors will be discussed in greater detail later in this chapter, but the most important thing to know is that timing of any reinforcer is critical for it to be meaningful. Actually, you have about a two-second window for an effective communication to relate to a specific behavior. Rewarding a puppy with a treat 10 seconds after a desirable behavior occurs is just an indiscriminate treat and means nothing. Worst case, the mistiming could be unintentionally rewarding an unwanted behavior.

TEMPO is the speed at which you are conducting training or interacting with the dog. If a dog is lethargic, you may want to use a higher energy level and speed in your training approach. If a dog is excitable or impatient, you may need to slow the tempo. For example, if the dog is too excited while waiting to be sent for a retrieve, don't reward that behavior with the retrieve. Require the dog to be calm and deny the retrieve until patience is evident. Your personal energy level should be calm and deliberate and the lessons should be administered slowly. Control the dog's energy level either up or down to your desired level with tempo.

TONE is similar to the discussion of tempo, but intent is reflected in your tone of voice. An excited tone can ramp up a dog just as a very quiet and even tone can calm down a dog. Your tone must match the reward or correction—an enthusiastic, high-pitched "good" or a sharp, low-pitched "no" will convey more than the words themselves. The tone of what you are saying is vastly more important than what is actually being spoken.

hunt. You should use the whistle much more than the voice. Using verbal communication, hand signals (body language), and the whistle (tone) combined in layers will make sure you have a good foundation in all three communicators for advanced gundog training.

UNDERSTANDING CANINE BEHAVIOR

A good canine leader understands how to communicate at the dog's level. Dogs don't talk, but they are always communicating with us and other dogs. Knowing how to interpret the subtleties and innuendos of canine communication is vital to a proper relationship. Communication begins with never compromising the trust and respect built into your relationship with the dog while still establishing a position of leadership.

Strengths in a Leader

Leaders are clearly assertive, in control, and decisive at all times. With clarity in their communication, leaders establish boundaries and

A dog's foot placed on the handler indicates avoidance or disrespect.

rants, or loss of control. Dogs trust and follow stable leaders. Instability and inconsistency denote a lack of confidence on the part of the leader and may invoke fear, apprehension, and mistrust in the dog.

Leaders establish and maintain the pack order and enforce boundaries for behavior. The role of leadership is reinforced through training as leaders instruct and followers respond. For instance, if a troubled dog is dominant over your children, you can manipulate the hierarchy of the pack by teaching your child how to work the dog. At that point, the role will be reversed, establishing the child as a leader with the dog as the follower.

Leaders don't repeat commands, which indicates a lack of confidence; they expect a prompt response to a known command. In addition, leaders don't converse with their dogs with meaningless chatter. They give one command and then reinforce that command with a positive, neutral, or correctional response (see the section on reinforcement later in this chapter for more information).

Leaders don't allow a dog to put his body or body parts on the leader. If a dog is leaning against you, placing his paw on your foot, or jumping on you, it is a sign of disrespect and perhaps assertiveness by the dog. If a dog is mouthing you, you're not the leader. In addition, leaders don't become involved in dominant games like wrestling, chase, or tug-of-war. The dog is going to win these escapades and the leader's respect will be compromised.

Leaders determine the dog's job and all dogs need a job, a purpose, a mission for proper stability. Dogs need to earn rewards. Food, affection, and attention are all based on job performance, desirable behaviors, or response to a command. For example, the pack leader decides who gets the retrieve. Retrieves are rewards for good behavior.

Leaders also control the food. Leaders should always require a behavior before food is given. "Sit," "down," and left and right hand signals all

expectations while applying them consistently, not just in training or afield, but in all elements of the dog's life. Leaders are fair, predictable, and even-tempered, without emotional tantrums,

Place training is an important, essential habit.

Posture, expression, and eye contact are key leadership communicators.

can be taught at feeding time using the pup's food. Place the food down and then release the pup by name. The leader should get a behavior before the follower gets the reward.

Leaders provide dogs with a defined place in the home, car, and lodge. Stable dogs do not control territory. Leaders control territory and that space has enforced boundaries. The dog should not exit a truck or trailer until instructed by the leader, nor should he bolt as soon as you open

his crate or gate to the kennel; he should exit only on command while remaining calm.

Leaders maintain an erect, bold body posture indicating a position of strength. Bending or leaning over is more submissive. Remember, body language is at the top of the canine communication hierarchy. If you're working with an older dog, your posture becomes a real indicator of your leadership. Stand tall to receive a proper delivery. When first working with a puppy on retrieving, though, it's encouraging to make yourself small, smile, and look inviting. You want the puppy to think his leader looks kind and approachable. The affection and attention of the leader is instrumental in encouraging a young pup to come consistently.

Weaknesses in a Leader

A dog can perceive a variety of behaviors as signs of a weak leader, including indiscriminate petting or any reward provided for no apparent reason, whether it is food, a treat, or meaningless tosses of the tennis ball. Who grooms whom in the wild? Followers groom the leader. What we try to do during the entire Wildrose training process is progressively change, alter, and modify behaviors. You'll get no behavioral modification with indiscriminate rewards, as they lose their value. If the dog is misbehaving and you're touching or petting him, or offering treats or food, you could be unintentionally rewarding a behavior that you don't want to capture. Indiscriminate petting or rewards will be seen as a weakness by the dog.

Inconsistency—in commands, in the dog's daily schedule, in your emotional state of mind, and in not enforcing boundaries in the home— is a sign of weakness from the dog's perspective. If you say "sit" and the dog doesn't comply, you need to respond. If the dog doesn't receive a response from you, you're not the leader. Actually, you have passively reinforced willful disobedience. If you put your dog in his designated place and he willfully leaves, the dog will lose respect for you if you do not take immediate action. Consistency is paramount in canine leadership (it might even work for kids as well).

Deke, one of the Ducks Unlimited mascots, is on his mat at all times in the home, at the lodge, and in the truck, and he doesn't leave until instructed to do so. The rules and the boundaries are clearly established and always applied, so he has developed a predictable habit. He enjoys the stability in his lifestyle. What the uninformed observer may conclude is that poor Deke has a

> ## The four Cs of effective canine leadership are:
>
> - ✦ Calm
> - ✦ Confident
> - ✦ Controlled
> - ✦ Consistent

restricted life, with no fun or individual freedoms. In reality, because of his calm social graces and exceptional performance afield, he is welcomed on any hunt and in any lodge. He actually gets to do a lot of really cool stuff because of his social behaviors, opportunities that other, less controllable dogs would not experience. Not a bad deal.

PROBLEM SOLVING

Great dog trainers are problem solvers who look first to themselves as the source of any problem, then to the circumstances of the situation or their training methods, and last to the dog. When you do run into problems with behaviors or in field training, you need to approach the problem in a logical and organized way.

To systematically solve training problems, the Wildrose Way has developed a problem-solving matrix. The first quadrant is genetics. Remember that like produces like and that problems may be inherited. Certain things can be overcome through training and certain things can't. For example, is your dog whining in the duck blind? Do you have a retriever that hates water or a pointer that eats birds? You need to think about the possible sources of the problem before attempting to solve it. Is the problem genetic— something the dog inherited from his parents— or does the problem stem from the way the dog has been handled by his owner or trainer? If the latter, the issue may be corrected through training. Hereditary problems are more problematic, while conditioned dysfunctions may be rectifiable over time. Training can overcome instinct.

The second quadrant is the relationship. Are you a calm, assertive, focused, and confident

Problem-Solving Matrix

GENETICS	RELATIONSHIP
METHODS	HANDLER'S ABILITY

Any problem—steadiness, aggression, focus, fear, or hard mouth—will fall in one of the four quadrants. Interestingly, any success you're having with a dog will also fall into one of these quadrants. Problem solving is much easier when you analyze the problem not by the incident, but by defining the core elements of each problem using the quadrants. This matrix exercise will help you drill down and find solutions at the root of the cause.

Once you define the possible causes to the problems you face, you should attempt to analyze what the dog is truly thinking by examining the circumstances from the dog's perspective, not yours. You should begin by looking at yourself first and foremost. Could it be that the handler, the family, or others are the cause of the problem? Your attitude, for instance, matters a great deal. Dogs are very perceptive. If things are bad for you at the moment, avoid trying to train the dog. Dogs have been reading body language for thousands of years. They can see your expression, perceive your lack of confidence, and detect your anxiety, stress, fear, or tension by scenting your sweat and reading your face. They know whether you're paying attention or distracted. The dog is constantly reading your eyes, posture, and body language. He can detect your mood, mindset, and focus, and those of other pack members. Is there instability in the family pack? Is there inconsistency or lack of balance in the dog's lifestyle or training? The dog can effectively read other animals and will read you as well.

Dogs often take on the personalities of their owners and families, mimicking their behaviors just as they do other dogs. Canines of all breeds can perceive things that humans can't imagine, not just by scent, but also by sensory perception. Be aware that your dog is constantly interpreting your attitude, body language, and mindset.

Energy can be a problem when training. If a dog has excessive energy, you have to burn that energy to reduce the level of challenge. High energy results in a lack of focus and inattention. As you will see in the discussion of the cyclical training model in Chapter Four, one of the key

leader? Is the dog the follower? Does he fit into the family's lifestyle and know his place in the pack order? Is your companion calm, patient, biddable, disciplined, and controlled? Is there a bond of trust between dog and handler, an established bridge of communication? Is the dog's daily lifestyle stable and balanced? These considerations fall in the relationship quadrant.

The third quadrant is methods. Are you using the correct training methods to produce the desired results? For example, if your dog is not steady, it could be because your kids are throwing balls and Frisbees for the dog to the point of exhaustion. That evening when you come home and go out for a lesson, you may find your prospect completely unsteady and having no particular interest in your boring instruction! Think about the way you are training your dog. Are you doing things too fast, throwing repetitious bumpers, testing instead of training? Are you approaching introductions properly? Do flaws exist in your methodology?

The fourth column is the handler's ability. Are you a skilled handler and an effective communicator? Clarity, timing, being seen and heard, eye contact, and predictable consistency are just a few of the responsibilities of the handler. Do you maintain the dog's trust and focus? The handler must also know how to train properly—what to do and when to do it. Your dog will disregard unclear hand casts or whistle signals. If the handler's ability to communicate is flawed, the dog's performance may be as well.

components is burning excess energy first to gain control and focus before you ever move into the day's training lesson or problem solving. Excess or misdirected energy can be a major contributor to a problem. Your approach should include a daily structured exercise routine. Establish a place for time out—a pen, the crate, or tying the dog outside—to reduce the stimulus derived continuously from the pack (you and your family).

Dealing with the dog's energy first allows you to address the real problem progressively and in a positive way.

No problem is going to be solved if your dog does not perceive you as the leader and if the pack's lifestyle does not remain stable. Does the dog have rules and limitations? Or does he have unlimited freedom for most of the day, with his only structure being the limited time you set

A young, field-bred English cocker makes a spirited pick of a woodcock.

aside for training? Your training sessions will likely encompass 20 to 40 minutes each day for older dogs, but only two to four minutes for a pup. What's going on with the dog the rest of the day? Make sure your dog has consistency and structure.

As previously mentioned, leaders are Calm, Controlled, Confident, and Consistent in every interaction with the dog. Until a productive relationship is established, no problem is going to be solved. When we receive a dog for training at Wildrose, we spend several days building a relationship with long walks, exploring the grounds, and establishing trust. Before you attempt to solve any problem, look at the matrix and then look at yourself. If you really examine it, only 25 percent of the model addresses the dog directly—genetics. The other 75 percent is you—relationship, method, and handling ability.

Five Reasons a Dog Will Do What You Want It to Do

There are five distinct reasons a dog will do what you want. The reasons are important to remember because they may offer an antidote to problems you may encounter. Also, they serve as a guide to your positive training experiences by allowing you to recognize, capture, and reward naturally reoccurring behaviors which can be of use to you.

INSTINCT: Choosing a dog with the right genetics should provide a package of desirable behaviors. Retrievers have a built-in prey drive to grab and hold. Spaniels love to locate prey in thick cover. Pointers instinctively stalk, but lack the carry-and-grab instinct, which is why they lock up on point. The trainer's job is to awaken natural instincts in a puppy through simple techniques—such as easy retrieves in a hallway, tossing a piece of kibble into cover for a spaniel, or dancing a bird wing on the end of a string for a pointer. Capture it, shape it, reinforce it, and reward it, and the desirable behavior will become entrenched. The pup will keep repeating behaviors he enjoys.

PLEASURE: Dogs are pleasure seekers, out for fun and enjoyment. If a behavior you desire is fun for the dog or it happens to coincide with an activity the pup likes, that's great. If a pup picks up something in the house, don't scold. Call the pup to you, collect the item, and reward the star with affection. There—you have a retrieve to hand. Capture the behavior. Dogs do things they instinctively want to do and many may coincide with the behavior you desire. Just reward, share, and shape it.

TRUST AND CONFIDENCE: When you build trust and confidence in the relationship, the dog begins to realize you can provide what he wants. A very biddable dog will do this much more readily than a hard-charging, independent-minded canine. The reason my trained dogs stop on the whistle and look at me for direction is because they know I'm going to put them on the bird for their ultimate reward. They have learned that to become interdependent and work with me gives them a better chance at a reward. It becomes a mutual respect between partners.

PATTERNING: This means entrenching a behavior in a dog to the point of mindless reaction. For instance, as you walk, toss the bumper and blow the sit whistle repeatedly in various situations. After numerous repetitions, the dog will sit on his own when the bumper flies. Sitting to the flying bumper is a reaction, a conditioned response that has become an entrenched behavior.

AVOIDANCE: The threat of force, fear of punishment and pain, and avoiding discomfort are all powerful reinforcers. The dog becomes conditioned to react to avoid discomfort. The problem with avoidance training is that without the threat of the force, the dog may well respond differently.

■ Behavior Modification

Modifying a dog's behavior and establishing essential skills is training the Wildrose Way. Besides awakening those instinctive abilities lying dormant in the young sporting pup, you will be working to apply the necessary control factors for the Gentleman's Gundog through behavior modification. That is, you'll be establishing the fundamental behaviors you want and eliminating the ones you don't.

Modification involves two approaches: *shaping*—molding a desirable behavior the way you want it—and then taking those behaviors and *patterning* them into an entrenched response.

SHAPING is capturing a small piece of an overall desirable behavior that you want to retain. Reward it and slowly modify it to get the desired results. For instance, a young pup returns quickly from a retrieve. You do not want to allow the pup to drop the bumper, so you should encourage the pup to come by making yourself small and inviting. Upon return, put your hand underneath his jaw and lightly stroke his back to encourage the dog to sit slowly while holding the underjaw and bumper. If you stand above the dog and just say "sit," the dog will certainly drop the bumper as he responds to your command. You are shaping the pup's behavior to bring back the bumper, hold it, and remain calm by rewarding a piece of the overall delivery to hand skill.

PATTERNING is the progressive repetition of a skill or behavior to the point of an entrenched reaction. This is a broader concept than shaping. What you're looking for here is a series of actions that become an absolute and predictable habit—in this case, bringing the bumper straight back to you. During hold conditioning, you put the bumper in the dog's mouth, walk away, and call him for a delivery to hand, then put the dog back in the same spot and repeat, each time with enthusiasm and praise. (In this case, you should not use a treat as a reward as the youngster will invariably drop the

This is an example of shaping the delivery.

bumper to retrieve the treat.) Through extensive repetition, you'll pattern the behavior into an absolute habit. You can progress even further by adding distractions until you know this small piece of delivery to hand is solidified.

THE REINFORCERS OF WILDROSE DOG TRAINING

The Wildrose Way is based on positive reinforcement. This is directly opposite to avoidance-based training, which often employs the use of electric collars, heeling sticks, and force-fetch conditioning to achieve results. Our method emphasizes positive reinforcement of the desirable behavior and performance as opposed to using force to condition the same. Setting the dog up to win, then reinforcing that desired behavior with a reward is the key. You want to capture and reward desirable behaviors to the point of a predictable habit. When teaching a new skill, repeat the activity with properly timed rewards to the point of habit formation.

The dog must value the reward itself to encourage a repeated action; it is important to understand what your dog considers a high-value reward. Some dogs prefer to retrieve rather than eat; some put a higher value on food. Others love affection. Many are bird crazy. You need to know going in what the most valued rewards are for your student. We pointed out earlier the importance of timing, and this is where it becomes crucial. If you're rewarding an action too late or out of sequence, the dog won't understand why a reward is being given and thus the reward loses its value. Worse yet, you may be unintentionally reinforcing something of which you are not even aware. Timing is the biggest challenge for the owner, novice handler, and even inexperienced trainer to get exactly right. Of the three methods of communication—timing, tempo, and tone—timing is the most challenging and the most critical.

At Wildrose, we use a system of variable reinforcers. In other words, the type and frequency of the reward vary, but not when we're first teaching a skill. Every time the pup sits, we reward with a "good" and praise. Each time the pup goes into the crate on command, he receives a treat. Over a period of time, we begin to vary the types and frequency of rewards. When first teaching any behavior or command, the reward should come exactly when the correct behavior occurs. Once the dog learns the skill, though, only the best responses get the reward. If the pup goes into the crate quickly, we quickly give the reward. If he goes in with hesitation, there is no reward.

As you progress with new and more complex skills, only the best behaviors should be recognized with the higher value rewards (that is, retrieves, ball catch, or affection). As known behaviors start reoccurring, begin to eliminate certain rewards like treats. For example, when the dog waits patiently on a retrieve, say "good" and send the dog. Later on, you may fade out or eliminate the "good" completely as the dog progresses to consistently quiet behavior. Go straight to the high-value reward, which is the retrieve. If the behavior is not exactly what you want, the dog does not get the retrieve. Simply walk out and pick up the bumper or bird. When rewards start to vary, the dog becomes quite motivated to self-initiate behaviors or offer quick compliance to discover just what will get a reward.

Occasionally, you should revisit older known skills and provide rewards if they are completed exceptionally well, like a really fast sit to flush. If a dog sits quietly while you put out the bumpers, you should reward the dog with equal enthusiasm for remaining still as you do for retrieving. Not reinforcing known or previously established behaviors is a common mistake. You need to recognize previously entrenched skills occasionally to let the animal know the behavior is still valued. Don't forget the small stuff or the actions are likely to fade.

All rewards have to be earned and properly timed to hold any meaning for the dog. Rewards may be physical—such as petting, food, or a retrieve—or they can be less direct—such as a tone, an audible marker, a smile, body language, or clapping of the hands.

The 12 Deadly Errors

There's one last thing to know before you put your hands on a pup and start training: understand that at this early age, it's as much about what you don't do as what you do. You can easily create problems by committing errors, but you can just as easily avoid problems and eliminate having to deal with the negative results at a later date with an ounce of prevention.

1– HUNTING THE DOG TOO EARLY. Taking a pup up to 12 months old to the field or the blind is a waste of time and could even prove detrimental. Premature exposure to hunting can create a young dog that is gun-shy, water-shy, bird-shy, and shy around other dogs. Much can go wrong and the dog can learn very little at that age. Dogs learn best through repetition and consistency. They're not going to watch and learn how to become a proper hunting dog. When should you expose your gundog to the first hunt? When you have completed a basic training program with the dog. (See Section Two for more information.)

2– OVEREXCITEMENT FROM MEANINGLESS AND INDISCRIMINATELY THROWN BUMPERS OR BALLS. It should not be necessary to build drive or hunting enthusiasm in a properly bred pup. Drive is instinctual and you can actually enhance it by minimizing the number of retrieves the dog receives. Anticipation is a great motivator. Spinning a pup up into a rage by throwing meaningless retrieves is counterproductive to steadiness and patience and accomplishes nothing.

3– BOREDOM. Too many repetitious drills, meaningless lessons, and working too long creates boredom. Puppies have very short attention spans of two to three minutes. Teach short lessons rather than long workouts. End on a positive note and always at the peak of excitement;

this is a good rule to follow throughout the dog's training. A dog that loses interest in training and quits is tough to restart.

4– PUSHING THE DOG. One step leads to another in progressive training. Don't jump around and try various techniques that have no relevancy or relationship to the techniques you previously used. Stick to the plan and make haste slowly. Trying to advance too fast will eventually cause the learning chain to break down. Ensure that each lesson is learned well before progressing.

5– TESTING AND PREMATURE EXPOSURES OR INTRODUCTIONS. Retrieving live birds too soon, tossing the youngster into the water or exposing him to cold water, or taking a prospect to the gun range to see if he is going to be gun-shy—these are common, often devastating mistakes.

6– LOSING YOUR TEMPER. Not only does this devalue your trust; impatience, anger, and frustration are also not indicative of a stable leader. And dogs do not voluntarily follow unstable leaders.

7– HUMANIZING YOUR DOG. Canines are not humans in little dog suits. Dogs are pack animals and we have to communicate and motivate them in that way. Do not project irrelevant human emotion onto a dog. They do not understand the concepts of love, compassion, honesty, sharing, or commitment. They do understand trust, respect, affection, bonding, territory, possessiveness, and loyalty. Think like a dog.

8– NOT DEVELOPING FOUNDATIONAL SKILLS AT A YOUNG AGE. The notion of letting a pup run free so he can just express himself and be a pup without any structure establishes unwanted behaviors and limits mental development. Imagine taking a child—not developing him or her intellectually or nurturing the child in any way, never talking or reading to the child, and never providing exposure to social settings—and then throwing the kid into first grade at age six. The result would be disastrous, but many people do just that with their pups. Your puppy needs to be wired to begin learning at a very early age.

9 – WAITING TOO LONG TO STEADY THE PUP. Steadiness to bumpers and balls tossed about is one of the most important lessons a young dog can learn. No worries here, as denials will not compromise interest in retrieving or drive. You should pick up 50 percent of the bumpers in training and 50 percent of the birds on the first hunts. Also, condition in patience for food or any type of reward. Anticipation actually builds desire in a pup.

10 – TESTING INSTEAD OF TRAINING. Nothing is learned from failure in the dog world. It is vital that the pup learns to succeed in training to develop confidence in himself and you. The dog's attitude matters. Don't push young dogs beyond their ability and physical capabilities. For instance, if a problem occurs on a retrieve, walk out and help a pup if he can't find a bumper. Simplify the exercise and build trust through success.

11 – COUNTERPRODUCTIVE INTERACTIONS. The pup may be calm and well-mannered while in training sessions, but during periods in the home or wherever you are in public, well-meaning friends may create opportunities for dysfunctional behavior. Kids, neighbors, affectionate friends, and other dogs may unintentionally create unsteadiness, disobedience, and bad habits. You may be mindful that the dog is always learning, but others may not understand, so remain vigilant.

12 – POOR OR INCORRECT TIMING OF REWARDS OR CORRECTIONS. You must apply reinforcement exactly at the time the behavior you want to capture or eliminate occurs and at the exact location where the behavior takes place. If a pup moves from sit 10 yards, return him to the original spot. Do not let the student get away with the cheat.

Use shaping to encourage proper delivery to hand through repetition and consistency.

SPECIFIC REINFORCERS

Reinforcers change canine behavior. Think of a gearshift on a car. The five positive motivators are the drive position; they are what move the dog forward in his development. Corrections are the reverse position; they eliminate the undesirable behaviors. Neutral responses, which correspond to the neutral position, are designed to disregard a behavior without giving it value, causing it to self-eliminate or fade away.

Five Positive Motivators

1– Affection and physical touching are excellent reinforcers when used in moderation, but they are the most overused and misappropriated owner activity, which make them subject to the most dilution. Petting, hugging, stroking, and touching—as well as expression and tone—can unwittingly reward a dysfunction. For instance, whining in the duck blind is a common problem and hunters unintentionally reinforce it by petting or touching to quiet the dog. Petting can reinforce fear of loud noises. Trying to calm an excited dog by petting can reinforce hyperactivity. Indiscriminate petting becomes dysfunctional very quickly in the canine world; in fact, it may be regarded as a weakness

Time out discourages an unstable pack member.

on your part as a leader. Affection is a powerful, high-value motivator and overuse will compromise its meaning and effectiveness. Don't dilute its value with indiscriminate petting.

2– Food is an extremely high-value reward, but be careful about what the dog is doing when you offer food. Again, you could be unintentionally reinforcing a behavior. It is productive to require the dog to perform a behavior such as sit or even casting with a hand signal to get a meal or treat. Dinnertime is an excellent time to train a valued skill, but offering food or treats in an attempt to quiet a dog is reinforcing the impatient behavior. If a dog is barking for his food and you provide the meal, what do you think you are reinforcing? Indiscriminate feeding of treats significantly dilutes their value as well.

3– A marker, normally a verbal cue or a clicker, is a powerful tool that immediately marks the behavior you want to capture at the exact moment it occurs. I use a verbal marker, such as "good." Other people use "yes" at exactly the time the behavior

Food is a primary motivator.

A clicker reinforced with treats is an effective event marker.

occurs. In the beginning stages, match the "good" verbal marker to a treat, then you can eventually fade out the treat. Verbal markers are quite useful afield to timely reward a correct action.

"Clicker training is a system of teaching that uses positive reinforcement in combination with an event marker," explains the Wildrose Diabetic Alert Dog trainer, Rachel Thornton. "The most commonly used 'event marker' is a clicker, a device that makes a quick, unique sound. This sound marks a desired behavior in real time and is followed by a motivating reward. The marker is a very precise way to communicate to the dog exactly which action earned the click and its reward. This method produces dogs that learn new behaviors quickly, easily, and enthusiastically. It is also a method that is easily passed on to the new handler."

Verbal markers are more applicable for hunting. Clickers in the gundog world are most effectively used in the training of basic core skills, like "sit," "down," and "kennel." Most gundog trainers wean their dogs off the clicker tool as it is not effective at great distances to capture or mark a correct behavior, whereas the verbal "good" marker can be projected at a distance precisely as the action occurs. In all cases, timing is crucial.

4– The retrieve may be a powerful motivator, particularly for dogs with a high prey drive, like retrievers and spaniels. You can use the retrieve as a positive reinforcer. Place the bumper a short

The retrieve and affection are high-value reinforcers for hunting breeds.

distance from your position and ask the dog for the desired behavior. If the dog complies, he gets the bumper. That's the benefit of sight and trailing memories, which require patience from the dog before the reward of the retrieve. Place the bumper, walk back, turn the dog around, and then wait to see self-initiated, quiet behavior before you allow the dog to get the retrieve. This is a great way to ensure steadiness and avoid noisiness or whining (squeaking) due to excitement and anticipation. The concept also works to train other behaviors, such as stop to the whistle. If the dog stops quickly, he gets cast to the retrieve. If he does not, the dog finds nothing.

5− Association is also a powerful motivator. Dogs place a high value on being with their pack. If the dog's conduct is unacceptable, he doesn't get to hang out with me or the group. If he's not focused, patient, quiet, and obedient, he's not going to stay with the pack (the family, the hunting party, the training group, whatever is going on at the time). If the student is whining, creeping, or running in after other dogs in training, the correction is banishment as an outcast. Association embraces the concept of pack mentality. The pack in the wild will drive out or isolate an unstable, disorderly member. Similarly, I remove the dog from the group and make him watch from a distance; he only returns to the activity when the desired behaviors are evident. If alone, I remove the dog from my proximity—time out, if you will—affording him no attention, not even eye contact. Over a period of time, the dog learns to stabilize and be in balance with the leader or the group, and accomplishes this with self-initiated behavior.

Neutral Responses

Positive motivators are used to retain and encourage the repetition of a desired behavior, while punishment or correction is used to eliminate an unwanted behavior. Neutral responses work best when an undesirable behavior cannot be corrected. For example, perhaps the infraction occurred at a distance. Never give a command that cannot be reinforced. Perhaps the dog did something partially correct, but not completely, such as running around with the bumper before eventually returning and delivering. You can't correct because the dog finally returned the bumper, but you can't reward either because the dog did it poorly. Another example would be a young dog showing overexcitement when you approach. Standing perfectly still, paying the dog no attention until he remains quiet, is a neutral response. Once appropriate, calm behavior is

displayed, engage the dog. One more example is a dog not coming when you call. You can't correct because the dog is at distance ignoring you, but when he does come back you can't reward because he didn't come when called.

A neutral response is also applicable when a dog is marginally misbehaving, jumping, or being ungentlemanly, demanding attention. Ignoring the plea is often the best response when a correction is not appropriate. Occasionally, when a dog is misbehaving at a distance to get my attention or reaction, I will simply put my hands in my pockets, turn, and walk away. Generally, the dog will show up at my side, unreinforced by attention, and I simply move on. If the dog is barking and you are constantly saying "Be quiet," the dog is thinking "Hey, I can get this person's attention or response anytime." Do not engage until the dog is quiet. This also applies when a young dog is noisy in the crate. By going to the crate and telling the dog to be quiet, you are giving him what he wants, your appearance and attention. Only go when he is quiet.

Negative Reinforcement

Corrections for inappropriate behaviors should be discussed at length, as this is an area where it is easy to make huge mistakes. Correction or punishment is designed to stop an unwanted behavior that cannot be eliminated or redirected in any other way. The moment a correction is administered you must be sure that the dog understands what the punishment is for and how to avoid the infraction in the future. At the same time, you should consider how to encourage the dog to replace the undesired action or inaction with a preferred behavior that may be rewarded. There are two types of negative reinforcement:

AVOIDANCE: The dog has been conditioned to avoid the punishment by doing the correct thing. The power of avoidance training lies in the presence and threat of the force. In its absence, the dog may choose to act in another way.

ELIMINATION: To gain compliance from the dog, discomfort is applied as a known command is given or behavior is expected. The discomfort or pressure (such as a lift of the lead tightening the slip collar) remains until the dog complies, in effect turning off the discomfort. Wildrose does not use a force-based training methodology to teach skills, which would include force-fetch, whip-fetch, or the popular electric collar training techniques. Force is only used to stop and eliminate unwanted behaviors when no other method has proven to be effective. Force must be applied exactly at the point when the unwanted behavior occurs. Mistiming can result in confusion and distrust. Force must be used only to reinforce a *known* command. Any behavior must be taught first and thoroughly understood.

Punishment is not a retaliation to get back at the dog, nor is it an emotional response. Revenge, frustration, impatience, and anger are not productive traits in a canine leader. Even when a correction is necessary, your goal is to replace the force with a positive reinforcer. Too much force and the dog will shut down. Too little and the dog will ignore it and become desensitized to its effect. Inappropriate actions must be corrected with consistency, not only in the field, but in all locations and situations. Punishment can't be indiscriminately applied and the handler can't overreact. Negative reinforcement requires leaders to give the dog enough time to process the command and make choices before applying the correction. The correction needs to be fair; the punishment needs to fit the infraction.

There should be no inappropriate emotion— no yelling or screaming—but your body language and tone must match the intent of the correction. Express displeasure with expression, posture, and tone, but remember stability. Humans are quick to apply force to make a dog do something, as opposed to conditioning a dog to do something correctly and then rewarding successes. Watch yourself objectively. You may find that you are quick to correct and scold, but forget to reward. You must be able to switch gears rapidly from negative to positive for the Wildrose Way to be effective.

◆ ELECTRIC TRAINING COLLARS

E-collars in an untrained handler's hands can be highly destructive, creating a long list of dysfunctional problems in a dog. If a person is not

E-collar training is the correction of last resort for the Wildrose Way.

trained to use an electric collar, he or she shouldn't touch one. If a handler can't train a dog without using an electric collar, he or she most likely can't train a dog with a collar. Training with an e-collar is strictly avoidance or elimination methodology. The collars are effective only as long as the threat exists. Plus, you could end up with two dogs—one with the collar on, one with it off.

E-collars in the hands of a professional can achieve good results when reinforcing at distances that would be hard to accomplish otherwise, and they can be highly effective problem-solving tools. Unfortunately, they often end up in the hands of people who don't know how to use them properly, or don't spend the time to teach the command first and then polish the known command with the e-collar. The dog must understand how to get rid of the shock; he needs to know if he sits down, the pain will go away. The dog will also learn that with a quick compliance to the command he may avoid the pain altogether. This approach must be taught very carefully, highly structured, and at the lowest stimulus level possible if you want to avoid damage to the dog.

The e-collar is a problem-solving tool of absolute last resort at Wildrose, and then only one single command is reinforced: sit or stand still. Done correctly and repeatedly, the dog will opt to eventually do the right behavior to avoid the shock. When the dog does sit on command and misses the correction entirely, reward instantly with a high-value motivator to establish a habit. As soon as you begin using an e-collar, the process has already begun to get rid of it. It's a temporary step only. Eliminating the collar's presence is important, as it is preferred to hunt a dog without any type of correction tool or collar, since the collar can become entangled, proving hazardous to the dog. Also, the limited use of force should always be applied in such a way that the dog has the option to choose the right behavior and receive an immediate reward.

The use of force is applied on a gradual escalation continuum. Referring to my years in police

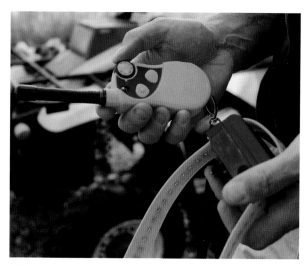

This is an example of an electric training collar.

training, it is best described as the escalation of force. On the street, the minimum level of force is used to accomplish results. At Wildrose, we practice the same, starting with the word "no," then a lead correction, then a rubberized slip collar, choker chain, check cord, prong collar, or, finally, the e-collar. To reiterate, we do not consider the e-collar's use as a training method; rather, it is a tool of last resort in the force continuum to stop an unwanted behavior.

Other accepted limited uses of electric shock collars include de-snaking, stopping activities like chasing vehicles or unwanted game, bolting (that is, running away out of control), and suppressing barking when no other methods have proven effective. In each of these instances, the dog is taught to eliminate and avoid the shock, except in the case of the snake. In de-snaking, the dog sees and smells the snake, then immediately receives a powerful shock with no introduction as to how to avoid the pain, which creates a fear factor relating to the snake.

By using positive techniques, you'll get fewer side effects than will result with force-based training. Force application will likely show up as a dysfunction somewhere else in the dog's progressive development. Force is fear-based; reward is pleasure-based. Use force of any type sparingly to eliminate unwanted behaviors and only as a last resort.

⚔ The 20 Wildrose Laws of Dog Training ⚔

Wildrose has developed a set of undisputed laws of dog training that are the foundation for the Wildrose Way of positive gundog development.

1 – Dogs are looking for a leader. From the second you pick your prospect, despite his age, the dog will want to know who's in charge and where he fits in the pack.

2 – If dogs can't find a leader, they will attempt to become one. Often the pup will do so in very dysfunctional ways, such as chewing, resistance to housebreaking, possessiveness over objects, and becoming territorial. Older dogs may ignore commands and destroy things, even becoming aggressive or territorial.

3 – What is conditioned in the pup between six weeks and six months of age won't go away. That's the way nature set it up. Canines are genetically predisposed to imprint their mother's behavior right out of the den. As the pack leader, you need to imprint the behaviors you want from day one. Put in the good stuff and avoid the bad. You and others entrench behaviors during every interaction with your pup. Sometimes what you don't do is more important than what you do.

4 – Don't condition in a problem that must be trained out later. Things such as chase, tug-of-war, chew toys, games like fetch that promote unsteadiness, free swimming, romping with other dogs, and free running are all undesirable behaviors that must be trained out.

5 – Make haste slowly. Make sure that each level of your training is thoroughly understood before moving to the next level. Establish good foundational skills. Be progressive; link lessons together in causal relationships where one skill automatically involves the next. Don't exceed your pup's capacity to understand and retain lessons. If you want to train a dog fast, go slow.

6 – Solve one problem at a time. If the dog has several problems, address the most basic problem or core skill and solve that first. For instance, if you have a dog that breaks, is spooky on the

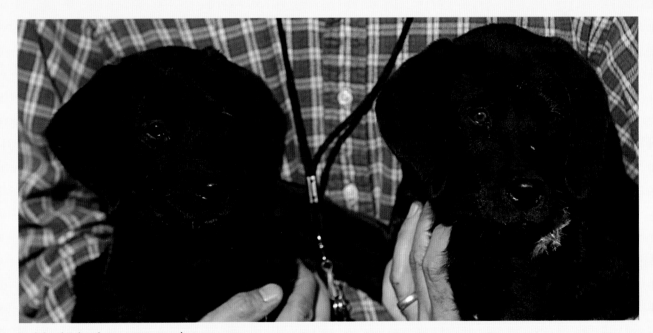

Training begins the moment you select your pup.

gunfire, and won't bring the bumper back when sent for a retrieve, the first thing to resolve is bringing back the bumper. If you try to resolve all the difficulties at once, you may overwhelm the dog. Stop worrying about the other two and correct the most basic problem, then proceed.

7 – If it's not right at heel, it won't be right in the field. This is a simple concept. Core skills need to be solid very close to you first, in yard work, including sit, recall, sit to flush, and steadiness to denials. As an example, if you're walking with your dog at heel and you blow the sit whistle and the dog won't stop or sit as you keep walking, then he's not going to stop at a hundred yards, particularly if there is some stimulus like a bird, gunfire, or another dog present.

8 – Get it right on land before going to the water, unless you're really fond of swimming. How do you teach a skill, provide assistance, or correct the dog in the water? Master any skill on the ground before going to the water.

9 – Dogs are place-oriented. This works in a positive and negative way. Dogs live in the present, the "now," but they have great recall on being in a particular location even though they don't transfer skills well from one place to another. You have to train a skill at multiple locations to ensure that a predictable habit has been established. You can use this concept to your advantage to entrench a behavior. You can also return to a place of success if necessary to reestablish confidence or simplify a lesson. That said, if you encounter a problem or have a bad experience in one place that proves to be negative or even traumatic, the dog will remember that location as well. Move to another place to resolve the issue. A negative experience in one location will not be forgotten for a long time. Change the place, the environment, and the situation.

10 – Memories before hand signals, hand signals before marks. This is almost the opposite of typical retriever training methods. The concept may apply to pointers and setters as well. Accomplish the harder things first. It is easier to develop memory in a younger dog than in an older one. Throwing a bumper and immediately sending the dog gives him independence and promotes unsteadiness. I want the dog to be interdependent, working with me first. Memory retrieves, including doubles and triples, create situations requiring the dog to be more dependent on your relationship and to rely on his own memory. Hand signals, casting, and whistle work are interdependent actions with the handler and should be introduced at younger ages. The last skill you should concentrate on is the independence of marking or free hunting. The order to follow is dependent first (memory/obedience), interdependent second (whistle/handling), and independent last (hunting/marks).

11 – Dogs live in the present, so match their mindset. Focus on the dog and stay in the moment. Dogs know when you're not paying attention. A handler needs to work in the present. Although dogs have great place recall, they're not worried about the past or the future. They live right in the moment. If you're thinking about something else while interacting with your dog, you may compromise your communication. Dogs need to see your eyes. Forget sunglasses, texting, and multitasking; hide the cell phone and engage your student.

12 – Dogs are pleasure seekers. They will repeat behaviors that bring them desired rewards. You control the pleasure or rewards. The dog will associate a particular performance with a desirable reward and likely repeat that behavior again. What you don't want is a dog out on an independent frolic receiving pleasure from the experience. A prime example is a dog that breaks, runs about unresponsive to the handler's commands, and then is rewarded with finding a bird. In training, dogs will continue to offer behaviors that bring rewards. Capitalize on the concept.

13 – Training is habit formation through repetition, consistency, and reinforcement with rewards. That's the direct opposite of avoidance training with force. Over time, your youngster will stay on his place mat because he is rewarded, not because it fears punishment. Later, the behavior becomes entrenched as a predictable habit. Reward behavior you want to retain or it will fade out. A dog that honors another retrieve, sits quietly and calmly in the blind, and doesn't whine should be rewarded just as much as a dog that made a great retrieve. Always reward the most valuable behavior.

14— **A dog will not follow unstable leaders.** As a reminder, the four Cs of leadership are Calm, Controlled, Confident, and Consistent.

15— **Instinct can be overcome by training, but instinctive behavior needs to be replaced with something of value to the dog.** A retriever may not automatically deliver to hand, but he may have an enormous prey drive—the desire to run out, get something, and carry it or run with it. Through training, you can reinforce the return, hold, and delivery by modifying the natural instinct of pick up and carry, then rewarding the delivery. Pointers may point, but may not back. Flushers without training may run up birds or not remain steady to flush. Proper training can modify instinctive behaviors.

16— **First trust, then respect.** You must establish the leadership relationship first through trust,

Canine leadership is established through trust first, then respect—never force.

then respect. A canine-human relationship is not about love or compassion; it is about respect. Dogs follow leaders in whom they have confidence.

17— **Under stimulus or excitement, animals revert to the most familiar behavior or habit that has been entrenched.** The dog's proper response becomes an absolute, predictable reaction despite the presence of stress, distraction, or confusion. The performance or reaction you're going to get under pressure is the most entrenched behavior, the default behavior. In these situations, a well-trained dog will perform by mindless reaction. His default behavior under stimulus will take precedence. Be sure that each skill is trained to absolute habit, a reaction.

18— **Train, don't test.** Repeat each skill to the point of habit. Dogs don't learn through failure. The goal in training is to set the dog up to win, repeating the lesson in different locations to establish a predictable habit. You do want to challenge the dog's performance occasionally, but if the fundamental skills are not present the dog will fail. Challenging is acceptable as long as skills are in place for the dog to be successful.

19— **If what you're doing in training is not working, back up.** When faced with a failure, a common mistake is to keep trying, which often results in repeated failures. Then frustration sets in, a lack of trust develops, and the training session breaks down. The tendency is to come back out the next day and attempt the same technique again. Wrong! If a couple of attempts to complete an exercise don't work, back up a few steps to the familiar. Revisit the last known skills that the dog thoroughly understands, and then armed with success, build out. Simplify the task, change locations, change the bumper, and change from whistle to voice. Change the orientation, get a success, and then push ahead.

20— **Never give a command that you cannot reinforce.** A correction should only be given at the place and time of the infraction. If you are in a position in which you cannot reinforce a command, don't give it.

CHAPTER 3

Starting Your Pup the Wildrose Way

■ Putting in the Essential Behaviors

Many people ask me, "When should I start training my pup?" My answer is always, "The second you acquire the pup." So, let's get started. The selection process is complete and you now have your new prospect. Your plan is in place and everyone is filled with anticipation for what the future holds. Now it's time to enjoy the dog you searched for so diligently. From the moment you say "I'll take this one," you should start focusing on the end result. As a reminder, begin with the end in mind.

This discussion about starting your pup is based on the Wildrose Puppy Seminar, which is given when clients come to the kennel to pick up their pups. It is a comprehensive look at the crucial first six months of the pup's life and what needs to be done to establish the essential behaviors that will be imprinted for a lifetime. This chapter is the blueprint for those first six months. You are creating a balanced, consistent lifestyle for your pup, as well as introducing him to the world as part of your pack. Your goal is to develop a fearless and enthusiastic pup that will become what I call a super learner. You are fostering a desire in the pup to interact with people, explore new things with boldness and confidence, and establish valuable skills to the point of habit.

The first six months of the puppy's life is considered the backgrounding period, which is broken into two age groups: from seven weeks to three-and-a-half months (first 14 weeks) and from three-and-a-half months to six months (the next 12 weeks). At Wildrose, we introduce the basic fundamental behaviors and commands during the first phase and entrench those behaviors and skill sets to the point of habit in the second phase. There are three main areas of focus during the backgrounding period: socialization, desensitization, and establishing core fundamental behaviors. Pups have an exceptional capacity to learn at this age and what they retain will likely be imprinted for a lifetime. Take advantage of this opportunity.

■ Socialization and Desensitization Produces Fearless Enthusiasm

Socialization and desensitization (desent) tend to overlap and are part of an ongoing process throughout the pup's development. Essentially what you are doing is gradually over the 26-week period exposing the pup to a variety of environmental and social experiences: people, places, and things. You are introducing your pup to the world and getting him used to all the things he will face as he goes through life as your companion. There is no set list of requirements to follow; just use your imagination as to the possibilities while remaining careful not to overwhelm or frighten the youngster. This should become a daily thought process on your part, always keeping the dog's development in mind. The outcome: confidence, stability, and balanced behavior.

SOCIALIZATION

Socialization is the ability to interact with people and other dogs, at any place and under any conditions. Proper socialization is crucial to any dog's future ability to fit into the social atmosphere of the home and maintain a calm, good-natured demeanor with other hunters and dogs. One of the most important aspects of Wildrose-trained gundogs is their ability to project the attributes of a gentleman or a lady as well as a focused hunting dog. Socialization involves continuous exposure to variables outside the pup's normal surroundings and leads to civil etiquette no matter what the situation. It creates a canine companion you will be proud to take anywhere.

DESENSITIZATION

By slowly exposing your dog to new environments, people, places, and things—from the urban landscape to farm animals, cars, trucks, ATVs, boats, or any other situations the dog may encounter in the future—you can minimize the problems of fear and distrust that can lead to dysfunctional behavior. Placing a dog in a boat for the first time on the way to a duck blind in predawn darkness is not a logical thing to do, nor is expecting your dog to understand how to climb on a water stand in flooded timber if the student has never seen one.

The key to desent is to proceed slowly and with the same thought process you would apply when introducing other high-stress exposures, such as large birds or gunfire. You want to be progressive, but gradual. The youngster must trust you and be self-confident. Make haste slowly. A perfect example of a poor introduction would be tossing the pup into deep water. Common sense should tell you that won't work, but people do it. You need to introduce your student to any new experiences in a way that inspires confidence, avoiding any element or approach that could startle the dog.

By controlling how you make introductions and proceeding with caution, you do not violate the pup's trust or negatively affect his confidence, but you also keep the puppy's development moving forward—encountering new noises, places, people, and things. These are lessons that can take place anywhere and anytime an opportunity presents itself.

A good example would be a canoe. You wouldn't throw a young, inexperienced dog into a canoe and take off anymore than you would throw a pup in the water as an introduction. It might work, but it could also result in a difficult

Progressive introductions to new things such as watercraft should begin on land before moving to water.

problem. A more logical approach would be to place the canoe in the yard; let the dog see it, sniff it, and explore it with you. Get in the canoe and make a game of getting in and out until the pup shows the confidence of acceptance. He trusts you, not the canoe, and it's up to you to maintain that trust. Sit with the dog in the canoe and rock gently to get him used to the motion. Train your student to sit quietly and not move around. Have the paddle with you so the dog gets used to seeing it. Take it slow, make it fun, and progress in stages. Soon you will have a pup that hops in the canoe and sits quietly, and you will be ready to progress to shallow water.

Use the same approach to introduce your student, despite his age, to anything new he may encounter as a future traveling wing-shooting companion—motor vehicles of all types, ATVs, people, small children, other dogs, aircraft, farm animals, water, city streets, public places, the mall, the list goes on and on. It bears repeating that every interaction between you and the dog is a learning process for the youngster. You are the guide to the world and its experiences. Read your pup and understand what he is communicating. Use that information to gauge the dog's development and once again—make haste slowly.

■ Core Fundamental Behaviors: Seven Weeks to Three-and-a-Half Months

Establishing core fundamentals is where, in effect, you put in the footers of the foundation for your gundog-building project. Fundamental behaviors will support your overall training efforts long-term. If they are strong, the behaviors will endure forever. If they are weak, holes will develop in your dog's performance and conduct. There are no shortcuts in dog training, no way to speed-train a gundog, but the resulting sporting companion will be worth the extra time and effort.

HOUSEBREAKING

One of the first tasks at hand is housebreaking, but rather than "breaking" the pup, the best approach is to avoid a problem by never giving him a chance to make the mistake in the home. Dogs are place-oriented and will tend to select one location to relieve themselves. Dogs are indeed complete creatures of habit. This will work against you if the pup establishes his "spot" in a corner of your home. But, you can also use this tendency to your advantage by encouraging the pup to select a spot of your choice.

Housebreaking is accomplished through a combined use of place training, crate training, controlling food and water, and not giving the pup free reign of the house. A crate is a crucial tool and should fit the small size of the pup; in a big crate, the dog may turn it into a condo, relieving itself in the front and living in the back. Scheduling becomes important as well. Create a feeding and watering schedule and allow no free access to food or water.

The first order of business every morning is to take the puppy out of the crate and directly

Place training is an essential skill that is beneficial in the home and later in the blind.

to one specific spot for relief. The pup's house-breaking is quite easy to establish if everyone is consistent. When not under supervision, the dog should be on a place mat, bed, or in his crate. Each and every time the pup comes out of the crate, awakens from a nap, is taken from his place, or eats and drinks, you should take him to his designated spot. If you are busy, this is a great time to tie or stake out the pup near his relief spot with a 10-foot snap wire cable. If you are diligent and consistent, the pup will adapt quite easily to the routine and housebreaking will be simple.

PLACE AND CRATE TRAINING

Place training is best established on a small, elevated platform, a padded mat, or a soft dog bed, which provides the puppy defined edges or boundaries. This process begins the day you pick up the pup. Anytime your dog is traveling in your vehicle or sitting with you in the home, he should be on his mat. Initially, your pup will try time and again to move off his place. Simply replace the youngster and say "place." You can attach the puppy lead and have the dog sit on his mat on the floor next to you as you relax in your favorite chair. Your dog can fidget and roll around all he wants on the mat, but with the lead you can ensure he remains in place.

The dog crate becomes your pup's personal haven, a place of safety, security, and rest.

No one should bother the pup when he is on place. The dog can do what he wants on place within reason, but he cannot violate the boundaries. Wherever you go, take that specific mat with you. This may seem inconvenient and difficult to maintain at first, but stick with it. Later, when the dog is fully trained, you will be able to take his mat and drop it anywhere and the dog will be comfortable on place and remain patient as a rock. You've ingrained that behavior to the point of habit.

As for the pup's crate, it should be a plastic shipping type with mostly solid sides and nothing that is chewable. Also, do not put a mat or blanket in the crate with the pup or it is likely to be consumed. The crate needs to be easy to clean and the type that offers the pup a "cave," which becomes the pup's own little domain.

EYE CONTACT

The ability to capture and hold the youngster's gaze before an interaction is an important step in early training. Gaining eye contact from the pup ensures attentiveness and indicates respect for you as the leader. In these early days of immaturity when the pup is easily distracted, holding his eyes and attention won't be instantaneous and success will occur for only a brief duration. Capture and reward it. Every interaction begins with getting the pup's eye contact by using his name before proceeding. This is a primary indicator that the youngster is focused, attentive, and ready to respond. The habit of eye contact preceding any command will pay huge dividends later in training.

LEADERSHIP PATTERNS

In Chapter Two, you learned how to become an effective, confident leader. As a reminder, leaders eat first; they go through the door first; they offer direct eye contact in communication. Now, you can actually put these concepts into practice with the young pup. For example, when it's time to feed, you are in control of the food, an excellent time for a leadership lesson. To reinforce eye contact, the food should come from a position close to your eyes. With the pup at sit, patiently waiting, hold the food bowl at your face and wait until you obtain eye contact. Ultimately, you will get the puppy's attention. When you put the bowl down, condition the dog to wait briefly. This simple lesson involves eye contact, patience, and response to a release command all reinforced by food. (Use the dog's name for the release, as this is what you will do later when sending the dog for a retrieve.) At feeding time, there are many simple skills that can be taught, including hand signals, sitting, coming when called, and entering the kennel—all using the food as a reward.

In everything you do with the youngster, always require a behavior before a reward. The pup has the mental capacity even at this young age to begin to understand boundaries, tones, and simple rules like not chewing your hand. Review the list of canine leadership traits outlined in Chapter Two. It is now time to put them all into practice.

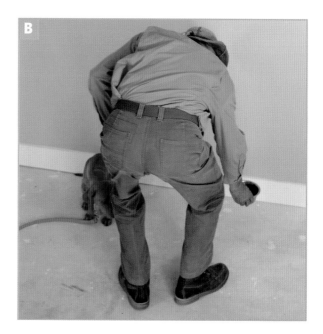

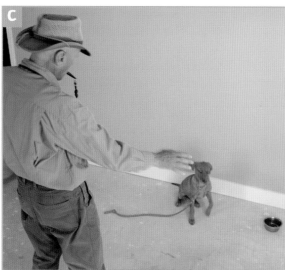

A: Before giving a pup a command, make eye contact using the food as a lure. **B:** Place the food as the pup waits patiently. **C:** A blast of the whistle gains the pup's attention, with a hand signal to follow. **D:** Food is the motivator and ultimate reward.

COLLARS AND LEAD

Place a small, flat collar on the pup as soon as you pick him up. This might be an irritation for the little one for a day or so, but he will get used to it. Then, it's time for the puppy walker, which is simply a basic slip lead, not a choker collar or pinch collar. This is a non-intrusive lead constructed of nylon material, which contracts when the lead is lifted and applies a slight constriction around the neck. It's nothing painful, just a bit intrusive. It is an excellent tool for teaching your pup to lead and to sit on command. Don't expect the pup to heel precisely at this young age. You simply want him to walk on your left or right side, in the correct position, in a calm, patient manner. I personally want the dog on my left at all times. Whichever side you choose is OK, but be consistent. In the hunting field or in the blind, I'm concentrating on a lot of things, from gun safety, to the bird, and even not falling down. I don't want my dog switching sides and getting in the way. This starts from day one and anytime your dog is with you he should be in that spot, left or right.

LEAD WORK

Verbally instructing the young pup to heel when he is out of position is meaningless. Give the "heel" command only when the pup is in the correct position. If the dog is pulling and you give the command, you're associating "heel" with the action of pulling. Associate the proper behavior with the proper verbal command and your student will quickly begin to realize where the correct heel position is. The lead should be loose when the pup is in the correct position and snap with quick bumps of the lead (never pulling) when out of position. Associate the "heel" command with a comfort zone. When your dog is out of position, don't say a word; just bump the lead (causing discomfort) to encourage the correct position.

Don't allow sniffing. That behavior is a total inattention and a distraction. Keep the pup's nose up with his eyes and attention on you. Dur-

This is a puppy walker, the perfect lead to start any pup.

ing this period, simply walk the youngster on the lead on the side you prefer and correct when he is out of place. Reward when he is in position.

SIT OR STAND IN PLACE

An easy way to teach sit is when the pup is by your side. Gently lift the puppy walker lead straight up and encourage the dog to sit. A light push on his rear may be in order initially. The moment he sits, the pressure of the lead will disappear. Young students will learn that the

Excellent eye contact encourages the pup to stay in the heel position.

Encourage sit by lifting on the lead and pressing on the pup's rear simultaneously. The second the pup sits, relax the lead.

command will be followed by discomfort, and sitting will release the pressure (elimination). Very soon, your pup will act as soon as he hears the command to avoid the discomfort altogether (avoidance). Once the pup understands the command, during your walks with the dog in the correct heel position, stop occasionally, say "sit," and lift the lead. You are developing a conditioned response; when you stop, he sits, ultimately without the lead prompting or command. Later, this routine becomes the base for sit to the flush. One thing to remember: If you're working with a pointer, don't reinforce sit. No one wants a pointer to sit on the point. Instead, reinforce "whoa" when you come to a stop at heel, allowing the dog to remain standing.

EARLY RETRIEVES

Your dog's first retrieves should be made with a knotted sock in a hallway of the house with no distractions. Kneel down with the puppy between your knees and toss the sock. When he picks it up, scurry backward to encourage the pup to come. Collect the sock and throw it again. You're not training for patience now. You're awakening instinctive drive. After a couple of retrieves, advance to the puppy bumper. Use a small bumper, either canvas or fire hose, but never plastic. Plastic promotes chewing and plastic bumpers are harder to hold and carry. Only a couple of repetitions are necessary each day. Avoid boredom. Keep the puppy interested.

The next step is a very simple memory. Place the youngster on the puppy lead, walk him down the hall, and drop the bumper. The pup is going to want to go, but you should encourage him to walk away with you. Establish a calm behavior at sit; only then take off the lead and send for the

A: With the memory placed, encourage patience before the release. *B:* Release by name and a hand signal. *C:* Just as the pup makes the pick, begin encouraging his return. *D:* Encourage delivery to hand by keeping your posture small and accepting the bumper immediately.

bumper. At first, the delay should be momentary. Slowly lengthen the delay. There is no change in complexity, just a change in duration. This is a trailing memory. Walk the youngster out, drop the bumper, walk him back with you, encourage him to sit quietly briefly, and then send him for the retrieve.

Once successful, move the retrieve to new locations, but do not add distractions. Go to the garage, along a fence, anywhere there is a confined area. Keep the line straight and minimize the opportunities for the dog to run around.

When the pup returns to you with a bumper, do not allow him to drop, but share the prize. Occasionally, give the bumper back to the puppy, let him hold it, and then take it back. Hand it to him again and take it back. Develop a shared relationship with you, the puppy, and the bumper. He will develop an understanding that the bumper is a shared experience and you're not just taking it away. You'll discover that this approach will encourage the pup to return to you willingly. It's important not to let the pup drop the bumper at delivery. Get the bumper in

Suggested Commands

The following list is a suggestion of commands. No matter what verbal command you choose and condition to a corresponding behavior, use that single command exclusively.

HEEL: Dog remains at the handler's side in loose lead or off lead whether sitting, walking, or running.

SIT OR WHOA: Dog sits or stands in the same position without movement. Dog may be called from position during training.

STAY: Dog is never called from position. More permanent than sit. Used when sit is not appropriate, e.g., in cold water.

HERE OR COME: Dog is recalled to handler.

PLACE: Dog remains at a designated location.

LOAD: Dog gets onto something, e.g., a ramp, stand, or vehicle.

OUT: Dog exits or jumps off of something.

KENNEL: Dog enters or goes inside something, e.g., a crate, trailer, or dog hide.

WATCH: Dog should be aware of his surroundings—an action is about to occur; take notice.

DOWN: Dog lies down and remains down.

NO: A de-select used to indicate a wrong decision has been made; the dog should not take action; or the dog should leave an item alone.

GOOD: A positive, verbal marker; a reward; indicator of a correct decision.

GIVE, DROP, OR DEAD: A release command for the dog to give up an object to hand.

BACK: Used with a hand signal to tell the dog to turn around and go in the opposite direction.

GET ON: Used with a hand signal to cast left or right.

GET OVER: To jump an object (like a fence or log) or cross a barrier (like a ditch, stream, or river).

DOG'S NAME: The release command for a retrieve; should also precede any command to which the dog should respond.

DEAD BIRD OR HIGH LOSS: To hunt cover closely to locate lost game; to track.

hand, but do not expect a stylish finish at this young age.

COMMANDS

Avoid chatter and meaningless conversation with your dog. Dogs don't talk. Use single-syllable commands like "sit," "place," "heel," and "stay." "Come on, let's go" doesn't work if he has been taught that

"heel" is the correct command. Everyone in the family should know the proper commands and use them exclusively. Any term you use is OK—for instance, "load" or "kennel"—as long as the command is clear and consistent. Always repeat the command as you're teaching its meaning. Once the command is known, don't repeat it. Say the command and expect compliance.

WHISTLE

At about three months of age, begin incorporating the whistle, replacing voice commands. Generally, you should use one single whistle blast as the sit command and a series of very quick whistle blasts for recall. When a puppy is doing something you want to be attached to a whistle command, such as running back to you, blow the whistle quickly five to seven times as he performs the behavior. If the pup is in the yard and he sees you with his food and comes flying toward you, blow the recall whistle. As the pup sits, blow the whistle once. It becomes a pleasurable event and the action occurring voluntarily becomes associated with the whistle. When the pup is complying with sit without lifting the lead, give the verbal command "sit," followed by one whistle blast, and repeat "sit" again. Gradually, fade out the verbal command and allow the whistle to stand alone.

SUMMARY OF THE FIRST 14 WEEKS

If there is one overriding factor in your success—particularly at this age—it will be consistency. In all early start fundamental areas, don't expect perfection and realize that the pup will not understand a physical correction or punishment. Force is not applicable at this stage. Shape, capture, and encourage behaviors while rewarding correct performance or compliance. Make haste slowly. Build the foundations and don't overextend the pup's mental capacity and atten-

Incorporate the whistle when the pup displays the appropriate behavior.

tion span. The essential behaviors, if properly entrenched, will follow the pup into adulthood and endure a lifetime.

■ Core Fundamental Behaviors: Three-and-a-Half Months to Six Months

To continue the building metaphor, if you will, the footers are in place. Now you can build the foundation walls of your gundog structure.

LEAD WORK AND INTRODUCTIONS

With the pup walking on lead, you should begin to offer valuable introductions. Start working on agility at this early age with the pup on lead. Walk-

ing up ramps and across planks from one level to another prepares dogs to negotiate elevated platforms and duck blinds. You can easily create realistic structures with several one-by-six-foot boards and a picnic table in your backyard. A pup needs to become comfortable being off the ground on a platform, but be careful not to let the pup fall.

RETRIEVES

Once the dog understands the short trailing memory, introduce a split 180 trailing memory. Trailing means placing the bumper with the dog watching, then turning and walking away, in effect creating a trail. The name 180 originates from the way the double retrieve is set up, 180 degrees apart or in opposite directions. Walk

Elevated platforms and ramps may intimidate the dog; it is best to provide these introductions early and frequently.

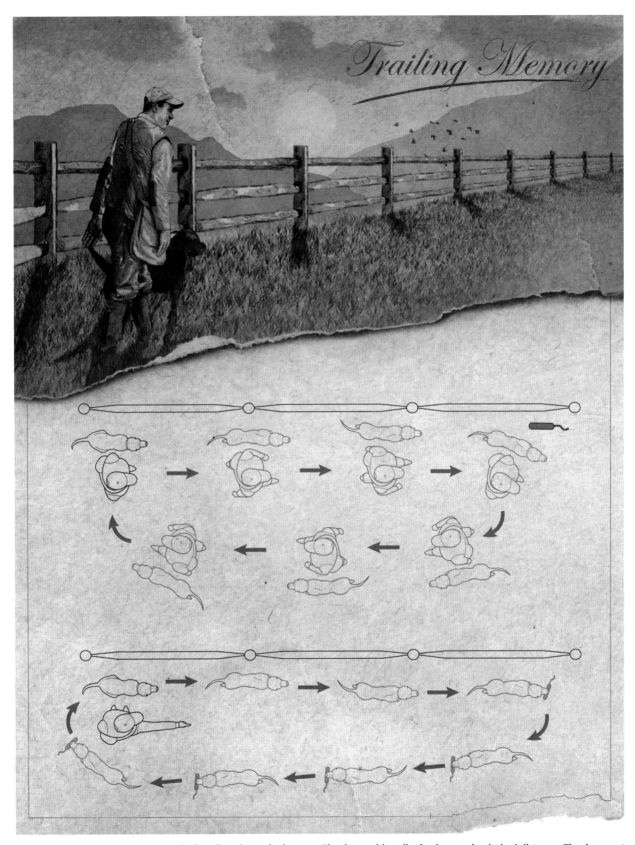

The dog walks patiently at heel as the handler places the bumper. The dog and handler heel away the desired distance. The dog must display patience before he is aligned for the memory. The fence encourages straight lining.

Established with the dog walking at heel as the handler places the bumper, this is similar to the trailing memory. The dog and handler turn and walk in the opposite direction of the first memory to place the second. Heel the dog away from the second memory and line him for the first. Upon completion, line for the second memory, completing the double.

Own the Eyes

With the pup's advanced maturity level and longer attention span, you can now expect to hold the pup's eye contact and focus for a bit longer before a command or activity occurs. You are ready to condition voluntary eye redirection.

Each command should be preceded by the pup's name and three-second eye contact. All good things originate from the eyes: food bowl, bumper, treat.

Building upon this conditioning, you can establish a voluntary redirection of the eyes. For example, with a pup at sit expecting you to offer a treat, hold the prize in front of your face. Then, just extend your arm to your side. Remain motionless and quiet as the pup stares at the treat.

When the pup's attention voluntarily returns to your eyes, immediately reward by saying "good" and offer the treat. The pup will soon learn that eye contact will be rewarded. Using the food bowl at feeding time, a bumper, or the dog's coveted tennis ball can achieve the same results.

Later, when you toss the bumper, the pup will focus on the fall. Reward when his eyes return to yours by saying "good" and give the next command.

A: Encourage eye contact with the presence of a treat. *B:* Extend the treat an arm's length away. *C:* Wait until the dog's eyes voluntarily redirect to yours. *D:* Quickly reward the eye contact with the treat.

the dog out and drop the bumper in one direction along the fence or building, walk him back, drop a bumper in the opposite direction, and then return to the middle of the straight line. Send him for the first bumper, the oldest first, and then the second. Next, do a triple retrieve. Use the same setup, but while the pup is out for the second bumper, toss the first bumper back to its original position. When the pup returns with bumper number two, turn and send him for number three, the unseen. The fence or wall will keep the puppy running straight.

What the pup learns is that there's always something out there, so a quick return gets another retrieve. If the puppy runs off with one of the bumpers, don't give him the next retrieve. Walk out and pick it up yourself. Give a neutral response and walk away, paying no attention to the pup. Again, you're not correcting, you're just not rewarding. Your attention and energy will not

Water introductions should be made on warm days with you standing in the water with the pup.

become a reinforcer. The dog will eventually return. If not, a check cord may become a temporary necessity until the dog establishes the habit of returning.

By establishing the trailing memory pattern, you can drop bumpers just out of sight in taller grass or across a small ditch and increase the complexity of the retrieve. The 180 trailing memory becomes the foundation for many other types of exercises in the Wildrose Way. One important note: Fun bumper retrieves are just thrown around for entertainment with no discipline required. They are commonly used in many programs for rewards. Avoid fun bumpers. Why wreck a perfectly good training session where patience and calm behavior has been encouraged, valued, and rewarded with a tossed bumper that encourages the dog to break and run? At this early age, the retrieve itself, affection, and the tone of your voice will be reward enough. Using a treat as a reward for a retrieve is also not advisable; the puppy will commonly drop the bumper to accept the treat, which creates another problem.

INTRODUCING WATER

An excellent way to introduce a very young pup to water is in a child's wading pool with the water warmed by the sun. Once accustomed to the water in the pool, progress to the shallows of a pond. The first exposure to open water should be a fun experience. Walk in with the pup and allow him to splash around only up to his knees. Use a shoreline to set up a single trailing memory retrieve. Ensure success by keeping the retrieve in the shallow water, and then follow up with a 180 double.

Once the pup is accustomed to short retrieves in shallow water, you can create a few retrieves in which the pup will lose footing, requiring a swim. When the pup seems confident in the water, wade out with the youngster to just where he can still stand. Toss the bumper a few feet farther into slightly deeper water, just enough that two or three swimming strokes will reach

This is a Wildrose bumper feather-laced with a game-bird wing.

the target. Wade back a few steps, turn, and send him out. When the pup bounds out, he will gradually run out of footing and swim a few strokes, get the bumper, and return. Slowly increase the distance, but again do only two or three retrieves a day. Keep the interest keen and build anticipation, but always demand quiet, calm behavior before you release for any retrieve.

INTRODUCING BIRDS

Using a puppy bumper, tape on a couple of game-bird wings. You want to see how the pup reacts. You should only introduce feathers and the pup's first bird in a confined area. Set the dog up to win and avoid mistakes. Get him accustomed to the feathered bumper before you introduce a bird. Use small puppy bumpers for short single trailing memory and 180 double retrieves, and then hide the feathered bumpers in cover for a bit of an enjoyable hunt. Make it a game, but play it infrequently to maintain keen enthusiasm and interest. Also, using too many feathered bumpers or birds may result in disinterest in regular training bumpers. Be selective in your use of the feathers.

Next, introduce a small, partially frozen bird, such as a teal, quail, or pigeon. Frozen birds discourage chewing. Do not use doves, as their feathers come off easily in the pup's mouth, and avoid large birds that are too heavy for the youngster, which may promote mouthing or dropping. Never offer a soiled or bloody bird; the taste may be displeasing. Pigeons are great on land, but never in the water. Again, don't overstimulate the puppy with too many birds.

For retrievers, only infrequent experiences are necessary for introductory bird retrieves and scenting development. For flushers, a bit more hunting of cold game in cover is in order. Perhaps try a flush of a planted bird (released or tethered), but not to the point of overexcitement. For pointers, plant live birds to establish game finding and the point. Use cold game for retrieves.

COMMANDS

Every command should now be preceded with either the dog's name or the word "no." Examples: "No, sit," "No, heel," "Deke, sit," or "Deke, heel." What's the difference? "No" is a de-select, a command to leave an object alone, to remain still, or to heel away. The dog's name becomes the indicator for action and the release for the retrieve. When you go out with your pup to place a bumper as a memory, say "No, heel," to indicate that the pup should not go in for the pickup at that time. Then, turn and walk away. At the appropriate distance, face the bumper and wait

a few moments. The dog should not move until he hears his name. The dog's name is the call for action, the retrieve command. This practice will be extremely helpful in developing steadiness and manners during group work. The dog retrieves by name only. If he doesn't hear his name, he should be rock steady. Practice name recognition skills in group work with other dogs. Perfect name recognition to the point that no dog in the group moves other than by name, as each is called out of line to their handler.

WHISTLE

By this time, your puppy should be responding well to both verbal commands and the whistle for recall and sit. Now you can begin to eliminate the verbal command by adopting a transition sequence. As you walk along, stop and instruct the pup to sit using the whistle and the verbal command in this order: whistle blast, "sit," whistle blast. The student will associate the whistle tone with the known word. Soon, you can fade the verbal "sit" and use only the whistle. Similarly, you can fade the verbal command "here" in the same manner, using only the recall whistle. The same process applies to pointers for "whoa" and "come" to the whistle.

SUMMARY OF THE SECOND 14 WEEKS

By now you should have an eager learner on your hands. In the past few months, you have introduced him to the life he will lead and the skills he will use to lead it. You have established trust and leadership and set parameters; now begins the process of refining the pup into the sporting companion you envisioned. There are some imminent physical changes in the pup that you must address, but these next few weeks present an opportunity to further strengthen the foundation of the relationship and the core skills of sit, stay, here, and heel.

Teething

At around four-and-a-half to six months old, youngsters begin to cut their adult teeth and their gums become quite sore. They lose their teeth in the jaw exactly where they will be carrying the bumper. A sore mouth will cause the pup to drop, which is a problem that you'll have to train out later. *Stop retrieving!*

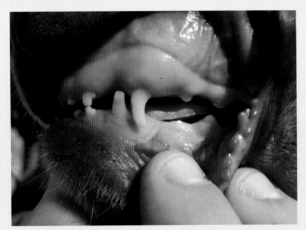

Stop retrieving when teeth begin to emerge.

The first sign of the change generally appears in the jaw with redness of the gum or a touch of blood that may appear on the bumper. Stop retrieving until all the adult teeth are in. The last teeth to appear will be the canines. During this period focus on other essential skills, such as obedience, socialization, and desensitization. Continue to build upon early starts, emphasizing an increase in the duration of the core obedience fundamentals and introductions. Work on place training on platforms, water stands, ATVs, and dog hides. Emphasize steadiness while other dogs work. Tie the dog out and add distractions.

By this point, the puppy walker has been retired and replaced with a cloth slip lead or the rubberized Wildrose combination lead. Move heel work to realistic conditions, such as fields where you vary the speed, change directions, zigzag, and negotiate obstacles. You are working with a slip lead to emphasize the correct position in heel (see the Off-Lead Heel section in Chapter Four for more information). You want the pup to stay in position because it's comfortable for both the dog and the handler. The correct position is on the left or right side of the handler—your preference—with the dog's shoulder at your leg. The dog's head should be out front a bit so he can see to the right or left and keep up with the action.

You don't want the pup sniffing the ground. Discourage this by gently pushing his nose up with your foot and getting him to watch you as opposed to sniffing. Dogs with great scenting abilities are distracted by scent and want to use their powerful noses on the ground. That is not a sign of hunting; it is a sign of distraction.

Use this period of non-retrieving to further solidify the dog responding only to his name. Say the dog's name, and then get eye contact for about three seconds before the command "heel." Give the dog time to process the command. If you don't give him adequate time to think, interpret, and respond, he's really just emulating your body language and not responding to the verbal command.

Incorporate denials. With the pup sitting at heel, throw out a bumper and say "No, sit." Then, walk out and get it yourself. Denials build steadiness. Toss bumpers around different sides of the pup. With every toss say "No, sit," redirecting his eyes back to you.

Begin to introduce sit to flush by using denials. As you walk along with the pup at heel, throw the bumper, stop walking, and blow the sit whistle. This is the beginning phase of training for sit to the flush and steadiness to flyers.

Obedience training spills over into other areas, including whistle stops, recall, place training in the field, redirecting eyes, steadiness, focus, and patience. So many things boil down to four basic core skills: sit, stay, here, and heel. This month-and-a-half in which retrieves are not allowed is a great time to refine core skills and expand valuable introductions.

During this time of yard work the pup can learn many valuable behaviors: the lessons of immediate response commands; developing the pup's self-confidence by accomplishing new things in many different environmental settings; solidifying a relationship of trust and confidence with the pup; establishing that all birds are not his; and reinforcing the concept of steadiness and patience in all things before a reward. Then, when those teeth are in, you are ready to return to the retrieving skills of gundog training and begin the final phase of backgrounding (six to eight months of age).

The correct heel position should be with the dog's shoulder parallel to the handler's leg.

CHAPTER 4

Foundational Excellence

■ Refining the Essentials: Six to Eight Months

More than a decade ago I had the pleasure of training with Bill Meldrum, then the head retriever trainer for the Queen of England at her estate, Sandringham. I asked him how he started his young dogs. His very crisp British response was, "Six weeks on lead obedience and six weeks off." He was referring to "starting" with a pup at about 10 months of age! Now, that *is* making haste slowly compared with most hunters' expectations in the Americas.

Very simply put, if you're going to produce a great sporting dog the positive way, one that is consistently steady, patient, focused, and willing to honor in the field, you're going to have to lay down an exceptionally strong foundation of obedience and allow the pup to mature a bit. Meldrum's 12-week concentration on basic obedience before proceeding further into gundog training would be a big commitment for anyone. Are you prepared to commit the necessary time between six and eight months of age to build foundational excellence? Your objective in this valuable time period is to solidify obedience under a variety of conditions and afford time for the pup to mature.

Almost every control skill expected in the field has something to do with obedience: stop to the whistle, steady to shot, ignoring diversions, delivering to hand, steady to flush, backing a dog on point, or taking the correct hand signal. If these skills are not obedience, then what are they? The puppy is now six months old and you have laid down a solid early foundation of essential behaviors. Now is the time to refine these skills and build toward excellence.

Six to eight months of age is the period in which you refine and formalize obedience skills to the point of a predictable habit. You are also introducing a system that Wildrose refers to as causal relationships, or linking and chaining behaviors together. This process requires remaining true to the spirit of the Wildrose Way, a positive, slowly progressive way of training where one set of skills is built upon another. Introduce the skill or command, set the dog up to succeed, repeat the behavior to the point of habit, then introduce another related behavior, creating a chaining concept.

Although the Wildrose training approach is largely positive, occasionally a correction of an infraction will become necessary. During the early stages of background training, you should avoid the use of physical force, but now moving into the six- to eight-month time frame, you may judiciously begin to use corrections if necessary to stop an unwanted behavior, reinforce boundaries, and ensure compliance when the dog ignores known commands.

CORRECTIONS

The Wildrose correction philosophy was discussed at length in Chapter Two. Review that section, as you have now approached the age at which the youngster will have the capacity to understand reasonable, well-timed corrections for an infraction, and can learn how to avoid that behavior in the future. Your dog needs to learn that there are consequences when he disregards or ignores commands and corrections for behaviors that violate established boundaries and etiquette. But remember to never correct for an unknown command or make a correction when the dog is confused. If the dog doesn't know what to do in the first place, force would be inappropriate, not to mention damaging to your youngster's trust and confidence.

Also, don't correct failures in performance. Ignoring a known command deserves a correc-

An effective correction may entail only a stern look, direct eye contact, and a gruff tone of voice to get results.

tion. A mistake in training does not. Failures are frustrating for you to be sure, but they are for your student as well. Back up a couple of steps in your training to the familiar, simplify, reteach the basics, and set the dog up to succeed to get the intended result. Recognize the difference between "can't do" and "won't do." Nothing is gained by using force to teach a lesson or skill.

Corrections build boundaries as well as stop unwanted behaviors. Consider place, for example. Place establishes a boundary. If the dog gets off place, he should be punished and put back on place. If he creeps off, he gets put back. If he jumps off a water stand, he gets put back. Each time, return the dog to the scene of the infraction. You are always establishing boundaries. Unacceptable behavior reaps discomfort; acceptable behavior reaps pleasure. The dog will learn to make the appropriate choices. Remember, dogs are pleasure seekers. If the punishment is properly timed and severe enough to cause discomfort, the dog will avoid the displeasure associated with the unwanted behavior in the future. Contrarily, with positive training and positive habit formation, the dog simply learns no other option and behaviors become predictable habits. Think of this comparison in human terms. Why does a person drive the speed limit? Respect of the law, safety, and lower insurance premiums (reward), or fear of getting caught violating the law and receiving a hefty fine (avoidance). The dog has a similar mentality: respect/reward or fear/avoidance.

THE WILDROSE CYCLICAL TRAINING MODEL

Over the years, Wildrose has developed a highly effective training model referred to as cyclical training. The cyclical training concept is based on how canines think and learn as opposed to humans. Humans usually approach things in linear fashion—with a beginning, middle, and end. Humans have not always lived in this manner, though. Before the encroachment of modern, urban lifestyles, we too lived in balance with the cycles of nature like the creatures around us. Farmers lived by these cycles, as did Native Americans. "Modern man" has largely forgotten the laws of nature and similarly the natural learning patterns of animals, but dogs have not.

Dogs live in a cyclical world and think in cyclical patterns, quite dissimilar to their human partners. The Wildrose approach to teaching canines involves the concept of those cycles. Many of the training patterns are set up using loops, circles, and even S-shapes, concepts totally understood by canines.

Initially, for retrievers, you'll want to overcome their tendency not to run at distances in a straight line for the very reason just mentioned: dogs work, hunt, think, and travel in cyclical patterns. While these patterns are desirable for a flushing spaniel or walking hunters' pointers that you want to keep in close range, the initial drills for retrievers should condition the dog to run in a straight line to make those longer retrieves. The most common of these exercises are the trailing memories and sight memories. Once proficient, you can move to cyclical configurations to enhance the dog's memory.

The circular patterns create a better approach to the dog's mindset and enhance the dog's ability to remember and learn. The concepts at this stage of the dog's development are completely applicable for pointing and flushing breeds as well.

The second application of the cyclical approach is the structure of the daily training plan. The cyclical training plan has three distinct sections. Each section may vary in duration, location, topic of instruction based upon the time available for training, and the needs of the dog. For example, a four-month-old pup's attention span requires a shorter, more focused session, while a starter's attention level may involve longer sessions with more variables.

Part I: The Ramp-Up

The ramp-up has multiple purposes:

1– Reaffirming leadership—who leads, who follows.

2– Reinforcing patience and known obedience skills.

3– Burning energy first to facilitate learning.

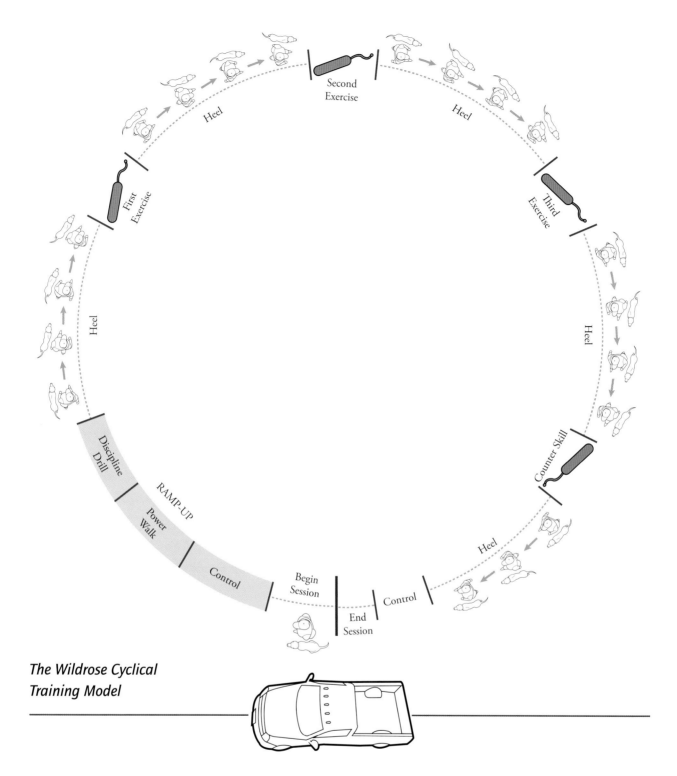

The Wildrose Cyclical Training Model

✦ RAMP-UP COMPONENTS

CONTROL: Every training session begins with the dog under control. Establish patience right from the start, at the pen, crate, or vehicle. The dog should sit quietly while you place the lead, wait to be invited out, and then exit under control.

You should remain still and quiet, waiting patiently while the youngster calms on his own initiative. You want a focused attitude before you begin. The student wants to go, but to get what he wants, he must give you what you want— calm, controlled, patient behavior. Once he is

The ramp-up power walk burns excess energy.

quiet, begin slowly walking at heel for 20 to 25 yards. You will be surprised how quickly the pup will mimic your stable behavior. Your energy level should be slow, patient, and quiet—exactly what you want to see in your dog.

POWER WALK: Walking at heel on lead reinforces leadership and control. Next, take a long, brisk, energetic walk without stops, retrieves, or any other activities. You're burning the dog's energy to gain focus. It's far better to deal with explosive energy now than trying to deal with it while teaching a lesson. At Wildrose, we discovered long ago that taking pups straight to the field for training is problematic. They are too full of energy and excitement to truly focus and learn. One thing to remember: When working with a young pup, burning energy is a much greater percentage of the overall training session than with an older dog that has more self-control.

DISCIPLINE: The discipline component reinforces obedience skills and promotes patience and concentration at the beginning of the session. Involve denials (thrown bumpers you pick up yourself), tennis ball rolls, reverse heel, heel work in square patterns (see Chapter Five), sit to the flush, sit to the whistle, and agility exercises all to reinforce steadiness, known commands, and leadership. You should be seen as in control. Read the dog. Patience, eye contact, and focus will tell you when the dog is ready to learn.

Part II: Training Exercises

At Wildrose, we normally present three individual training exercises or lessons each day following the ramp-up. For the young pup, each lesson will be short. Over time, duration and complexity will be gradually increased. Heel work is accomplished between each session to

This starter takes an excellent line as a counter skill for the day's training.

bring energy and excitement levels down as you move to new areas. Walk with the dog to the first area. Complete the exercise, then move on to a new location, then to a third. Lessons may be similar or varied depending on the needs and objectives of the training for the day.

Part III: Counter Skill

After completing three learning activities, use a counter-skill exercise to conclude the training session. The counter skill revisits a known, familiar skill, often one that the dog enjoys, but is unrelated to the three training activities experienced on the day. The counter skill ends the training session with a win, a success, and it helps to reaffirm the value of previously taught skills. Since it is dissimilar to the exercises previously performed, it establishes the dog's ability to easily switch from one skill to another. For example, perhaps you have completed three dif-

ferent lining activities that day. The counter skill might be a hunting cover exercise. If you have taught quite a bit of handling, you might end with a familiar long-line trailing memory.

Finally, return back to the pen or the truck. Expect patience while kenneling. It is very important not to allow the dog to be out of control at the end of a session, as it destroys the concept of patience in all things. This is the final behavior of the session, and the dog will remember it.

This cyclical model is effective because it is logical to the dog, is designed to entrench behavioral patterns that deal with high energy, and establishes your control right from the start. Also, you may realize that it duplicates the hunting experience: beginning under control at the vehicle, getting to the field, and requiring discipline and patience as decoys are set up or blockers get into position for the walk-up. That's the ramp-up. Next, action and excitement are intertwined with expected calm, patient behaviors. This is established with training lessons separated by heel work. On the hunt, shooting action is also separated by periods requiring patient behavior from the dog, exactly as established in your daily training routine. Last, the counter skill may be experienced when a dog has actively quartered a field, then must use a separate set of skills to run in a straight line to retrieve a wounded bird. This model was developed by hunters for hunters and is suitable for all four phases of training—yard work through the first hunt. It offers flexibility, reduces the likelihood that corrections will be necessary due to excess energy and inattention, duplicates the hunt, and, most importantly, the dog understands its cyclical format.

OFF-LEAD HEEL

The pup is between six and eight months old and can understand the lessons of consequence so now you can begin to solidify the proper heel position. Not remaining in position while walking or pulling on the lead results in discomfort, a correction. The lead and slip collar should remain as loose as possible at all times around

The Wildrose combination lead has three distinctive parts: the slip collar, steady tab, and detachable lead.

As the pup progresses at heel work, the long lead is detached from the steady tab, which can be dropped in a progression to off-lead heel and may be retained while the dog makes a retrieve without interfering.

the dog's neck. Do not tug on the lead to pull your dog back into position. This never works. It is the snap of the lead that is effective. A slip lead that remains loose around the neck can be easily snapped sharply to mimic the biting sensation of the pack when the dog is out of position. If you have a tight lead around the neck, a fixed collar, or a device across the bridge of the dog's nose, you will not duplicate the necessary snap.

At Wildrose, we use a very strong synthetic rubber lead and collar called the combination lead. It's actually a three-piece, British-style slip lead. The collar section, a steady tab, and the lead are all connected with easy-to-release latches that allow you to use all or part of it for the desired result. For instance, just using the steady tab clipped to the slip collar allows the pup to run along without stepping on it. When you snap the lead for a cor-

rection, snap it in front of your body as if to pull the dog sideways. Snapping or pulling to the rear creates a resistance that the dog will naturally pull against. You are not training sled dogs here. The ultimate goal is off-lead heel, so working the loose lead approach is important to master.

In advancing to off-lead heel, train to heel along a surface that the dog will not want to sniff,

A: *This shows proper heel work and lead position.* **B:** *This shows a correction across or in front of the body.* **C:** *The pup returns to the proper heel position.*

such as concrete or pavement. Grass offers a lot of scent distractions. Use a straightedge like a curb or sidewalk where you can keep the dog moving in the right position. Encourage the pup to stay in position with cues and verbal incentives. If he strays from the straightedge onto the grass, snap the lead to correct. The edge is initially a useful guide to help slowly fade the lead's use.

Keep the pup's eyes on you. To begin, use a lure such as a bumper or a treat to keep the dog's eyes on you. Tap your whistle on your belt. Keep the pup checking in. When he's not watching, that's when you change directions.

Make abrupt 90-degree turns, walk across the road, and go up the other side. Anytime the dog gets out of position, reverse the direction or make a 90-degree turn to get him back to focusing on you and where he should be. If he drifts ahead, turn and go the opposite direction, each time with the correct snap of the lead.

A: *This shows proper position at heel while moving forward.*

B: *This shows proper position for reverse heel.*

Your pace should vary. Referring to the three Ts of communication from Chapter Two, here's where tempo again becomes important. If the dog is highly excitable, you should be slow as molasses in wintertime during every interaction. The dog will gradually begin to mimic your behavior. The opposite is true for a lethargic dog. Introduce some excitement and enthusiasm. Use tempo to modify the dog's energy to the desired level.

Precede every command with the dog's name, and get eye contact before you give the command. Reinforce sit, stay, and whoa (standing motionless), and remember that stay is intended for the long-term; never call the dog to

The combination lead may be flipped around the dog's body and draped over the shoulders as a progression to off-lead heel.

Proper Placement of a Slip Collar or Lead

The slip lead is placed on the dog in the shape of a P for left-side heel.

The slip lead is placed on the dog in the shape of a 9 for right-side heel.

This is the proper placement of the British slip lead for left-side heel.

you from stay. Go back and collect him. Remote stay requires that the dog remain in place for a longer period as the handler leaves the area. Disappear around the corner of a building, then reappear to see if the pup is still at stay. Always return to the dog and position yourself so the sitting dog is in the heel position, make eye contact, offer a reward, and heel away.

Gradually loosen the lead by letting your dog carry it rather than drag it. Flip the lead to the outside of the dog's body, which encourages him slightly toward you. Gradually, you can move one step closer to off-lead heel by dropping the lead across the shoulders and allowing the dog to carry it as you walk. If you need to grab the lead to correct the dog's position, it is in easy reach. The flat combination lead will lie perfectly balanced right across the shoulder. Soon, you will be able to use just the steady tab, which can be dropped and allowed to hang free because it is short and won't drag. Progress to both on- and off-lead heel work in different locations: grass fields, woodlands, shallow water, or negotiating ditches and obstacles, including as many situations and environments as possible.

REFINING STEADINESS

WALKING AWAY: This is a simple exercise to evaluate a dog's steadiness to your body movement. With the pup at sit or standing still in the heel position, abruptly walk away without saying a word. Without a command to do so, the pup should not move. If he does, replace him in the exact location, correct with a stern, "No, sit," and walk away. Return to the heel position and walk away again. Circle the dog again, returning to the heel position. Walk away. On the third or fourth repetition use the same exact body language, but this time say the dog's name, get eye contact, instruct "heel," and move with the dog at your side. Your prospect is learning to distinguish between responding to the command versus responding to body language.

APPROACHING THE DOG: If you are returning to your dog in a stationary position, do NOT walk straight at the dog. Do so and he's likely to stand up and move toward you. Either circle all

the way around the dog in a loop ending up in the heel position or approach the dog from the front and make an abrupt hook into the correct position. The dog should not move at your approach. This level of steadiness will be highly valued in the duck blind. Again, the dog should not move unless he hears a command, even with your approach.

AFFECTION: Where you touch the dog for a reward is important. Petting the shoulders or under the jaw are the two preferred locations when encouraging the dog to remain calm. Petting on the shoulders with the leader's arm across the dog's back is more of a pack-dominant position. Petting underneath the jaw causes the dog to lift his head, which is important for delivery to hand.

Sit down by the dog. In many hunting situations, you will be sitting by the dog rather than standing. If you have only trained standing up, the dog will have a completely different reaction when you're sitting. Eventually, whether you are

Hook   Circle

There are two options for the proper approach to a dog in a stationary position: the hook or the circle.

Give praise by stroking the dog under the chin or across the shoulder.

sitting or standing, there should be no difference in the dog's behavior or response to commands.

STEADY TO FLUSH

By now, the dog understands sit to the whistle, but you want to get a conditioned response of steady to the flush. You are going to build on the foundation you've established with the pup to sit or stand when you stop at heel. Every time you stop and throw something, or stop abruptly, the dog is conditioned to sit or stand motionless. It requires time and repetition, but the training will pay huge dividends out in the field when a bird flushes. A dog that breaks is a distraction and a danger on a hunt, potentially putting itself in the

Early starts for sit to the flush: As the bumper is thrown, stop, lift on the lead, and blow the sit whistle.

This shows steady to the flush using live, tethered pigeons.

command. (As a reminder, sit requires the dog to sit down, while whoa requires the dog to stop but remain standing.) If the dog doesn't sit, lift on the lead. With repetition and consistency, the dog will learn to respond in a variety of situations. Throw a bumper, a ball, even a Frisbee. Variation creates solidity.

Each flush is a denial. Always pick up the bumper, bird, ball, or whatever you're using as a distraction. With a pointing breed, use "whoa" since you don't want a pointer to sit. Walk along and throw out a bumper, stop and let the dog focus on it, walk out, and pick it up. Walk back to the dog, reward steadiness, and move on. Establish this routine as an absolute reaction, and later in training it will be easy to progress to the use of live birds and gunfire.

line of gunfire. Steadiness to flush and birds in flight is a valuable behavior for pointers, flushers, and even retrievers.

As you're walking during heel work, pitch a bumper abruptly and stop, giving the sit or whoa

REMOTE STEADY

Remote sit and stay are important in keeping the dog rock steady when distractions occur and you are not positioned next to the dog. When bumpers are thrown or when other dogs, chil-

Early starts for remote steady: Two students sit patiently as a short retrieve is made in front of them.

The ultimate test for remote steady: Prepare your dog to sit motionless outside the blind or boat as birds approach and only retrieve on command.

dren, or small animals run by, the dog should not move, even when sitting at a distance. Distractions don't always occur when the dog is next to you. Initially, you can make remote steadiness a bit easier for the youngster with the use of a platform, building on established place training behaviors, but ultimately you'll need your dog to remain steady in any location, even in the middle of a field, outside the blind, or on the front of a boat. Remote steadiness will be a foundation for a number of advanced skills.

Remote steadiness conditioning should involve: denials of thrown bumpers, tethered birds in flight, other dogs working, and any type of distraction that one may encounter afield. Whether you are in sight of the dog or not, the behavior should be predictable. You are developing the patience that will help prevent breaking

and noisiness from overexcitement. If your dog sits patiently and does not anticipate every retrieve even when alone, the result will be a much quieter and more patient hunting companion.

RECALL WITH DISTRACTIONS

It's important to condition a dog to recall despite any distractions. In the initial stages, this is best accomplished by reverse heel. As you are walking a straight line with your young dog at heel, just reverse directions, use the recall whistle signal, and back away with the pup on lead. As you back away, toss out a bumper or ball, but keep blasting the whistle to encourage the dog to come while ignoring the diversion. Another approach is to call the young dog to come along a chain-link fence. As the pup approaches, toss the bumper over the fence to

A: Back away with the pup on lead while blowing the whistle for recall, steady to the flush. *B:* As the pup approaches, toss the bumper as a flush. Simultaneously lift on the lead for a sit and blow the whistle. *C:* Maintain steadiness to the flush. Pick up the bumper as a denial.

the far side while continuing the recall. The fence prevents any chance of a switch and, over time, the dog will begin to ignore the bumper toss.

RECALL, STEADY TO FLUSH

Once the recall with distractions is solid, move on to recall/sit to the flush. Use the same approach, but incorporate off-lead heel along with stop/sit to the whistle and a hand signal just as you toss the bumper. At first, make an abrupt stop as you walk backward. The body language, whistle, and hand signal indicate that the dog should stop and sit just as the bumper flies. Next, while heeling forward, abruptly back away and continue at reverse heel, then toss the bumper. Encourage the dog to stop or sit at the sight of the tossed bumper without any other signal. Eliminate using the hand signal and keep backing away; only use the stop whistle in association with the tossed bumper. You're minimizing the tendency for the dog to follow your body language, making the

whistle and the bumper flight more significant. Much later, after gunfire introduction, use the same procedures to have the dog sit on the shot and thrown bumper rather than on the whistle. In all cases, the flushed bumper is a denial.

The lessons suggested above are specific refinements to the early start of heel, sit, stay, and here. Once the dog is fairly consistent in the basics of obedience, many handlers tend to move on too quickly. But with canine training, being fairly consistent will fail consistently when the dog is faced with complexity and distractions. Under pressure or confusion, a dog will revert to the most familiar entrenched behavior or attempt to escape the situation. A predictable desired reaction must become the default behavior, an entrenched habit, if you want a fine shooting companion in any situation. Take a lesson from the Queen of England's own retriever trainer—commit the extra time to allowing your youngster to mature and perfect the fundamentals of obedience to the point of refinement.

■ Canine Communication

This two-month bridge between backgrounding and the start of basic gundog training is a great time to concentrate on evaluating your dog's behaviors to discover what he is really thinking and communicating through actions and body language. Your dog is always communicating, but what is he telling you? As pack leader, it is your job to know. In reading your dog, here are things to look for:

TAIL: Recognize tail position, where your dog normally carries his tail. If a dog's tail is higher than normal, that can be an indication of dominance or assertiveness. A lowered tail can be an indication of concern or worry, and if it drops severely between the legs, that can be an indica-

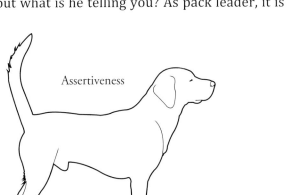

Assertiveness

This dog is assertive, dominant, in control.

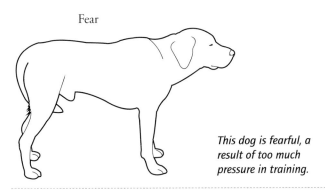

Fear

This dog is fearful, a result of too much pressure in training.

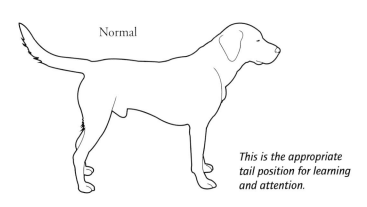

Normal

This is the appropriate tail position for learning and attention.

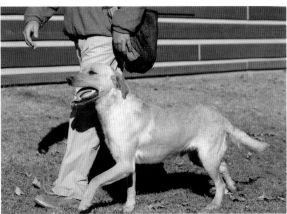

Trainers can shape eye contact with praise and consistency.

Licking lips after an interaction is indicative of submission.

tion of fear or too much pressure in training. Determine the normal position and use the tail as an indicator of the dog's mindset. If it has dropped just a bit and is wagging in short, fast little strokes, that's a good indicator of what you want—biddability, focus, and attention.

EYES: This one is fairly easy. Eye contact is an indicator of attention, an attempt by the dog to read and interpret you. When a dog looks away in training to avoid the command or detach himself from the lesson, this is an avoidance behavior. The dog looking away when you attempt eye contact indicates that you are not in charge of the situation. Direct eye contact indicates focus or seeking information.

LICKING THE LIPS: If you give a command, make a correction, or are working on building a boundary and you see the dog drop his head and subtly lick his lips, that is a sign of submissiveness and biddability. That lick means the dog understands the instruction, has retained the lesson,

or has understood the correction and is accepting you in a leadership position.

RISING HACKLES: We've all seen this one. When the hackles or hair on the dog's back stand straight up it is a sign that he is attempting to assert dominance over or intimidate another dog or a person. It is easy to see this behavior coming, so you can make the appropriate correction or divert the dog's attention away from the situation. Snap the lead and say, "No, heel," or "No, sit." Interrupt and divert attention by making the dog do another behavior, a redirect (see Chapter Six more information).

ROLLING OVER: If the dog is at heel and suddenly tries to stop and roll over on his back, the inappropriate thing to do is stop. Just keep moving at

Rolling over is an avoidance strategy.

Although dogs don't talk, they are always communicating. Raised hackles communicate dominance and assertiveness to the approaching dog.

Leaning against the handler or placing a foot on top of the handler's foot indicates a lack of acceptance of the leader's position.

the same pace, not snatching or grabbing the dog directly. Use the lead and just keep moving. If you stop, the dog is in charge. Leaders lead. Granted he might resist, but he will pop up and return to the heel position if you don't allow the tantrum to work.

LEANING AGAINST OR PLACING A FOOT ON TOP OF YOURS WHILE YOU'RE STANDING: The dog is communicating that he devalues your leadership position. Leaning against you is not affection. Push his foot off and push the dog away. If the dog is at home and he puts his head in your lap, that's affection and you should not correct that. Learn the difference between the dog's intentions.

MALES MARKING REPEATEDLY: Marking by peeing repeatedly is a sign of assertiveness and inattention. Male canines can retain small amounts of urine for marking purposes. The practice has nothing to do with the elimination needs of the animal; the dog is simply marking territory. Stop the behavior at the first sign.

As much as you are using your communication skills of timing, tempo, and tone, you also need to understand what the dog is communicating to you and those around him:

RELATIONSHIP PROBLEMS: If a dog jumps on you, mouths your hand or your arm, bursts through the door ahead of you, or stops to sniff on every bush when walking with you or performing an exercise, the dog does not respect you.

POSSESSIVENESS: Taking something and not giving or releasing it, or playing "keep away," is possessiveness. That's dominant prey mentality; you're not in charge.

Dogs will test leadership. When at place, you may see the dog stretch and move around so that half of his body is off the mat or just one paw is on the mat. Is this because the dog is too warm? Or is it a test to see at what point the leader will react? The same challenge may occur with stay. A dog will slide or readjust from the point where he was left in place. This is a creeper; your authority is being tested. Make a correction and replace the dog all the way back to the original spot.

Canine communicators are powerful indicators for the handler. How else will you know what your dog thinks? Dogs don't talk. Every dog differs and so will its body language. It is imperative that you learn what normal behavior is for your dog in order to recognize the changes when they occur.

Fix the Problem Now

When you have a problem there is always a cause. The source could be man-made—a mistake made in training or perhaps a step skipped in the developmental process. Sometimes the problem is the result of the handler not paying attention. Other problems the dog develops on his own, and occasionally the problems are genetic.

There are numerous possible problems you may face, but there are several very common challenges specific to a sporting companion that you should be aware of and prevent before the behaviors become entrenched.

THE CREEPER: The creeper is a dog that is too anxious or perhaps lacks the discipline to remain rock steady at place, sit, or stay. If you leave the dog at sit and walk away and he moves to follow, you have a CIT (Creeper in Training). Generally, the cause of the problem stems from calling the dog too frequently off sit. In the early stages of development, when you put a dog at place or sit, it is better to go back and get him. Later, make it a habit to not call the dog to you from sit unless you are conducting a training exercise, and then only infrequently. The correct response to creeping is to walk back with a scold, pick the dog up by some of the loose skin on the side of the face or a shake of his collar, and physically put him back where he started. A kind voice and leading the dog back will not provide a severe enough correction to overcome the pleasure of creeping. Always return the dog to the original point. It could be 100 yards away, but you must make the trek to be consistent. Be reasonable with the young pup and don't expect him to remain in place for too long a period.

HARD MOUTH: A dog that chews and mangles birds has a hard mouth, a highly undesirable trait in a game dog. Starting a pup too early on real birds with blood and dirty feathers can cause a pup to chew. Plastic bumpers may also encourage chewing. Giving the pup chew toys is a prime culprit, and playing tug-of-war games is detrimental as well. Dogs playing together and tugging on objects really promotes two dysfunctions at once. Finally, improper hold conditioning or a failed attempt at force-fetch can cause hard mouth. Mouthing issues can also be genetic, but the best approach to the potential problem is through prevention.

WHINING: The British call it "squeaking." Too many thrown bumpers and overexcitement create a lack of patience that can cause the dog to become vocal. Sometimes it's genetic. If the parents whine, chances are the pup will, too. Trying to calm a whining dog by stroking or touching is a common mistake. The act—affection—becomes an unintentional reinforce-

This shows an appropriate pack leader correction.

ment. It is best to correct the behavior with a quick, forceful snap of the lead and a verbal correction. If working with other dogs, exile the squeaker from the pack and require him to sit quietly away from the action. Once quiet and patient, he can return to the exercise or shoot. Providing too many thrown bumpers, known as marks, likely will overstimulate anticipation and excitement. Concentrate on memories, which

require patience for each retrieve. In the field, the whiner is always denied a retrieve.

BARKING: Like whining, barking can be a genetic issue, but it may also arise due to enthusiasm, anticipation, or even fear (the alert barker). Your response depends on the situation. For example, do not unintentionally reinforce an alert or nuisance barker by attempting to quiet the dog with a touch, food, or a treat. Divert the dog's attention by getting him to perform an alternate behavior (see the section on redirects in Chapter Six for more information). Barking can become an attention-getting method for the dog. Do not respond to or provide the dog attention when he is barking.

GUN-SHYNESS: This too could be genetic as like produces like, but far more often it relates to the dog's poor introduction to gunfire. Taking a pup on a hunt or the sporting clay range too early—and anything under eight months of age is far too early—or unintentionally startling a pup at an early age with a shot is a sure way to induce gun-shyness. The list of totally inappropriate ways to introduce gunfire and the mistakes people continue to make in this delicate area is long and continues to grow. At this point, just know this: If you test a young dog to see if he is gun-shy, he probably will be. Gunfire introduction should never be a surprise. It's a progressive method that occurs once the starter is well within the basic gundog program, is displaying self-confidence, and is retrieving to hand extremely well.

NON-DELIVERY TO HAND: A dog that runs off with a bumper is displaying possessiveness. This is a pup with a high prey drive, or one that hasn't been properly taught to return at an early age. Examples of situations that promote non-delivery include: a youngster that was allowed to play chase with other dogs or tug-of-war over objects with kids; a pup that has had the spoils of many chew toys or one that has been allowed to run independently, left to his own indulgences; or the "water freaker," a dog who gets in the water and won't come out because of his enjoyable months of free swimming as a youngster. By not training for proper delivery on land first, the starter will learn disobedience in water and will just swim around ignoring commands. Think about the consequences of every interaction with your pup. What is being taught?

AGGRESSION: This can be genetic but can also be situational, patterned behavior or may arise from association with an unstable family pack. Dogs without a stable leader can become territorial or possessive over food, toys, or people. They may become aggressive toward other dogs and try to become pack dominant by picking a fight or raising hackles. Good leadership from you—which means immediately correcting such behaviors—and early socialization are the keys to avoiding the situational aggressive dog.

CHASING GAME: This may begin in the backyard when a pup is running free and chasing squirrels, chipmunks, or rabbits. These behaviors, if not corrected, may become entrenched. One way to correct is to seize any opportunity to confront exciting situations from house cats to park dogs at play. Even pitching a Frisbee across a field in front of the young dog as you walk around is an excellent way to simulate a bird flushing. Allowing the dog to run free and chase other creatures is very detrimental. Don't condition in a behavior that must be trained out later.

FEAR: Situational fear of public places, noise, or people is likely the result of improper social exposure at a young age, or being startled in a certain situation. Remember, dogs are very place-oriented. Anything that the pup is not acclimated to can create a fear factor and he will likely remember the event or place.

Again, at all times you must be thinking about what the dog is learning. If you want a sporting companion that performs well in all situations, become a problem solver, and, most importantly, avoid dysfunction in the first place. Make haste slowly.

Gun-shyness is largely man-made. The practice of surprising a pup with gunfire introduction is inexcusable.

UP TO THIS POINT, THE FUNDAMENTALS *of the Wildrose Way have been largely universal between the breeds. At an early age, canine behavior and basic obedience are the same for all. You may now find a divergence beginning to occur in the applications of the methods as they relate to specific breeds such as retrievers, flushers, or pointers. A bit of refinement in the application of the methods may now be in order. The Wildrose Way is applicable for retrievers and flushers, but with slight modification the methods can also benefit close-working pointers—dogs that will remain under control, handle well, retrieve to hand, and remain steady to the point, back, and flush. The Wildrose Way is a highly flexible approach to gundog development. You are encouraged to modify the methods discussed to fit the specific needs for your dog and hunting situation.*

FIELD TRAINING

CHAPTER 5

Gundog Basics: Part I

f you and your gundog prospect have completed Section One of this book, you have likely made tremendous progress. You have established a working relationship based on trust and respect. Essential foundational skills are entrenched and your dog has become a super learner, an eager and willing student. Your learner is now seven to eight months old and ready both mentally and physically to enter the most significant phase of his development—training and preparing for actual hunting situations. Until now, you have focused on obedience and acclimating the dog to the world around it. For the next five to six months, the primary objective of the Wildrose basic gundog course is to produce a classic sporting dog hunting companion—specifically a game-finder—a dog with virtues of high value to the wingshooting enthusiast. Once completed, you will have a dog that is ready to transition into the hunt and will have the skills necessary to move into advanced training after the first hunting season.

The Seven Core Skills

In this chapter, you will focus on the first four skills: obedience, steadiness and honoring, delivery to hand, and lining memories.

1 – OBEDIENCE: The basis of all phases of field work. What is steadiness, honor, delivery to hand, casting, and recall if not obedience? Obedience is the cornerstone of the skills you will be developing.

2 – STEADINESS AND HONORING: Sitting quietly, not running in, not interfering with another dog's retrieve, steady to flush and shot, or backing a point.

3 – DELIVERY TO HAND: Picking and delivering a bird gently to hand without dropping or mouthing it.

4 – LINING MEMORIES: Taking an initial direction of travel for an unseen or seen bird and carrying that line to the fall area without distraction.

5 – HANDLING: Responding to whistle signals and taking directions by hand signals.

6 – HUNTING COVER: Aggressively searching cover to locate game.

7 – MARKING: Visually sighting with pinpoint accuracy a bird that has fallen and going directly to the location when sent.

■ Core Gundog Skills: Obedience through Lining Memories

There are seven core gundog skills vital to the development of a wingshooting companion; these skills should become the guide for your Wildrose basic training. This chapter addresses the first four—obedience, steadiness and honoring, delivery to hand, and lining memories—and explains the methods necessary to develop these skills, many of which build on the essential foundational behaviors that you have focused on since the pup first entered your home. People often ask, "When can I take my dog hunting?" The answer is when your dog has been thoroughly introduced to, and proven competent in, all seven core gundog skills.

OBEDIENCE

Impeccable obedience is a must in the development of a polished hunting dog. While this may seem redundant considering all the work you've completed previously, it is actually a further refinement of the basic skills established early with your pup. What you have accomplished with close control on lead must now be perfected at distances off lead. Refining obedience is the perfect ramp-up in the cyclical model—after the energy burn has occurred and the tone for the day's training has been established. The harmony of your handling and the dog's obedience make up the glue that holds all the hunting skills together. Make sure it's superglue.

Heel Work

Remaining in the proper position at heel at all times is now mandatory whether on the lead or off. The dog must remain steady, in the correct position, and focused on you despite any distractions or terrain changes. Your objective is off-lead heel with the dog remaining in the proper position no matter what he encounters or what direction you take. You cannot heel a dog on lead effectively or safely while hunting.

The fourth core skill is lining directly to a bird despite any barriers.

Off-lead heel begins on lead with the lead slowly being faded out with the use of the steady tab, then just the collar. Incorporate all types of terrain; cross ditches; practice going under fences, which will involve sit and recall; vary your pace; and switch directions frequently. The dog should remain focused on you in the field or marsh. The first objective is to have no tension on the lead. The lead is only a correctional tool, not a steering device. Flip the lead over the dog's back as described in Chapter Four. Next, drop the lead across the dog's shoulders and continue to walk. Then, use only the steady tab. With the dog in position and attentive, simply drop the tab. Avoid dragging a lead or a check cord, which would apply resistance around the collar, making the transition to off-lead heel much more difficult.

The final step is heeling off lead with only the Wildrose slip collar in place. Even after your dog is performing well off lead, frequently revisit heel work on lead. Too much off-lead heeling can make a dog a bit sloppy. Now that you have estab- lished a progressive method of working from on lead to off lead, you can use that method to progress to other exercises that will further refine heel work off lead.

Reverse Heel

The best way to reinforce recall without creat- ing a creeper is reverse heel. As a reminder, a creeper is a dog that moves around when left supposedly still in one place. Calling a dog off sit, stay, place, or whoa repeatedly produces a CIT (Creeper in Training). Avoid contributing to this problem by not calling the dog off sit. Practice recall with a whistle or voice commands by using reverse heel rather than calling the dog off sit or place. With your dog at heel, move forward and abruptly begin to walk backward. The dog will turn to follow. Continue to walk backward away from the dog at the same pace and give your recall command. You are teaching the recall com- mand without compromising steadiness.

A: Move forward with the dog at heel. B: Back away at a 90-degree angle while maintaining the same pace. C: Turn into the dog to change direction. D: Walk forward with the dog at heel. E: Change direction once again at a 90-degree angle and back away.
F: Continue to back until you reach the starting point, then change direction and continue.

Polish the dog's ability to stay on the correct side of your body in the heel position using reverse heel squares. If the dog is heeling on your left, heel forward, then back away from the dog at a 90-degree angle to your original path. He should turn 90 degrees to his right and come as you continue to back away. Then, turn 90 degrees again toward the dog and walk forward in the opposite direction from where you began. Teach the dog on lead to wheel around in front of you to the proper heel position. Next, back away again at a 90-degree angle and repeat the sequence. You'll find you are making a big square. A reverse heel square is an excellent method to perfect off-lead heel work.

Perfecting Sit to the Whistle Off Lead

Once your dog is doing well heeling off lead, polish sit to the whistle by heeling forward and blowing the whistle as you keep walking. The dog should sit immediately, even as you walk away. Ultimately, you want consistent stops with the whistle only—no signal, eye contact, or body language involved. The body language says continue, but the whistle says stop. The whistle has become more important as a communicator. Again, begin on lead and progress with success until you can fade out all signals but the whistle.

Walk Aways

Introduced in Chapter Four, your goal is to walk away from the sitting dog that is off lead without a command and the dog should stay put, watching your movements as you walk around. Repeat the exercise three times, giving the heel command once; two times the dog sits still, once he moves off. The command sequence is the dog's name, eye contact, and the command "heel."

By now, you should be approaching your dog consistently as discussed in Chapter Four; either the loop back to the heel position or the hook. This is the perfect opportunity to polish this steady behavior.

The dog should remain still as you walk completely around his position in ever tightening circles. You should see no movement. The more eye contact the dog offers, the better. On long-term sit or stay, even at your side, if the dog lies down, it's no problem, as long as he remains still and quiet. This behavior is indicative of a dog that is relaxed and not going anywhere—good stuff. No need to make the dog sit up. Encourage the patience.

Energy Level Control

Remember timing, tempo, and tone. Match your body language to the desired level. Slow, calm, and deliberate behavior will bring a high-energy dog down, just as more enthusiasm will bring a lethargic dog up. A good way to increase interest in a lethargic dog is to train along with a high-energy dog. Competitive nature will often spark the interest of the more laid-back dog.

THE TURNOFF: An effective way to regain control of an excited dog is to develop the "turnoff," a cue that means be quiet, still, and settled. The turnoff is established by placing your hand under the jaw of the dog, cradling the muzzle in your open palm. Your demeanor and tone should be relaxed as you attempt to establish a calm behavior. Gain eye contact, and require quiet. At first, the youngster will move when you put your hand on the muzzle. Use both hands to regain control, capture just a few seconds of quiet, and then reward. Repeat the command "quiet" very softly. Gradually lengthen the amount of time. Use the turnoff to relax your dog, maintain calm, or settle him after an exciting retrieve. Through repetition, the dog will react to the turnoff and voluntarily relax and demonstrate self-control.

The turnoff serves as a calming stop for an excited dog.

The Three Ds of Steadiness:
Denials, Delays, and Diversions

Steadiness training can be divided into three categories:

DENIALS: Simply denying the retrieve. In training, either you or another dog should pick up 50 percent of all bumpers or birds thrown. The youngster learns to anticipate that not every shot or mark results in a retrieve. Denials transcend all training levels from basic to advanced, and even extend to the hunt. If denials have been used in training from the beginning, the results will be obvious.

DELAYS: The amount of time between the fall of the bird or placement of the bumper and the release of the dog for the retrieve. In training, the duration of the delay is gradually extended to facilitate the dog's memory. On the hunt, you may wait until several birds are down before sending a dog for the retrieve. Every delay situation requires patience and quiet behavior before the release of the dog, whether the retrieve is a memory or a mark. Training with memory patterns builds in a time-lapse between placement of the bumper and the retrieve—a built-in delay.

DIVERSIONS: Diversions are forms of steadiness; that is, no switching from one downed bird to another. In training and on the hunt, a dog will encounter countless distractions. In each situation, the dog should remain focused on the retrieve at hand, not the diversion.

Denials reinforce patience and quiet behavior in training.

Sit to the Flush

Building on off-lead heel work and steadiness foundational skills, you may now perfect sit to the flush. While backing away at reverse heel off lead, toss out a bumper and blow the sit whistle. By now, the dog should be sitting well to the whistle. With the bumper down, the dog should be steady and focused, redirecting his eyes to you. Pick up the bumper as a denial. If there are any problems, put the youngster back on lead.

Remember to reward a good sit, a remote stay, or steadiness with the same enthusiasm that you would for a retrieve. On a flush of a sharptail in the Badlands, Deke made a brilliant flush of a single bird and remained steady to the shot and fall. I sent my other dog, Indian, who was walking at heel, for the long retrieve. Once Indian returned with the bird, I approached Deke, who had remained absolutely still, and shared the reward with both dogs. Value and reward steadiness or it may disappear. For example, reward a dog for a nice back of a point, for an honor of another working dog in a duck blind. Reward a dog that remains quiet and still at heel when a bird falls and other dogs get the opportunity for the action.

STEADINESS AND HONORING

This is a further progression of absolute obedience. To be reliable in the field, dogs must be rock steady. Steadiness is the dog's ability to sit still and quiet during any type of activity—a shot, a falling bird, or the distraction of another working dog or hunter. This is a supreme test of a dog's obedience and will be the conditioned result of all the work you've done since the dog was a small pup. The hundreds of little steadiness and patience exercises should now be entrenched, essential behaviors.

Three Types of Diversions

1–RETURNING FROM A RETRIEVE: As the youngster returns with a bumper, throw another bumper to simulate a secondary fall. Begin by tossing the diversion high and behind your position. If the dog tries to switch, simply cut him off. This procedure is best started as part of the delivery-to-hand conditioning along a fence line. As the youngster practices recall while holding an object, introduce a wide diversion to serve as a distraction. Gradually bring the diversion around your position to increasingly closer distances to the dog's returning path.

2–LONG BIRD/SHORT BIRD: Similarly, teach the dog to ignore a short bird and go for a long bird or a memory. After setting up the trailing memory and aligning the dog for the retrieve, toss out a

Introducing a diversion as the dog returns from each retrieve begins wide to the handler's position (1). Then, slowly bring the bumpers closer to the dog as he advances (2, 3, and 4).

short diversion almost behind you, point at it, and give the de-select "no." Line the dog for the longer bumper. This will happen often on the hunt. Two birds will fall, one quite close, which holds the dog's attention, while the second bird falls into cover or perhaps tries to swim away. You'll want

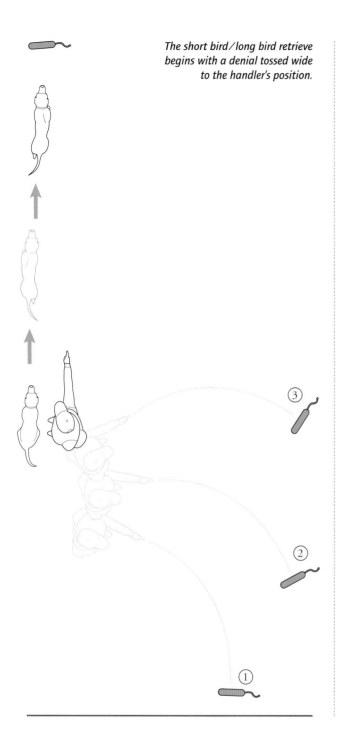

The short bird/long bird retrieve begins with a denial tossed wide to the handler's position.

The most challenging diversion is a secondary bird fall as the dog is lining or swimming for a retrieve.

the diversions at a rather wide angle to the dog's path and do not introduce this concept until your student has perfected the other two and handles well on land and water.

Steady in Group

If you hunt with others, it is important to train with others. Suddenly exposing a dog to a new pack the day of the hunt is a recipe for disaster. You can alleviate this by training with other dogs, particularly those with whom you hunt, but in any case the dog needs to be exposed to working with a group. This is best done on lead at first to ensure that your dog is under control and to avoid bad habits. It's much easier to correct a dog that is about to break than to deal with a dog that is already on the run.

to pick the longest bird first, requiring the dog to ignore the shorter distance of the two.

3– Bird Falls While Going Out for the Retrieve: This is the most challenging diversion. The dog is driving out and another shot and fall occurs within his sight, or perhaps another bird flushes. It will take practice to keep the dog driving out to the original bird. Begin by throwing

This is an example of group work using a live bird. Two gundogs are steady on point as the group honors.

In group work, you'll be training for several skills at once. Ensure that your dog responds to instruction only by name. You have been using his name before each command for months now, but you need to be sure it is 100 percent reliable when confronted with the excitement of the group. If the dog doesn't hear his name, he should remain absolutely steady and quiet. Your dog remains focused on you despite distractions and learns to sit quietly as bumpers are tossed and retrieves are made right in front of him. Simply build upon the skills that you have established in basic obedience and apply them to working around other dogs.

Line up the dogs in your group. Keep your dog focused on you as each dog weaves in and out through the line at heel. Then, advance to denials. Toss out a few bumpers in front of the dogs. All handlers should walk out to pick the bumpers up while keeping their young dogs in place. Then, move away and toss bumpers and balls over and around the dogs. Again, handlers make the picks. Dogs should remain focused on their handlers. Correct any movement or creep-

ing by lifting the dog and taking him back to his original position as described in Chapter Four. Grasp the loose folds of skin just under the ears firmly with both hands, lift so the dog barely loses his footing, and return him to his original spot. This is similar to the way the pack leader disciplines its followers in the wild. Don't let your dog get away with moving out of place.

Call each dog out of line to heel by name. No other dog should move. When teaching a dog to respond while in a group, initially stand only a few feet in front of the dog, and then gradually lengthen the distance. In time, your dog will learn that he should move and retrieve only when you call his name. With the group he will also learn when to remain steady and honor other working dogs.

Honoring in a group can involve a mark thrown or a memory placed as each dog is individually released by his name while all others remain quiet. Any whining, movement, or attempts to run in should be met with a quick snap of the lead, replacing the dog back on lead if he is off at the time, or possibly heeling the excited

The Three Secret Tools of the Wildrose Trainer

There are three secret tools for problem solving that have been used for years at Wildrose. When approaching any problem in training, first refer to the problem-solving matrix and the established Wildrose Laws in Chapter Two, and then attempt to identify the cause of the problem, not just the symptoms. Analyze what needs to be corrected, beginning with the possible contributing factors. Creatively applying the tools described below may help to solve a problem in a low-force manner.

SLIP-CHAIN COLLAR: The name choker chain is a poor choice for this tool. This heavy chain collar (four millimeters) involves no choking applications, only a snap to apply a fast direct pressure to the dog's neck. When properly used, the heavy chain delivers quite a bit of energy to the neck, mimicking the bite of another dominant dog, a normal correction made among pack animals, one the dog will understand. The chain delivers more bite through thick fur than rubber or cloth collars. The chain should eventually be replaced, as it is only a temporary problem-solving tool.

SCENTED TENNIS BALLS: Dogs with a high prey drive love them. Balls are great to increase interest in hunting cover or retrieving. Pursuing a bouncing ball down a driveway may be all it takes to awaken the prey instincts in a disinterested student. Also, tennis ball catch makes a great reward for an excellent performance. It is easy to scent tennis balls. Take the breast feathers from a game bird, place them in a plastic bag, and allow them to air-dry for a few days. Dampen the tennis balls and place them in the bag with the feathers for a couple of weeks. Now you have a training object that you know smells like a game bird.

BIRDS: Cold game or live flying birds can motivate a slow starter or a dog that has become bored with training. Birds improve motivation. To jump-start a reluctant youngster in some cases requires a chase or flush of live birds. The attractiveness of a tethered pigeon flying about or the scent of a fresh bird tossed into cover may be all that's necessary to awaken powerful instincts in the youngster.

Scented tennis balls can be high-value motivators.

The walk-up involves steadiness, concentration, and discipline when moving with a group.

student away from the action. No patience, no retrieve. Practice retrieves in front of the line very close to the dogs and finally straight through the line. Each dog gets a turn while the honor dogs sit steady and quiet. The retrieving dog must remain focused on the retrieve and should not engage the other dogs.

Walk-up

The dogs move forward across a field much like in a pheasant-hunting situation. It is one thing for the dogs to be steady at sit, and quite another when they're walking at heel. With the dogs off lead, if possible, the line moves forward and the handlers throw bumpers. Now is an opportunity, if you would like, to also practice sit to the flush as you toss bumpers. Use your whistle or hand signals if necessary. If the dog is conditioned to sit when he sees a flyer, he won't be breaking. If problems arise, use the slip collar and steady tab. This is a great benefit even for the duck hunter to hone steadiness. As the line walks forward and the handlers throw marks, each dog in the group receives one retrieve. Occasionally, leave the

dogs at sit and walk out and get the bumpers yourself. Honoring is obedience, as is steadiness. Find some pals and make sure your dog is rock steady in a group situation.

DELIVERY TO HAND

Delivery to hand of an undamaged bird, alive or dead, is a fundamental skill for a Gentleman's Gundog—no dropping, no plucking, no chewing. Reliable delivery to hand is accomplished the positive way through hold conditioning.

Throughout the early stages of training, the emphasis has been on getting the bumper to hand without requiring a stylish delivery. Since the early starts, you have shaped behaviors with the bumper; a delivery is a shared experience and bringing the bumper to you is a great way to get a reward. You have avoided snatching things away from the pup, playing chase or tug-of-war, or allowing chew toys. And you have diligently discouraged dropping anything anytime.

With the pup now about eight months of age and retrieving reliably, begin hold conditioning by stopping all retrieves and introducing the

Pressure Point Manipulation

There are three points of contact you will use to stimulate the sensitive nerve centers of the dog:

A– Place your fingers around the spine at the base of the skull. Use a slight amount of pressure with your fingers in a rotating manner to produce a massage sensation. Use your other hand

to brace under the jaw and massage in upward strokes lifting the head. Done properly, the dog will relax quickly.

B– This shows another view of the exact finger placement for the pressure point massage.

C– Massage below the ear canal, just behind the jaw. Again, place your fingers for inward stimulation on the pressure points. This is not a petting action; it is a direct pressure on

the nerve centers produced by the tips of the fingers.

D– This shows another view of the exact finger placement for the base of the jaw massage.

E– To massage the feet, stroke along the bone lines with your thumb in a downward motion while holding the dog's foot.

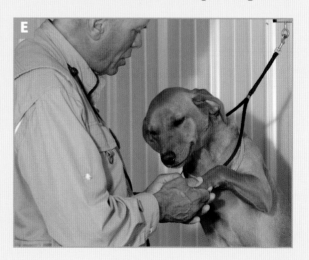

Wildrose hold-conditioning process. There are three parts:.

1– Acclimating the pup to the table or elevated platform and introducing the pressure point manipulation technique.

2– Teaching the commands of hold and release.

3– Holding objects properly while moving.

Hold conditioning should always be done at the beginning of the day's training session, just after the energy-burning power walk in the cyclical training model. The youngster should be fresh and alert, but not panting or hot. A platform such as a picnic table is best for beginning the conditioning steps. Elevating the dog places him in a more dependent position and puts you in a more comfortable working position. With the dog sitting up, tie him securely so he can't lie down, roll over, or avoid your manipulation.

Use an object that is unfamiliar to the dog, such as a small wooden dowel about one inch in diameter and eight inches in length, to prevent the pup from associating any initial displeasure that could occur as you begin hold conditioning with a familiar object, like a bumper. Match the command "hold" with the dog's behavior of grasping the object securely without chomping or chewing. The release command "drop," "dead," or "give" (your choice) will instruct the dog to release the object.

First, introduce the pup to the platform in a comfortable manner. A great way to get the dog used to being elevated is to feed him on the training table every day, making the table experience enjoyable. Once he is used to the table, begin pressure point manipulation. This is a massage technique designed to de-stress and relax the dog. It becomes a pleasurable experience that he will associate with hold conditioning.

Within a few days, your dog will anticipate the table with pleasure and delight. Some dogs will even lift their paws to encourage the massage. Use each of the three techniques interchangeably during every lesson. Now, use the massage of the pressure points to make hold conditioning a positive process. When the dog is holding the object correctly, the massage continues and your voice is a soft, patient tone. If the dog drops or chews the object, your tone sharpens with a scold of displeasure and the massage stops immediately.

The Conditioning Sequence

The hold-conditioning process begins with the use of a wooden dowel and ends with a partially frozen bird. The training may take just a few days to complete or it may require several weeks, but what's important is that once the process has begun it must continue until completion. Also, all retrieving work must stop during this entire period.

For the first few lessons, tie the dog securely on the table, which gives you the use of your hands so you can use the massage techniques. Place the wooden dowel in the mouth of the dog by reaching over the muzzle and opening the mouth. Place the dowel and clear the upper and lower lips from the teeth that could be pinched against the dowel. Place your fingers under the dog's jaw and your hand behind his head for manipulation.

Over time, slowly release your hand from under the jaw as the massage continues. Repeat the same sequence with the side pressure point technique. Once you can remove your hands and the dog continues to hold, move to the foot massage.

After you can walk away and your student continues to hold the dowel, repeat the lessons in several different locations with the dog sitting in place as well as sitting on the ground. Finally, progress to moving while holding at heel and reverse heel. Follow up with holding in and out of the water, first as the youngster heels, then move on to recall.

Repeat the entire process with a variety of bumpers at different locations, including a partially thawed bird to prevent chewing.

You are teaching two different commands in hold conditioning: "hold"—to take and hold

Causal Relationships

Dogs learn best when one skill or behavior is logically linked to the next. Each lesson causes the dog to recall a similar, previously well-established lesson, much like creating a popcorn garland for a Christmas tree. A long, beautiful garland is accomplished by carefully adding one piece of popcorn at a time to the string until a small section is complete. The next section is similarly produced, and then the two are tied together to develop the finished decoration.

Progressive training is much the same, adding subskills and behaviors together until a complete concept is assembled. One skill is linked to the next to create a chain of behaviors. Then, another subskill or a developed series of skills is carefully linked to create a concept or exercise. Training by developing habits linked through causal relationships leaves no holes in the dog's development or in his ability to multitask and remember complex patterns.

securely without chewing—and "drop," "dead," or "give"—to give up the object. In training, you should be able to reach and touch the object with your hand without the dog releasing it. The dog should hold until ordered to release. Never hit or strike the object, but you may touch it and slightly move it to test the dog's ability and understanding to hold securely.

Once successful using the dowel, repeat each step in the sequence again using a variety of objects, including a regular bumper, an oversized bumper, a feather-laced bumper, and a partially frozen bird. During the sequences using the bumpers, with the pup consistent on hold and delivery, begin to use distractions like decoys or diversions. Add complexity as well, such as walking up a ramp, climbing steps, or going into a dog

hide—all while holding. Finally, return to a simple trailing memory for an initial retrieve along your old friend, the familiar fence. Begin with just a short one to assess the dog's proficiency at delivery. As the young dog comes toward you, remind him to hold. If he drops or makes a poor delivery, change your tone of voice to express displeasure and replace the object. Do not hesitate to return to earlier hold-conditioning steps if necessary to achieve reliable results. Make haste slowly.

Delivery Styles

There are two different positions for delivery to hand. Select the one you prefer, but with either, encourage the dog to lift his head to present the bird. No lying down, no head swinging, no dropping to your feet. With either method, the dog should not release until instructed to do so to avoid a wounded bird escaping.

FRONT DELIVERY: This is most commonly used with spaniels and pointers, but it is a very functional style for retrievers and the one preferred at Wildrose. The dog comes straight to the hunter's front and sits or stands. This is an excellent style for flooded conditions, duck blinds, and thick cover.

*OPPOSITE: **A:** Place the wooden dowel in the mouth of the dog. **B:** Release your hand from under the jaw as the massage continues. **C:** Repeat the sequence with the side pressure point technique. **D:** Move to the foot massage. **E:** Walk away to make sure the dog will still hold. **F:** Repeat this exercise in a different location. **G:** Try moving while the dog holds at heel. **H:** Try moving while the dog holds at reverse heel. **I:** Repeat the entire hold-conditioning process at several different locations.*

This shows a front delivery.

This shows a side delivery.

SIDE DELIVERY: Dog returns to heel at the handler's side, turns, and sits while holding the bird.

LINING MEMORIES

The shortest distance between two points is a straight line. Lining is the retriever's ability to take and hold a straight path, despite influences, to a bird or bumper. At Wildrose, we build lining skills by using four types of memories. Memories are the cornerstones for the entire training program. The rule is this: Memories, not marks.

With memories, you can teach dogs to negotiate barriers, drive deep into woodlands, lengthen the distance for retrieves, and practice multiple retrieves—all without compromising the dog's steadiness as you might by teaching these same skills using marks. Memories provide built-in delays, which are a huge benefit to enhancing patience and steadiness. Memories also make it easier to progress to unseens or blinds. Marks don't. With marking, the dog is accustomed to seeing the bumper fall. With memories, the dog must remember the placement of a retrieve over a period of time, then line correctly in order to find the reward.

Sight Memory

The dog sits at a fixed point watching as the handler or helper walks out to place the bumpers. The bumpers are not thrown as marks, just tossed out at the reference point as the dog watches at a distance. Normally, you should place the bumper to begin these retrieves along a fence or other straightedge to assist your dog in holding a straight line. You can set up multiple retrieves along fences running at different angles in the same manner.

For a sight memory, the dog remains quiet and motionless while observing bumper placement.

Circle Memory

Circle memories may be used to establish a variety of multiple retrieve patterns.

Trailing Memory

Refer back to the trailing memory diagram in Chapter 3 on page 73. The dog walks at heel as you place the bumpers. Walk the route to the area, drop the bumper, and heel your dog away to retrace your path with the de-select "no, heel." Do not use the dog's name preceding the command to heel or he may think it means to go for the bumper. Walk the desired distance away from the reference point or memory bumper, then reline for the retrieve. The pup should be more than familiar with these patterns by now, as you've been using trailing memories and split 180 memories to introduce and teach him the essentials of early start retrieves.

Now, you may progress to more complex versions of the trailing memory as the maturing youngster is capable of understanding the applications. For instance, you can gradually modify a split 180 into a diversion exercise by bringing the second bumper of a 180 around your position for a tighter angle to the memory, much like the hands of a clock. Soon, your youngster will ignore the shorter wide bumper and go long for the first. You will be running a short bird/long bird diversion.

You may use sight and trailing memories to teach a wide variety of useful skills, even in shallow water. The dog understands the concept of the patterns, so you can incorporate complexity and distance without compromising confidence. Retrieves may be linked together to teach a variety of skills, such as introducing diversions, going under fences, negotiating obstacles, or driving through thick cover or deep into woods.

Circle Memory

Develop the dog's ability to run straight lines on doubles, triples, or even quads by walking in circles. Sound interesting? It's a special Wildrose technique called circle memories. Here's how to set up a simple double for the young starter.

Use a couple of fixed reference points like a tree, post, rock, or bush. Do not use man-made articles like cones, flags, or buckets. Such items will not likely appear on a hunt, so acclimate the dog to look for and focus on natural reference points that could be used in the field. Initially, the dog will need a reference point to line toward as a confidence builder. With your dog at heel, take a circle path to your first reference point (remember the discussion in Chapter Four about cyclical training). Upon arrival at the first point, stop, toss out a bumper, and allow the pup to focus a few moments on the fall area.

Say "no, heel," then walk on to continue your loop. Do not walk in a straight line or the effect will be lost. Place the bumpers a reasonable distance apart to minimize the chance of switching. Approach the second reference point and place the bumper in the same manner as the first, then circle back to your original starting point.

Line your dog directly for the first bumper. If the pup loses the line or switches, recall him and move your position forward between the two memory points, which will in effect widen the angle. Then, line the dog again. Now, you are ready to pick the second bumper. If you would like, you can toss out the first bumper as a short bird diversion wide to your side and behind. Turn your hunter away with a "no, heel," and line for the second memory. You pick up the diversion as a denial.

Once you complete the double patterns in several locations, you can progress to multiple retrieves set up as circle memories to include all types of terrain—heavy grasses, woodlands, and water. Circle memories promote steadiness and build memory all while teaching the dog to run a straight line.

Loop Memory

The fourth Wildrose memory is the loop. This is a variation of both the trailing memory and the circle memory. The shape of its path, with the dog walking at heel, is an oval rather than a straight line, yet the circle is not nearly as wide as with the circle memory. The loop is commonly used to set up retrieves when you don't want your dog to merely retrace the direct path as he would in the trailing memory or in a situation where the area's size or density would not

A loop memory is in the shape of an exclamation point.

accommodate a large circle memory, such as dense woods, marshlands, or thick grasses. Remember Wildrose Law No. 10: Memories before hand signals, hand signals before marks.

Dog Alignment

There are two ways to set up a dog for a line to a memory, multiple marks, or, later in training, an unseen.

CONTINENTAL-STYLE: The handler stands parallel to the dog's body. With an outstretched arm, the handler looks directly over the dog's head at the target and points to the area.

AMERICAN-STYLE: With the dog sitting at the handler's side, the handler extends his hand in front of the dog's head above the line of sight. The arm used should be on the same side as the dog.

In both styles, the hand is a pointer rather than a caster. The hand movement should not be distracting. The dog's body alignment in relation to the line to be taken to the bird is vital. Your hand should encourage the dog to look out and get the picture of the target area.

Too much hand movement or holding your hand out in front of the dog for too long a time distracts the dog's concentration. It also indicates to the dog a lack of confidence on your part.

Continental-style: The handler looks directly over the dog's line of sight.

American-style: Excessive hand movement will distract the dog's line of sight.

If the dog is not in proper alignment, heel him forward a couple of steps until the spine and nose are in line with the direction you intend the dog to run. When you achieve proper alignment and the dog is patient, bring your hand down and release the dog with his name.

Key Introductions

There are a few key introductions that are critical to your success. The following instructions will help you properly introduce your dog to gunfire, live birds, and a number of other external factors often present in hunting situations.

BIRDS

Up until this point, you have been using feathered bumpers, the occasional partially frozen bird, wings, and scented tennis balls. Now it is time to begin introducing the young dog to live birds.

Remember to get it right on land before going to water. This rule is especially true with bird introductions. Once your dog is picking cold birds on land and water, you want him to be able to pick live birds as well. A wounded bird thrashing around may put off a young dog, so get it right in training before the hunt.

Pigeons are great for this. You can bind one wing to the bird's body or use a bird sock to keep the bird from flying. Occasionally, dogs react differently to live birds than dead ones. Also, make sure your gundog has been introduced to the type of game bird he will experience on the hunt.

STEADINESS TO FLYERS

There are two fun and effective techniques to produce a quiet, steady gundog even when faced with the excitement of a live flush of a bird or ducks approaching the blind. Practice both techniques as denials as you walk with the dog at heel and again with the dog at remote sit.

THE FRISBEE FLYER: Dogs are very stimulated by the gliding action of a Frisbee in flight. With the dog at sit, throw the disc to a friend over the dog's head.

There is more to introducing dogs to birds than just retrieving a bird to hand.

With the Frisbee caught by the other person, there is nothing for your dog to retrieve should he break. Next, with the dog at heel, send the Frisbee unexpectedly ahead of your path, duplicating a flush. Your dog's response should be to sit to the flyer or to keep moving at heel with you, your choice. Again, pick the Frisbee up as a denial.

THE TETHERED BIRD: All that is necessary to add the stimulus of a real bird in flight to your training lesson is a pigeon and a small bird harness, which is attached to a pole by a string. Now you have a bird in flight that you can control. Should your dog break, you can retract the bird instantly. With your dog at remote sit, fly the bird around to assess steadiness. At first, you can expect that a bit of gentle reinforcement with a lead will be necessary. Once steady, practice

Birds in flight are the ultimate test of steadiness for a young dog.

recalling your dog. Just as the dog approaches, toss the bird to duplicate a flush. The youngster should stop and sit to the flush or continue toward you, again your choice. After gunshot introduction, add a popper shot to increase the stimulus. Also, make a few retrieves with the dog ignoring the flyer as a diversion. Often during a hunt a live bird will be flushed or land just as your dog completes a retrieve, so prepare for it.

NEGOTIATING OBSTACLES

An important step in training is to teach the game dog how to drive straight through or cross any reasonable barrier encountered. A barrier is anything that may disrupt a dog's line to a downed bird or influence his hunting pattern. Not all obstacles are physical. Some occur naturally in topography or abrupt changes in ground cover, but each can influence a dog's performance.

A *physical barrier* is something that blocks the dog's path but remains negotiable—a mesh wire fence, fallen timber, deep ditch, or stone wall.

With practice, dogs can learn to hurl themselves over or under such obstructions, but unprepared, your dog may not continue his pursuit.

There are also *environmental barriers*, which do not obstruct the dog's path or movement at all. It's only an obstacle from the dog's point of view. These include abrupt changes in ground cover. For example, a dog won't go from open ground into grass cover or may not leave cover to cross open ground. There's no real obstruction, but a significant change in terrain can influence the unprepared hunting dog. Other types of environmental barriers include row crops, plowed ground, steep hillsides, hedgerows, thickets, water, and even fog, rain, snow, or ice.

The third barrier is *psychological*. Frustrating for the unprepared dog and hunter alike, these influences exist only in the mind of the dog. Possibilities include shadows, a four-strand fence the dog could easily go under, clumps of grass, a stream or ditch, the field road, or perhaps a path. Each may disrupt a dog's progress much to the surprise of everyone around. The

Decoys of all types should be introduced first on land, then on water.

point is obvious. Incorporate as many of these factors as possible in normal training lessons.

The preferred way to teach a dog how to overcome influences and obstructions is with a trailing memory. You want your hunter to punch through and across all barriers to make a tough pick. Set the lesson up by walking through each influencing factor yourself with your dog at heel. Toss out three or four bumpers in a ladder pattern, no piles. Turn and re-walk the line.

Exit through the first of the barriers and turn and line for the first retrieve. While the dog is away, back up to include another barrier. Send for the second retrieve. Continue to back away gradually, lengthening the line with each retrieve. Your hunter is learning to punch straight through all barriers—cover, ditches, fences, even briars—all with confidence.

Flushing hunters and pointers must learn not to shun thick cover. Encourage young dogs to take to thickets, ditches, and creeks without hesitation. Right from the start, your pup should find all good things in tough places—their bumpers or birds should be hidden in brush

piles, ditches, and brambles. He goes in deep and finds a reward. Habits learned early will likely endure a lifetime. Obstacles, both actual and perceived, can have a drastic effect on your dog's successful performance in the field in both hunting and retrieving. It's best to train for them.

SPECIAL INTRODUCTIONS

The versatile gundog will encounter a wide variety of equipment and distractions during his hunting life. Early introduction is the key to the dog's success afield. As a reminder, make introductions first on land before going to the water.

Decoys

There are three things your dog must know about decoys: how to ignore them, how to avoid them to prevent entanglement, and how to react if he does strike a decoy line. First, heel the pup on land through all types of decoys large and small, even those that move, like spinners and flags. Next, do the same on lead in shallow water.

Finally, add a few short retrieves with the dog swimming through the decoys.

Enlarge the spread and use decoys often in training exercises on both land and water. The dog should find bumpers not only inside the spread of decoys, but beyond the spread as well. Condition your dog not to panic should he swim into a decoy line. Simply put on your waders and get out in the water with your dog on a long lead so you can maintain control. Attach a couple of decoys by a string to the dog's collar and allow the dog to swim around with you while pulling the decoy lines. Follow the lesson with a few very short retrieves with the decoy package still intact. Should he ever snag a line in the future, the dog won't panic.

Watercraft

Introduce the watercraft first on land. Teach entry and exit while the boat remains stable. Then, sitting in the boat, shake it and make noise to acclimate the dog to the noise and motion of the craft. Make a couple of retrieves from inside the boat. Then, proceed to the shallows. Here you can teach the dog entry and exit on water, but the dog will be able to maintain footing for the entry. Finally, take a boat ride together with motors and gear.

ATVs

Off-road vehicles must be introduced with caution. Tying a dog to the vehicle can be dangerous, but an unsecured dog may exit while the vehicle is in motion, causing injury. The best approach is to introduce the dog while the vehicle is motionless. Once he is comfortable, let another person drive while you hold the dog on lead. When the dog is totally familiar and accustomed to the ride, you can allow him to ride unsecured.

Dog Hide

Remaining patient in a small dog hide is another necessary preparation that you can complete at home. This is really an extension of crate training, acclimating the dog to enter and exit the hide and remain quiet inside for extended periods of time. Use the same technique to teach the dog to lay comfortably with you in a field layout blind.

Place Extension

The dog will be required to sit patiently and quietly in a duck blind for extended periods of time. Practice this at home or at work. Set up the dog's field stand and proceed doing whatever you planned to do. The dog must learn patience in the field for longer periods despite distractions.

Introduction to Gunfire

A very important step in training a gundog is the proper introduction to gunfire. Most gun-shyness

Dog hides will prove beneficial for open-field hunting conditions.

A primer revolver, using .209 shotgun primers, is ideal for gun-shot introduction.

in a well-bred pup from hunting stock is man-made. Go slowly here and take as much time as necessary. Introduce gunfire progressively after the youngster is more than eight months old, as well as:

◆ Bold in the field.
◆ Steady to thrown bumpers.
◆ Confident in the handler.
◆ Bold on the retrieve.

The most important thing to remember is *no surprises or testing.* The thrown bumper or mark becomes the distraction and the retrieve becomes the motivator, both redirecting the youngster's attention away from the noise of the shot. A few days before the first shot, carry a gun around while training to familiarize the dog with the object. Sit by the dog and have another person throw a few bumpers. To line for the retrieve, point the shotgun but do not fire it.

Make your first shots with a cap gun, blank pistol, or primer pistol (never a handheld dummy launcher). In all cases, the shot should be made well away from the dog's location to the front, and should be fired by an assistant, *not you.* The first shots should make a muffled pop, not a crack; you don't want the sound to be so loud that it startles the youngster. For the first few shots, the shooter should stuff the cap pistol in his or her training bag to muffle the shot.

You want the pup totally focused on the thrown bumper. The assistant gets the pup's

The shooter points at the bumper in flight with a toy gun as the thrower fires the shot.

- ✦ *Conduct gunfire introductions in a wide-open area to reduce shot intensity.*

- ✦ *Point muzzles of guns away from the dog's location to reduce intensity of the sound.*

- ✦ *In case problems develop, do not initially associate the sound of the shot with the visual of a long gun or bird.*

- ✦ *Do not introduce gunfire by taking the starter to a shooting range.*

- ✦ *Never introduce a shot in an enclosed area like a blind or a hide.*

- ✦ *No surprise shots. Have your youngster's complete attention.*

attention, tosses the bumper high, and then shoots. The retrieve should be made immediately.

If there is no negative reaction to the shot, slowly move the shooter closer. Only conduct three to five repetitions each day. Later in the sequence, begin to pick up every other mark as a denial to reinforce steadiness.

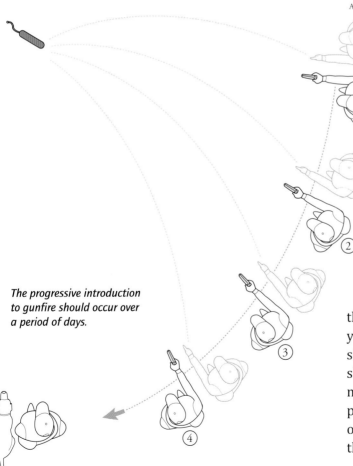

The progressive introduction to gunfire should occur over a period of days.

Over a period of days, you'll be able to bring the shooter with the pistol closer to your position. Begin the sequence again with a pistol out of the bag. After a few sessions, you should be able to handle a cap gun yourself. Remember Wildrose Law No. 5: Make haste slowly.

Next in the progression, you'll use a training tool called a retriever launcher. Never start a pup on gunfire with one of these launchers. The crack of the shot is powerful. Use special light-load shells to shoot the bumper and have your helper make the shot well away from your position. Use the same progression at the same location over a couple of days as accomplished in the other sequences. Gradually move the shooter closer. If your dog has any negative reactions, stop. Skip a couple of days, and then begin again at a greater distance in a different area with a less intense shot.

Finally, introduce the shotgun. Follow the same progression described above using a helper with a sub gauge like a .410 or 20-gauge with a light-shell load. Gradually bring the gun closer using marks as distractions until you can make the shot yourself. Use a progressive introduction to gunfire over time and you should experience little difficulty with gun-shyness. Throughout these sequences, do not compromise steadiness. You should pick up every other bumper as your starter watches. Maintain the standard.

CHAPTER 6

Gundog Basics: Part II

The term "meat dog" is often applied to a less-than-controllable hunting dog that aggressively finds and retrieves game birds, but usually does so on his own terms. "Meat dog" is descriptive of a totally self-employed gundog out on an independent frolic after birds to flush, point, or retrieve, with little regard for the wishes or instructions of his handler.

Contrarily, a Gentleman's Gundog is a controllable hunting partner, one that is an effective hunter with game-finding skills equal to the meat dog, but one that retains elements of refinement, including steadiness, patience, and handling ability. A Gentleman's Gundog is a "team player" that possesses the obedience, steadiness, delivery to hand, and lining abilities discussed in Chapter Five. With these skill sets well entrenched, you may now progress to the remaining core skills of a proper basic gundog: handling, the ability to control your dog at a distance in the field; hunting cover, the ability of your dog to thoroughly search an area to find hidden game; and marking, the ability of your dog to see a bird fall, remember its location, and retrieve it when sent.

◾ Core Gundog Skills: Handling through Marking

As a reminder, there are seven core gundog skills. This chapter addresses the last three—handling, hunting cover, and marking—and explains the methods necessary for successful development. Once you complete the exercises in this chapter, your dog will be ready for the hunt.

HANDLING

Whistle Commands

The importance of training a gundog to handle on both land and water cannot be understated. You want your dog to respond quickly to both hand signals and whistle commands under

The Seven Core Skills

In this chapter, you will focus on the last three skills: handling, hunting cover, and marking.

1– OBEDIENCE: The basis of all phases of field work. What is steadiness, honor, delivery to hand, casting, and recall if not obedience? Obedience is the cornerstone of the skills you will be developing.

2– STEADINESS AND HONORING: Sitting quietly, not running in, not interfering with another dog's retrieve, steady to flush and shot, or backing a point.

3– DELIVERY TO HAND: Picking and delivering a bird gently to hand without dropping or mouthing it.

4– LINING MEMORIES: Taking an initial direction of travel for an unseen or seen bird and carrying that line to the fall area without distraction.

5– HANDLING: Responding to whistle signals and taking directions by hand signals.

6– HUNTING COVER: Aggressively searching cover to locate game.

7– MARKING: Visually sighting with pinpoint accuracy a bird that has fallen and going directly to the location when sent.

---

all conditions. There are four basic whistle commands to teach along with corresponding hand signals. Wildrose prefers the English, pea-less whistle. This whistle is quite loud so the dog can easily hear it, yet it does not put off game as much as the commonly used pea-type whistles.

STOP: You've been practicing a shorter version of sit to the whistle since the early starts. The stop to the whistle is a single, continuous blast combined with the stop hand signal. Have your hand up high above your head before you blow the stop whistle. If you delay, blow the whistle, and your hand pops up just as the dog turns, it will look like a back cast from the dog's perspective. Put your hand up, and then blow the whistle. When the dog turns, he sees your hand in the stop position. It is your choice whether you want the dog to stop and sit on the whistle or merely stand steady.

RECALL OR COME: You've been practicing this as well since the early starts. The recall whistle is five or six multiple blasts combined with a recall hand signal. That's correct, you should use a recall hand signal. The hands are wide apart from the body at the handler's side, palms out toward the dog. This is a welcoming gesture, just in case the whistle signal is unclear due to weather conditions in the

The stop hand signal must be high overhead for visibility.

This is the recall hand signal to return fast.

This is the hand signal to return slowly while hunting.

field. If the dog turns to look back and sees the hand signal, he understands to come.

HUNT IN: Hunt in is a slow, repetitious, low-tone blow of the whistle with a corresponding hand signal that is pointing to the ground in front of the handler as if bouncing a basketball. This is an important whistle command to bring a dog back to a bird that was overran. Hunt in directs the dog to move toward the handler slowly while hunting cover, using lots of nose, as opposed to recall, which is to signal a quick return to the handler.

QUARTERING: This signal should not be taught until more advanced stages of training and is mentioned now only as a reference. It is excellent for an upland hunting dog working in front

Use two blasts of the whistle to signal the dog to bend (change directions) while quartering.

of the hunter. Two blasts of the whistle combined with a directional hand signal, left or right, instruct the dog to change direction when quartering a field.

Casting

Before getting into casting, it is very important to make sure you are using the correct hand when stopping the dog as you prepare to cast him in a certain direction. When casting back, either hand is correct as long as there is no diversion or distraction. If there is a diversion, use the hand *opposite* the diversion and step in that direction as you cast the dog back. Your body language and hand signal combined will assist in directing the dog away from the diversion.

When casting left or right, stop with the hand you intend to handle with and step in that direction as you make the cast. Keep in mind that much of the casting work will begin with stopping the dog with a hand signal. Be sure to use the correct hand to stop the dog so that you are not switching hands to make the cast.

Back Cast

This is the command and hand signal given to cast a dog 180 degrees behind his current position away from the handler. It is not necessary to use angle backs. To teach the cast, begin with a bumper placed as a trailing memory along your familiar fence. With the trailing memory placed, walk back along the fence 10 to 15 yards and leave the youngster at sit, continue your walk another 10 yards, then turn and face the dog. Raise your hand slowly in the air to the proper stop position and blow the whistle with a short "stop" blast to gain the pup's attention. Then, walk toward the youngster as you give the hand signal for back by dropping your hand

A: The stop signal is your hand held high and well away from your body. *B:* Position your hand so you can see the dog through your fingers. *C:* The hand signal for a back cast is straight up while stepping toward the dog.

The Redirect

A redirect defined is an action taken to divert a dog's attention away from one distraction or stimulus to focus on another. As you've seen in the pull/push exercise, it can be as simple as redirecting the dog's attention from the diversion bumper by getting eye contact and sending him for another bumper, but redirects can also be very effective problem-solving tools.

Occasionally, when working with a problem dog, you may need assistance getting the dog to focus on an activity or to disregard another stimulus (a fear factor). Using a redirect is one way to help accomplish this. A redirect is giving the dog a specific, enjoyable task on which to focus in order to move his attention away from another situation, or to better enable him to concentrate on the task at hand. You may choose to use a redirect in several training or problem-solving situations, such as when a dog shows hyperactivity, stress, nervousness, fear, or aggressive behavior.

With dogs of high oral fixation—those that enjoy carrying and retrieving objects—that passion provides an excellent platform for establishing a redirect. The most common redirect that we use at Wildrose is having the dog carry or hold something in his mouth. The dog must be excited by the whole experience. Find an item that the dog enjoys carrying or catching—a tennis ball, a wooden dowel, a Frisbee, or something special that he only gets on rare occasions. Avoid using a bird or bumper. You do not want to risk the dog dropping the bird or bumper, or associating the item with a stressful experience.

With a nervous, fearful, stressed, or aggressive dog, begin by having him carry the object around in a low-distraction environment. Make this a positive experience. Once he is comfortable carrying, slowly add the problem distraction or situation. For instance, with a dog that is nervous around new people, have him carry the object around. Then, while the dog concentrates on holding the object, have him walk past a new person. Gradually, get to the point where you can walk the dog straight up to someone new without him showing any signs of stress. If he drops the object, simply tell him "no," put the object back in his mouth, and remind him to hold it. Make haste slowly.

The redirect activity is excellent for dogs with sensitivity to gunfire, watercraft, loud noises, vehicles, storms, or new situations. When working on a new experience that may prove to be fearful for the dog, begin the process the same way. Get the dog comfortable carrying an object around or playing catch, then introduce the new experience slowly. Remember the discussion on introducing new experiences in Chapter Three under desensitization. Your objective is to get the dog to enjoy the experience or at least minimize noticing it by redirecting his attention away from the possible fear factor while concentrating on the prize.

Another use of the redirect is to retain the focus of a hyperactive dog or one that remains highly distracted during training. By introducing a secondary behavior—focusing on holding the object—the dog remains more settled and has an improved ability to concentrate on the training lesson at hand. Once the dog is successful and confidently completes the task, you can slowly remove the redirect activity.

This is the proper hand position before any cast.

Hold the dog's gaze briefly before the cast.

down and pushing it back up with a verbal "back." Your body language will send a clear message and the dog is accustomed to running lines along this fence, so teaching this lesson is easy. The dog will quickly associate the signal and the command with the desired behavior. In all cases of teaching the back cast, the bumper must be directly behind the dog.

All casting should be done in straight lines. Left and right should be at 90 degrees to the dog's position and backs should be 180 degrees behind the dog. No angles are necessary. You can pick any bird if your dog takes straight casts on a grid pattern. A second important point is that stopping with the hand you intend to handle with decreases confusion. If the cast is to be to your left, stop the dog with the left hand. Be clear and distinctive so the dog can understand your directions at distances. Slowly lower the stop hand down to eye level to the point that you can see your dog between your fingers. Hold the hand for a brief second to retain the dog's focus, and then push the hand straight out to your side for overs or straight up for backs. No waving. All hand signals should be made in a cross pattern to your body.

Pull/Push

The pull/push is the first step in teaching stop to the whistle at a distance the positive way. The dog is conditioned to sit to the whistle first on lead at heel, then off lead at heel, but now you need control at distances. The technique is set up as a trailing memory. Leave the dog sitting facing your position about 15 yards out with the bumper directly behind him. Rather than give an immediate back cast, pull or call the dog toward your position. With a stop whistle and hand signal, hold the dog's attention briefly, then back cast. If he stops promptly, he gets the retrieve. If not, deny the retrieve and simplify the exercise.

Next, begin to incorporate short diversions tossed wide to your position after the stop, followed by a back cast for the memory. The pull/push diversion is set up the same way as a trailing memory. Pull the dog toward your position. As you give the stop signal, toss the diversion. The dog's eyes will likely follow the bumper. Wait for his eyes to return to yours. This is a redirect. After the dog looks back at you, back cast with the appropriate hand opposite to the placement of the diversion. If you threw the diversion to the left, make sure to cast the dog back with the right hand.

OPPOSITE: A: *Hold the dog's focus to ensure patience.* **B:** *Blow the whistle and give a stop hand signal.* **C:** *Bring your hand to eye level and hold the dog's gaze.* **D:** *Give the back-cast signal and step toward the dog.*

Rotational Backs

To solidify the concept of backs away from a diversion, use the Wildrose rotational back exercise. The scenario works much like the face of a clock. With the dog placed in the center, a bumper is directly behind him at 12:00 while the handler is at 6:00. Toss a bumper as a diversion to either 3:00 or 9:00 on the clock face. Wait for eye contact and back cast with the hand opposite the diversion. Replace the dog in the center of the clock with the diversion bumper directly behind him. The diversion now becomes the pri-

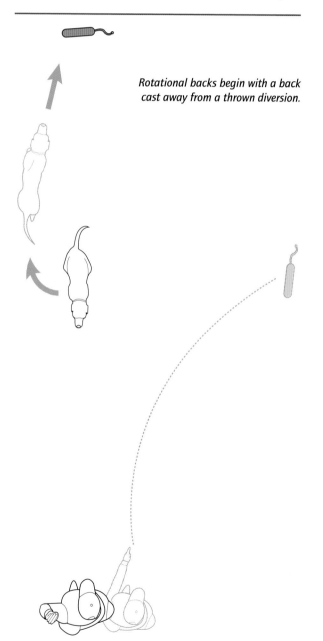

Rotational backs begin with a back cast away from a thrown diversion.

mary memory. Repeat the exercise with the diversion falling on the same side of the dog each time. Again, back cast. Repeat the rotation in the same direction around the clock until you're back at the original position, a total of four repetitions. This could be one of the three exercises in the cyclical training model for the day. Follow up the next day with the same concept occurring in the same location, but adjust the diversions and rotation to occur in the opposite direction.

You need to run back casts, pull/push, rotational backs, and stop-to-the-whistle backs for quite some time—a minimum of 30 days—to ensure that the dog fully understands the back command *before* introducing left and right hand signals. Be sure to practice back casts in all types of terrain—through ditches, over logs, and into water. Don't become predictable. Periodically pull the dog all the way to you with a recall. You can't have your prospect anticipating a back cast with every stop on the whistle exercise.

Stop to the Whistle Outbound

You have now accomplished two objectives that will make stop to the whistle as the dog is going out much easier. Your student is reliably stopping to the whistle coming toward you, anticipating an exciting signal to follow, plus you have added an attractor—the diversion. When the dog stops and looks to you for direction, something interesting happens—your pup learns that a quick response to the whistle results in a reward, a retrieve. If the pup does not stop, a helper quickly picks up the bumper and the dog does not get the reward. By making your dog proficient at stopping while coming toward you before attempting to stop him as he goes out, you're much less likely to need a lunge line or an electric collar to perfect reliable outbound stops.

For your first attempt at stopping the dog while going out for a retrieve, it's back to the same familiar fence. Set up the trailing memory. On the way back, leave the dog at sit as you would on the back-cast exercise, but this time call him to you. Line him for the memory. Just a few yards out, exactly where the dog was previously sitting, blow your stop whistle, and—just as the dog looks back to stop—throw the diversion as an attractor. At first, keep the stop very close to your position. If you have practiced the pull/push exercise long enough to form habits, you'll most likely get results. If not, return to that exercise. Remember, the diversion is always a denial.

If you get a quick stop, give the verbal marker "good" and a back cast for the reward. Set up properly and run frequently, the pull/push and backs with diversions exercises

The Stimulus Package

Developing a gundog properly involves training to the point of predictable performance under any circumstances. This is best established with the Wildrose Stimulus Package, a series of exercises that introduce both complexity and distractions in order to produce predictability. Teaching any behavior or skill requires both repetition and consistency. As previously mentioned, a dog must perform the specific lesson five times correctly in five different locations to create a habit. Each behavior or skill must be reinforced successfully at a variety of locations under different conditions for the trainer to assume that the dog will perform with predictability.

Next, the dog must perform reliably under any type of circumstance. Two variables are now introduced individually, not simultaneously.

+ **COMPLEXITY** is the increase in the difficulty of the task. This includes variations of the exercise in duration and distance.

+ **DISTRACTION** is a condition that diverts the dog's attention, interrupts concentration, increases excitement, or stimulates energy.

The dog must perform each behavior with both complexity and distraction individually with reliability before you combine both variables into an exercise.

For example, consider delivery to hand. The young dog reliably delivers to hand a single bumper in five different locations five different

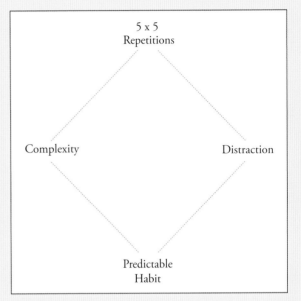

The Wildrose Stimulus Package

times. These could be five short trailing memory singles involving open ground, water, woodland, thick grass, and a pond edge. Then, begin to add more complex deliveries, which could involve a 180 trailing memory over a small log in one direction and under a four-strand fence into light cover in the other.

Next, separately introduce a distraction with delivery to hand out of water through decoys with two shots from a training pistol or throw a diversion as the dog returns. Once your dog is successful at several exposures, you'll be able to create a training scenario that will involve both variables simultaneously. Repeat the lesson in several locations to ensure competency. The stimulus package model is the best approach to developing any skill into a solid and predictable behavior.

A: The bumper is at a 90-degree angle to the dog's position. Gain the dog's attention with a whistle blast. *B:* Hold the dog's attention briefly. *C:* Ensure focused eye contact before the cast. *D:* Cast in the direction of the bumper from the center of your body with a verbal command.

will encourage your dog to want to stop to the whistle to receive that immediate gratification—the retrieve—and to see what you are about to do that could be of interest—like a tossed bumper, bird, or even a popper shot. Provide the dog a reason to want to stop and build the response to the point of habit. Again, don't be predictable. Once the dog is reliably stopping on the outbound, occasionally call him back to you and then send him straight for the retrieve. This ensures that he is focusing on your commands and not anticipating your intentions.

Left and Right Cast

Introducing left and right hand signals is easy if you return to your straightedge, either a wall or fence, to help set the dog up for success. Begin with a simple trailing memory along the fence using an easy-to-see white bumper. Walk down the fence 15 to 20 yards, turn the dog, place him at sit with his back to the fence, and walk out

about 15 yards. Turn to face the dog. Get the dog's attention with a blast of the whistle and the correct hand raised in the air—if the cast is to his right, raise your left hand. Slowly bring your hand down so you're looking at the dog through your fingers. He will be looking at your eyes and your hand as well. Shoot your hand to the left (or right) and introduce the verbal command "over" or "get on" as you step in the intended direction.

The straight barrier will encourage a straight line to the bumper. Repeat to the same side with the bumper set farther out, but still visible. Now, repeat the sequence in the opposite direction—two left and two right casts followed by a pull/push to reinforce the back command. This is enough for the day.

Pull Cast

Once the dog is able to reliably distinguish between the right and left cast along the fence or wall, add complexity by incorporating move-

A: Place the bumper as a sight or trailing memory. *B:* Throw a diversion in the opposite direction. *C:* The dog should redirect his eyes voluntarily or with a whistle blast before the cast.

ment. Think of a baseball diamond. From home plate, create a loop memory to place a single bumper at either first or third base. Continue the loop and leave the dog at second base as you walk back to home plate. Call the dog to you and stop him on the pitcher's mound. Make sure you raise the correct hand for the direction you want to send him. He should be looking right at you and waiting for a command. Cast him for the bumper and give him a verbal "good" just as he moves in the right direction. Remember your timing and reward him for the correct cast. Waiting until the dog returns from the retrieve is too late. Next, reestablish the pull-cast pattern for a hand signal in the opposite direction.

Left to Right with Diversion

Go back to the familiar fence or wall and set up your original casting drill as a trailing memory. With the barrier behind the dog's position and the memory placed, throw a diversion to the opposite side of the dog and then cast for the memory. Return the dog to the fence and get ready to cast for the diversion that has now become a memory. Repeat the pattern to pick the remaining bumper. Toss another diversion in the opposite direction and follow with a cast to the memory. Once your dog understands the concept, you will be ready to use the pull-cast exercises again, this time with diversions. Soon, you will be ready to begin casting in different locations, such as through ditches, over fences, and into the water.

Casting to Water

Using the pull-cast drill, walk your dog along the edge of the water and throw the bumper a short distance into the water. Continue walking for a short distance, turn, and put the dog at sit. Walk back past

A: Pull using the whistle and recall hand signal. ***B:*** *Stop and hold the dog steady briefly.* ***C:*** *Cast into the water.*

the floating bumper, turn, and face the dog. Call the dog forward and then parallel to the bumper, stop, and cast with the appropriate hand. Repeat this scenario in the opposite direction. As the dog becomes proficient, you can add complexity with diversions and by lengthening the distance of the retrieve.

You now have a dog with an excellent foundation in casting and stopping to the whistle, with complexity in movement and diversions. These subskills can now be built into training exercises and incorporated into training sessions using the cyclical model as the main exercises or the ending counter skill. Remember, train don't test, and step back to the most familiar skill if you run into problems.

Handling Exercises

We use a number of exercises at Wildrose to develop a young dog's handling ability, but there are a couple of things to consider before starting the exercises.

OVERHANDLING: Primarily handling exercises are developed using pull/stop—that is, stopping the dog for a signal as he approaches the handler rather than stopping him on the outbound. This helps to avoid overhandling with too many stops disrupting the dog's retrieve. Too many stops going out can reduce a dog's drive and cause the dog to anticipate the whistle stop. The pull/push and pull/cast techniques teach the lessons of handling with few negative side effects.

POPPING: This is a behavior in which a gundog begins to stop on a retrieve on his own initiative. The dog anticipates the stop or looks to the handler for encouragement or direction. Dysfunctional popping is when the dog spins quickly after he has been released for the retrieve or when the dog lacks self-confidence. This usually develops from overhandling or too much reliance on the handler's assistance. Functional popping, on the other hand, is a desirable trait in a hunting dog. For example, a dog goes on a long retrieve and disappears into the woods with great drive and searches diligently but to no avail. The dog returns to the edge of the woods and looks to the handler for further direction. This is a sign of teamwork and a good interdependent relationship. Now, on to the exercises.

Simple Baseball: This is a great drill to incorporate many of the casting skills previously taught to your dog. To set up the exercise, use a circle memory as discussed in Chapter Five by placing visible bumpers at first, second, and third base in a baseball field pattern. Walk your dog from home plate to third and drop a bumper, then on to second, and then first, and then place your dog on the pitcher's mound facing home. Go to home plate, raise the correct hand, and cast the dog to the first bumper placed. Once the dog has retrieved the

bumper, return him to the mound in the same position, blow the whistle, and raise the correct hand. Before you send him for the next retrieve, though, throw the first bumper picked back to its original position. Then, send him for the next bumper. Continue the exercise to successfully pick two rights, two lefts, and four backs. Remember that the back cast should comprise 50 percent of any casting exercises. Once successful on open ground, move the exercise to different terrain and incorporate ditches, fences, plowed ground, and the water's edge.

Walking Baseball Extensions: Using a large field of close-cropped grass, set up your baseball drill with the bumpers at least 30 yards away

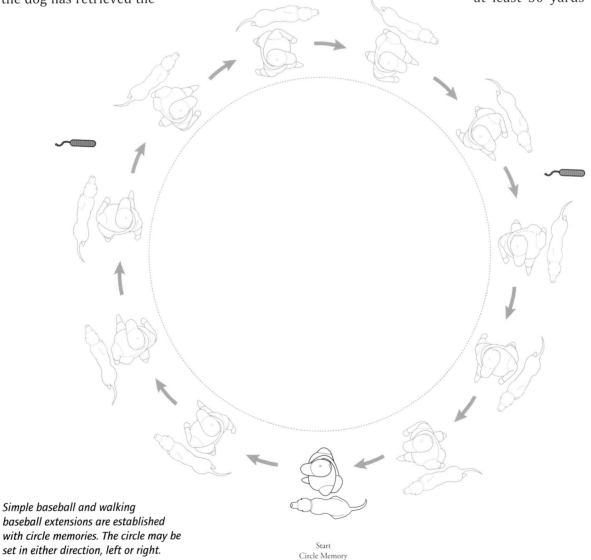

Simple baseball and walking baseball extensions are established with circle memories. The circle may be set in either direction, left or right.

Start
Circle Memory

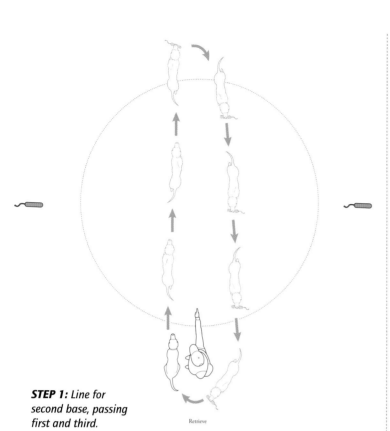

STEP 1: *Line for second base, passing first and third.*

Retrieve

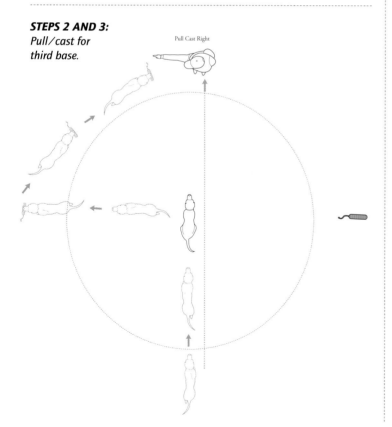

STEPS 2 AND 3: *Pull/cast for third base.*

Pull Cast Right

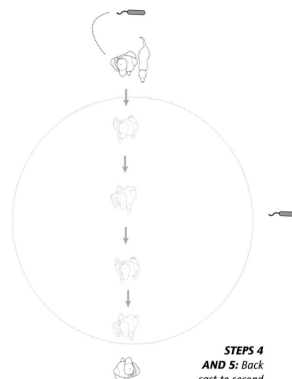

STEPS 4 AND 5: *Back cast to second base with the diversion in front.*

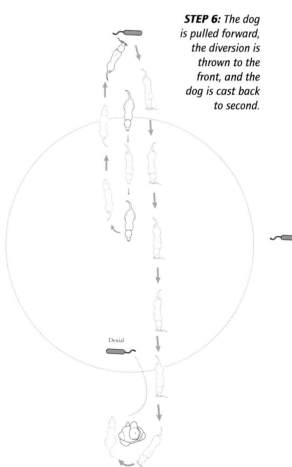

STEP 6: *The dog is pulled forward, the diversion is thrown to the front, and the dog is cast back to second.*

Denial

from home plate. Set the pattern up again as a circle memory.

1— Once you place all three bumpers, take your dog to home plate and line him straight down the middle of the field past first and third to make the pick on second base. Here, you are ignoring two short birds to pick the longest bird first. Should your dog pull to one of the shorter birds, stop him immediately and move forward closer to second base, which will widen the angles.

2— Once the second bumper is successfully picked, leave the dog at home plate and walk to second base.

3— Complete a pull/stop at the pitcher's mound and cast to third base.

4— Upon the dog's return, drop a bumper behind your position at second and heel the dog forward toward home.

5— When you reach the pitcher's mound, blow the sit whistle and keep walking toward home.

6— Now run a pull/push. Call the dog forward. As he approaches, toss a short diversion in front of the dog as you stop him to the whistle. Then, complete a back cast to the bumper on second. Pay careful attention to the hand you cast with, as a bumper still remains on first base.

7— Once the dog returns to home plate, toss a bumper a short distance behind your position, leave the dog at home, and walk back to second base, picking up the diversion you tossed earlier as you pass. Next, complete a pull/stop at the pitcher's mound and cast for first base.

8— Now you have a long single bumper remaining at home plate. Toss out a short diversion to the side and with the de-select "no" and line the dog for the bumper at home. When he returns, pick up the short diversion as a denial.

The walking baseball extension combines many handling skills into one complete exercise. You can modify the drill for advanced training later on to lengthen casts, handle for unseens, and even hunt with the use of scented tennis balls.

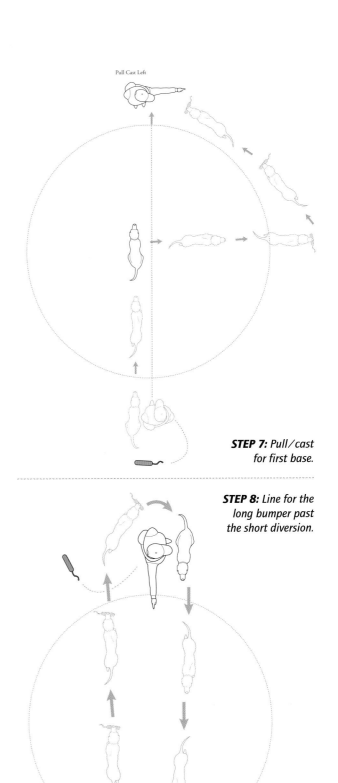

Pull Cast Left

STEP 7: *Pull/cast for first base.*

STEP 8: *Line for the long bumper past the short diversion.*

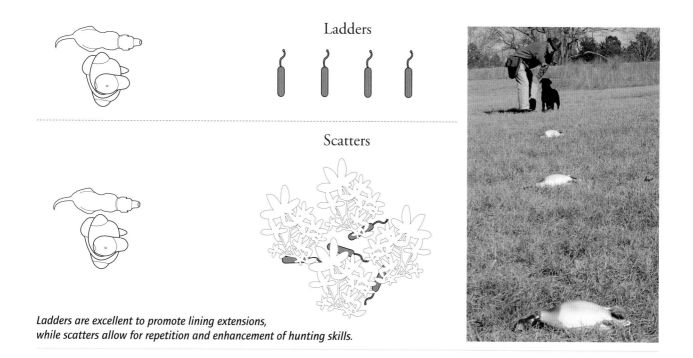

Ladders

Scatters

Ladders are excellent to promote lining extensions,
while scatters allow for repetition and enhancement of hunting skills.

LADDERS AND SCATTERS: There are two different ways to place multiple bumpers in the same area for repetitive retrieves, each with different functional purposes. Wildrose does not use the practice of piling bumpers—that is, placing multiple bumpers together in the same spot. This promotes shopping or switching, which will become a problem later. Ladders and scatters, or "salting," do not, as the bumpers are placed at a distance apart often not even visible to each other. Plus, the average wingshooter does not pile birds on a hunt. Realistically, birds are more likely to fall scattered around the area, so piled bumpers offer no benefit to the training experience.

Ladders is the practice of placing multiple bumpers 10 yards or more apart in a straight line to teach lining extensions. This forces the dog to run farther to find the next bumper.

Scatters is the practice of salting an area with scattered bumpers to provide multiple retrieves in a common place and offer the additional benefit of enhancing hunting skills by developing search patterns. Bumpers are scattered in an area and the returning dog must search that area for the next bumper. Place the bumpers at a distance apart based on the size of the search pattern you want to establish with your dog.

HUNTING COVER

A great gundog is a great game-finder, one that gets into the thickest cover or coldest water and roots out those hard-to-find birds. In the hunting world, the dog's nose knows.

Always be aware of the wind and scenting conditions. Sending a young dog on a hunting cover exercise with the wind at his back is going to make the find more difficult since the scent will be going away from his approach. Run your training exercise into the wind at first. If the

The most important attribute of a gundog is his nose.

Training Tools

FEATHER-LACED BUMPERS: Use small bumpers with game-bird wings taped securely to each. A variety of colors serve to enhance the hunt as well. Use yellow or green bumpers for lush green grasses and dark orange or black for woodlands.

SCENTED TENNIS BALLS: Place several green tennis balls in a bag of game-bird feathers for about two weeks. When you use them, you'll have some excellent objects to hunt.

TENNIS BALL THROWER: A Chuck-It is an excellent tool for launching tennis balls.

wind is coming from an angle (crosswind), adjust your line a bit to compensate before sending the dog. For example, if the wind direction is from your left, line the dog a bit to the right of the scented target and he will hit the scent cone on approach and turn left into the target. If you line him directly at the target, he may overrun.

Begin by placing scented tennis balls as sight or trailing memories in thick cover. Delay briefly and then send the dog into the wind. If your youngster has trouble with the small ball at first, use feather-covered puppy bumpers. They'll hold scent better than the ball and will be easier to find.

As the dog begins to hit the scent, you can see his body language change with excitement. When the dog has obviously identified the scent, repeat your hunt command: "hunt dead," "hunt dead." In time, your pup will recognize this cue and know your intentions to stop and hunt.

The Unseen

Drop the ball without the pup's knowledge, walk away a few steps, and line the pup back into the cover. At the appropriate time, blow your stop whistle and give the "hunt dead" command. To help hold the pup in a tighter

area, use a smaller body of grass or brush rather than a huge grass field. Circles of high grass left unmowed work great for this purpose. This defines the hunt area for the youngster.

As a final step, you want the young dog to mark by sound and hunt the area where he hears the fall. Cover the pup's eyes and toss the bumper into thick cover or shoot a launcher bumper. When the pup gets close to the fall area, give the hunt command. The Chuck-It or tossed-in scented tennis balls work great for marking by sound followed by a hunt. As the ball hits the ground, it may bounce or roll, providing great practice for a short track and hunting cover. Launcher bumpers

With his eyes covered, this gundog marks totally by the sound of the falling bumper.

Training for marks must include both sight and sound, plus marking off the gun.

tumbling through timber provide much the same. Dogs will quickly become good listeners as well as splendid hunters.

Later, these skills will pay dividends in the field. The game dog will mark by sight and sound and learn to hold a hunt area tightly, thoroughly searching the cover for scent.

MARKING

A versatile gundog must be a good marker. Marking is the dog's ability to accurately pick a bird that he sees fall despite the influences of terrain or environmental conditions. For the versatile sporting dog, the conditions can be quite tough.

First, you want to develop the dog's ability to watch the field and see the bird fall. An effective dog will watch the shooter and the direction of the shotgun's point when fired (marking off the gun), and will possess the ability to hold focus on the correct area of the fall (concentration).

When it's time to train for marks, add a bit of realism. Work in groups from a sitting position and involve a shotgun so the youngster begins to mark well by watching the direction in which the gun is pointed. This skill is beneficial in a dove field, duck blind, or on a pheasant hunt.

Using a feather-covered bumper, have an assistant walk out into the field to throw the mark. As the assistant walks, he or she should spin the bumper to hold the dog's attention. As he or she prepares to throw, begin to use the "watch" cue. Repeat "watch" quietly as the dog focuses on the spinning bumper. In time, the "watch" cue will have your dog looking to the sky or field for action.

Use a simulated gun or toy gun for early marks to teach your dog to track the movement of your gun barrel. Point the simulated gun at the thrower as the dog watches right down the barrel. As the bumper is thrown, track the trajectory of the mark with the toy gun and follow the flight path all the way to the ground. For a moment, hold the gun pointed at the fall area, allowing the dog to focus on the area while remaining steady. If your dog has the mark, just release him by name. Do not attempt to physically line if the dog

Negotiating any obstacle is an important element of effective training for marks.

has the mark sighted. Your hand movements will only interfere with his sight picture.

For the next sequence, hide your thrower out of sight of the dog. Repeat the drill in a more realistic location, such as woodlands, fields, or on the water. You can now use a shotgun with blanks for more realism. Obviously, you should not point the gun in any direction close to the thrower. Use your "watch" cue and point where the bumper is likely to appear in the sky. Your dog should be picking up on the idea of watching the gun for an indication of the bird's location in flight. Remember, deny your dog 50 percent of all marks. You pick them or allow an honor dog to do so.

Second, your dog must be proficient at distance estimation—how far to run. Otherwise,

your dog may run short of the fall area to begin his search or overrun the bird and disappear into distant cover. The best way to develop lining skills for marking is with memory exercises. The sight, trailing, and circle memories will improve lining ability without compromising steadiness, whereas too many marks will likely create unsteadiness.

Third, your gundog must have the ability to run a straight line to the area of the fall despite obstacles; influences or barriers, such as fences, logs, rough terrain, or thick cover; or environmental conditions, such as wind, rain, or snow. Again, memories are the best way to practice building these skills.

Last, a good marker must hunt hard once he gets to the area of the fall. Not all birds will remain

Marking by Sound

On a wingshoot, about a third of all birds are going to fall behind your position, so train for it. Using a training dummy launched by an assistant shooter directly in front of your position, have a bumper shot overhead into woodlands or heavy cover behind your position. Quite likely, your hunter will watch as you track the path of the bumper with the gun. Your dog will pick up on this scenario quickly—learning to watch the flight path of the bird as far as possible, then listening carefully to mark the fall area. Again, if the dog has the area marked behind you, forget lining, just release him by name and let him do the work. Get ready for this one. Birds are

A dog in a dog hide has limited visibility.

going to fall behind the hide on a duck hunt and behind your walk-up line on a pheasant hunt. Make sure to train for it.

exactly at the spot where they fall. In thick cover, you will need an aggressive hunter, a dog that will hold a tight search pattern using lots of nose—a real game-finder. Scented tennis balls are excellent for developing pinpoint marking. The helper tosses the ball high for the mark. The ball will be a much more difficult find for the starter. This is where hunting cover training pays off.

Marking training is much more than just tossing bumpers around or firing a launcher shot. On the hunt:

✦ You will be working in thick cover or deep, cold water. Visibility will likely be limited.

✦ You will often be working under high stimuli and confusion. Other dogs and hunters will contribute loads of distractions.

✦ Your dog will need to remember multiple falls (more than one bird down) with accuracy.

What about secondary flushes of an upland bird? For example, just as your dog takes a line out to the marked bird, he steps on another pheasant, which flushes and becomes a target for another hunter; or, when out for a retrieve on a duck hunt, another bird is dropped. Will your dog switch or stay on his original mark? Slowly incorporate these and other realistic conditions into meaningful training for marks.

It's also imperative that you practice realistic marking skills while your dog is in motion, like walking or hunting cover, not just as he sits beside you. Practice marks as you heel your dog through fields or woodlands. The marks, shot or thrown by an assistant, should come from all angles. All birds won't fall straight in front of you on the hunt.

You want your dog to concentrate on what's going on in the field while remaining with you at heel. This is multitasking so to speak, but don't throw the marks yourself. Birds originate in the field or over water, not from your bumper bag. As the game dog is hunting or quartering the field, practice marks as well. Effective marking when the dog is interested in hunting pursuits is quite different than when he is sitting at your side.

Prepare thoroughly well before the hunt for any circumstances that may challenge the dog.

Marking ability, which is largely a skill of eyesight and lining ability, should be practiced in realistic conditions just like you might find on the hunt. Marks should fall in all directions around your position, just like you would experience in the field or marsh. A good balance would be: one-third to the front, one-third behind you to the rear, and one-third to your extreme right or left.

Transition to the Hunt

Before taking your gundog prospect on a real hunt, I strongly suggest that you wait until he is at least 14 months old, nicely matured, and has total confidence in you as the handler. Also, the dog should have completed all the lessons of the basic gundog series highlighted in Chapters Five and Six. Additionally, before the first hunt, you want to complete several transitional training exercises—that is, "training as you will hunt." Transitional training scenarios are designed to

duplicate the conditions of the hunt as closely as possible. Transitional training for the gundog is similar to scrimmaging for a college football team or war games for a military combat unit—practice as you will play.

Obviously, the excitement and challenge of a real duck or upland hunt is hard to duplicate, but you need to evaluate your dog under these conditions before finding yourself afield with an unprepared candidate.

In transitional training, dress the part and use heavy shotgun loads. You may incorporate a few hand-thrown clays duplicating flyers to shoot, which are always very exciting. Incorporate the gear you will use on the hunt, and use the type of game birds that you will be hunting. Hopefully, you've saved a few birds from last season for just such an occasion. Even better, you could take in a day's shooting at a game preserve. Do not make the mistake of just running a few yard-work exercises, then heading out on a hunt and expecting excellent results. Remember, dogs don't generalize

Transitional training requires practicing as you will play in actual hunting situations.

well and training skills learned in the yard or in field training may not transfer easily to practical, real-time hunting situations. It is necessary to practice a few realistic scenarios just the way you'll hunt before the first field experience.

First Hunts

The young dog's first hunt is not a shooting experience at all for you. You are actually training. You will need to focus on a few goals for the starter:

✦ To keep the youngster steady, use a four-foot or six-foot tree-tie lead. This will guarantee no slipups. Only release the dog when it's time to make a retrieve.

✦ Maintain denials. Pick up a few of the short birds yourself or allow another dog to do so.

✦ Keep the rookie calm and watch for gunshot sensitivity.

Occasionally, multiple shots fired by several hunters using heavy load ammunition can be a bit much for a young dog. If hunting with friends, it is wise to sit outside the blind or walk at a dis-

tance, not quite so close to the action on the first few shots. You are there to continue the dog's training, not for the shooting. Your job is to provide the starter with an awakening to the understanding of what the field experience is all about, to move those repetitive lessons practiced so hard and so long into real time—the hunt. Concentrate on obedience. Do not compromise your standards for heel work, delivery to hand, quiet patience, and steadiness. Civility matters.

If you're an upland hunter, the same rules apply for the first bird hunt. Remember, the pup is still learning and nothing is learned from failure. Moreover, you do not want your dog to learn bad habits associated with the field experience. Make sure you set your dog up to succeed on his first hunt.

I find little more thrilling than when I see the "light bulb" come on in the mind of a youngster on his first hunt. You can see the expressions change in the dog's face, in his eyes, as he puts things together. The dog's very focus and intensity seems to mature instantly when he sees that first bird. Now your hunting companion understands what it's all about.

■ Parting Thoughts

The basic Wildrose Way training course emphasizes steadiness, patience, and control as very high priorities. You may find, as a result, that your starter is a bit "sticky," so to speak, when faced with new experiences on the hunt. By sticky, I mean a reluctance to execute when confused. For instance, the dog may not go when released for a retrieve under conditions he has not yet experienced. He could stop on a line out for an unseen. Perhaps he refuses to chase his first wounded bird or gives up on a pesky diver duck. That's OK for starters. You have heavily emphasized steadiness and other control behaviors rather than chasing game and independent behaviors for months on end in basic training, but I assure you the dog will "shoot loose." Like a brand-new over-and-under shotgun, which exhibits a very tight action, over time and with wear it will "shoot loose." And so will your disciplined hunting companion. Focus on the fundamentals and maintain realistic expectations for the first hunts; the journey afield has just begun.

A waterproof, tree-tie lead secures the dog to ensure steadiness for his first hunts without the use of a collar.

FINISHING WORK

LITTLE COMPLEMENTS A PASSIONATE WINGSHOOTER MORE than a dynamic yet well-mannered gundog. Such an animal becomes a source of pride for the owner and the envy of his sporting companions. A finished gundog is the culmination of several years of dedicated work and realistic hunting experience.

Finishing work takes basic training skills to the next level, turning a novice gundog into a versatile wingshooting companion—a true Gentleman's Gundog. It involves developing the dog to manage complexity, improve handling, extend range, and—most of all—to become "game smart." The waterdog develops distance, lining, and handling ability, while the upland game dog learns the art of hunting patterns and uses the wind to locate game. But in the end, there is no substitute for actual hunting experience. No game-bird exposure, no game dog.

CHAPTER 7

The Finished Waterfowl Retriever

D rake, Ducks Unlimited's first mascot, was an unusual retriever to train from the start. He was "soft" in nature, but highly intelligent. He possessed fantastic scenting abilities and a passion for birds—any bird. As his training advanced and public demonstrations of his talents became more frequent, he would often go "flat," disinterested in repetitious training routines and especially in the simple drills he performed so many times at events. What to do?

Mitchell Crawford, an Ole Miss student at the time, was a volunteer training assistant at the kennel. On one occasion, after a particularly unimpressive display of drive and style, typical of a bored Drake, Mitchell commented, "Drake likes new things." His observation was obvious and correct. Drake could easily become bored.

So began our development of training lessons to teach necessary, advanced waterdog skills while avoiding the application of force to make remote corrections and to prevent boredom. A highly intelligent dog with natural ability needs challenge and stimulation in the training experience to keep interest keen. Therefore, the trainer or handler mandate requires creativity. It takes a bit of planning to avoid excessive repetition in your instruction. The trainer or handler must also consider consistently setting up the dog for success, yet providing opportunities for the dog to think independently, and accomplishing these mandates without boring the dog to the point of disinterest.

The waterfowling experience engenders passion in hunters and demands a great deal from a working dog. Flocks of birds circle across the blood-red skies of dawn. The air is often icy and cold, and large decoy spreads are strewn in front of the blind.

This is Drake, Ducks Unlimited's first retriever mascot.

low water, and even plowed ground and row crops. Lessons may require:

- ✦ Wearing the gear and clothing that you'll wear on the hunt.
- ✦ Practicing lining the dog while standing in shallow water.
- ✦ Using calls, decoys, and gunfire.
- ✦ Incorporating blinds, hides, and boats.
- ✦ Using cold game, feathered bumpers, and scented tennis balls.

The difference between basic and advanced waterdog training at a minimum is the complexity of the retrieves and distances involved. In basic gundog work, activities were kept relatively short to maintain control and to ensure your young starter didn't launch into an independent frolic on a hunt. Now, you can gradually extend distances with lining and handling exercises. A 45-yard retrieve may become 100 yards or more. A 20-yard hand signal cast will extend to 40 yards or more on both land and water. Advanced waterdog training is preparing for the unexpected by training your retriever to do a few important core skills very well. Your purpose is to produce a competent thinker who remains under control and trusting of you as the handler.

Multiple shooters huddle in small blinds. There is no shortage of mud but sometimes a great shortage of visibility. Other dogs are working and there is scent everywhere from previously fallen birds.

These are some of the conditions that a seasoned retriever must face on an actual duck hunt, not to mention the necessity to sit patiently for hours on end on those slow bird days. Advanced waterdog training is more than throwing long marks or engaging your dog in complex pattern drills. It's preparing for real-time shooting conditions and developing the dog's ability to pick those difficult birds that could otherwise be lost.

■ Advanced Preparation

What training areas are available to provide the diversity and realism necessary? You will need large open fields with a variety of cover and contours, both large and small bodies of water, flooded timber, marshlands, both deep and shal-

EXTENSIONS

Developing your dog's ability to pick birds and handle at longer distances is the first step in waterdog finishing work. There are two basic concepts to understand before proceeding to actual training exercises:

1– How to develop lining ability without undermining the dog's steadiness or compromising confidence.

2– How to properly line the dog.

Back Chaining and Linked-In

There are two similar approaches for the first challenge, teaching long lines while enhancing confidence. Both use the Wildrose trailing mem-

Advanced training is preparing for retrieves of greater complexity and distance.

ories and work on the basis that the last behavior the dog accomplishes is the one he will remember most. The trailing memory allows the dog to be running toward the familiar, therefore gaining confidence for success.

BACK CHAINING promotes progressive learning by teaching a dog through working in sequences. Your training connects basic skills linked together one at a time, beginning with the last skill in the sequence and working backward to the first. You're developing multiple skills in sequence to perform a long retrieve despite influences or obstacles. You can accomplish this by breaking each challenge or task in the long retrieve into segments, with the last step introduced first. Each behavior in the chain reinforces the previous performed behavior. The final step is taught first and becomes the most familiar. As the dog accomplishes each segment, he is getting closer to the familiar, so he is running toward confidence, success, and reward.

LINKED-IN is similar to back chaining in its progressive linking of individual skills and segments to complete an overall exercise, but it differs in one way: you do not necessarily teach each required segment in progression. The trainer develops the behaviors and skills individually and then links them together in segments with a bit of overlap in each. This method is useful when teaching a complex scenario that involves areas that cannot be negotiated or back chained. A perfect example is an across-water retrieve with a long land exit and reentry on the far bank. In this case, you would teach each link necessary for the retrieve and then connect them together, similar to the way a modern construction crew assembles a large ship or aircraft; each component is individually constructed and then connected together. The result is that one sequence interconnects to the next. This causes the dog to remember the previous exercise, which will be the following sequence in the chain. You are developing causal relationships (see Chapter Five for more information) and all links are connected to complete the exercise.

PROPERLY LINING THE DOG

As previously discussed, proper alignment of the dog's nose, spine, and tail is important to establish a dog's initial line (direction of travel) to a

Primary and Secondary Reset

When confronted with a situation in which your dog does not perform correctly on a retrieve, what do you do?

PRIMARY RESET is when the handler completely scratches the effort, recalls the dog back to heel, and attempts another approach. It is a complete reboot and a fresh start. For example, the dog disregards the line given by the handler. Rather than handling out of the problem, recall the dog and reset. Or perhaps the dog refuses to cast properly. Either the dog is confused or he is ignoring your signals. Don't reward this dysfunction by allowing the dog to ultimately locate the bumper. In both cases, recall and reset.

SECONDARY RESET involves pulling the dog by recall closer to the handler but not all the way back, shortening the distance, regaining focus, and attempting the signal or command again. This process is quite familiar to the dog because of the numerous pull/push and pull/cast exercises performed throughout his training life. For example, the dog switches for the wrong bird. After repeated casts, the dog continues to pull to the distraction. Recall the dog closer to you and away from the suction. Stop, regain the dog's calm focus, and attempt a new cast. Both approaches are highly effective in addressing failures in training and even hunting situations.

Secondary reset pulls the dog closer to the handler, and then, with a brief stop, the dog is recast to the correct area.

memory. There are two parts to running a line to a memory or an unseen retrieve:

1–*Taking the initial line*—Running a straight line with confidence for the first 15 to 20 yards in the direction of the fall.

2–*Holding the line*—The ability to stay on course despite influences or conditions.

This sounds simple in concept, but there are a group of factors that exist in the field and marsh seemingly just to disrupt your dog's path. An astute handler reads the course. That is, he or she looks out to the area in the direction of the retrieve and the location of the fall, all the while considering the environmental factors, terrain, barriers, and suction influences, including:

A retriever takes an initial line while training in realistic conditions.

✦ **Environmental Factors:** Wind, snow, fog, cold, heat, and lighting.

✦ **Terrain:** Slopes and contours of the land, ditches, abrupt changes in cover, water, and moving water.

✦ **Barriers:** Both physical and psychological barriers (see Chapter Five for more information).

✦ **Suction:** Points of land protruding into the water, cover, scent from old falls, diversions, and distractions.

The handler must calculate the potential disruption to the dog's course due to these factors. He or she must attempt to compensate for their influence before setting the line and releasing the dog. I commonly say at workshops that the average golfer puts more thought into lining up a drive than the average hunter does when lining a dog. The big difference between the two is the dog has an opinion while the golf ball does not.

Take headwinds, for example. Dogs don't like running straight into a headwind. Compensate for this factor. Most dogs tend to fade with the wind just as they fade with the downward slope of a hillside. With a crosswind, there are two approaches to consider. Line the dog wide of and above the target into the crosswind, realizing that he will likely fade downwind as he runs toward the bird and will drift right into the correct scent zone. Or, you may decide to line a bit downwind of the target so that your dog arrives close to the bird in the scent cone area and turns into it.

> ⚜ **WILDROSE TIP** ⚜
>
> *The best way to adjust your dog's body alignment is with the turns, squares, and reverse heel movements taught in yard work. Body alignment is not achieved through touching or physically moving the dog.*

A powerful retriever lines for a long unseen.

Lining Extensions

Extension exercises develop the dog's ability to run long straight lines to a fall despite influences and enhance the dog's memory capabilities. There are many applications used at Wildrose to accomplish this goal in training, but all relate to the four types of memories: trailing, sight, circle, and loop. Just modify the exercises to fit the training scenarios you wish to accomplish. Here is where creativity begins in training. Memory patterns are like building blocks; once taught, you can construct any scenario you would like.

Remember Wildrose Law No. 8: Get it right on land before going to the water. This law certainly applies now, as you are teaching very long retrieves and how to handle multiple falls at distances. Get it right on land first, as it's difficult to make appropriate corrections or help a student when swimming in deep water.

I once asked an old Mississippi Delta farmer how he was able to plow very long straight furrows even on rolling ground before the inven-

tion of the geonavigation system used on today's tractors. "Easy," he replied, "Just pick out a tree, post, or any fixed object on the horizon and drive straight to it." This works for developing lining extensions as well—teach the dog to look way out to a reference point on the horizon. It works in training and it works brilliantly on the hunt.

> ### ⚔ WILDROSE TIP ⚔
> *Wildrose has a simple rule for the order in which ducks are picked on the hunt. Pick runners first, longest bird second, first bird down third. There are fewer chances for a lost bird with this approach. Remember, the Wildrose Way is to train as you will hunt and hunt as you have trained.*

Bumpers are placed at fixed reference points using a circle memory. Bumpers will be retrieved in the order of placement, first to last.

Circle Memory Extensions and Multiple Retrieves

Select a large field. I'm talking about acres here, an area that offers different factors, such as short cover, slopes, a ditch, or perhaps a field road. Select three or four obvious reference points that are natural in the field, such as trees, bushes, or large rocks, rather than using man-made devices, like flags, buckets, or cones. You won't see any of these types of crutches on a hunt. Realistic reference points will be the locations where you will place your bumpers. Train the dog to look at the points as you line, first at short distances. In time, when you set up your dog for a line in the field, he will look out for the point you identify with your arm or hand as you line. Remember, in lining, point with your arm, don't cast.

Set up the pattern as a circle memory, placing each bumper at the base of the reference point. Allow the dog a moment to contemplate each area, and then move on, maintaining a wide circle, to the next point. After all the bumpers are in place, line

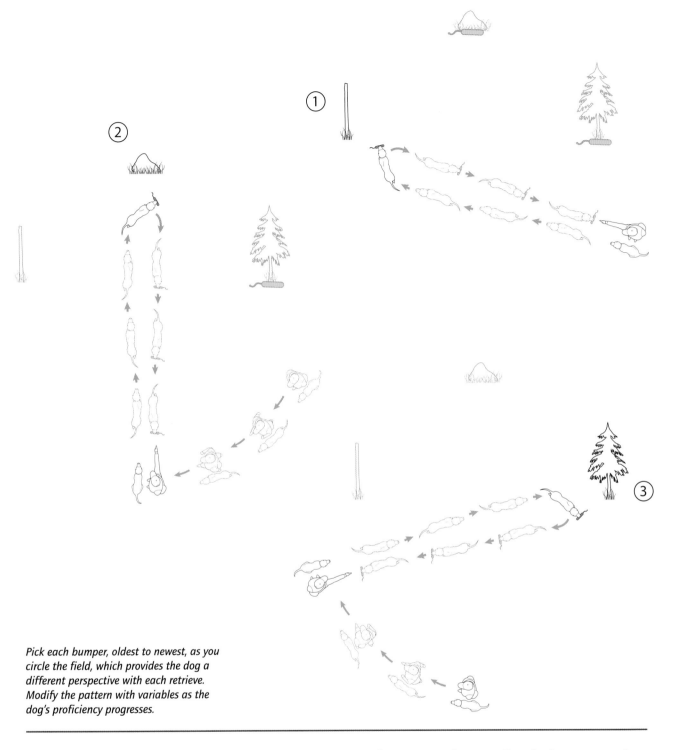

Pick each bumper, oldest to newest, as you circle the field, which provides the dog a different perspective with each retrieve. Modify the pattern with variables as the dog's proficiency progresses.

to the first. Once collected, move to another position and line to the second, continuing the circle and picking the sequence until completion.

Variables to the pattern are endless. As you circle, replace the bumper that was picked at a new reference point for additional retrieves as you continue the circle. Toss out short bumpers

as diversions when you line for long memories.

After the dog understands the concept of running to the reference point, begin to move the placement of feathered bumpers to different sides of the reference point, which will require the dog to hunt in a search pattern. Each time you send the dog, he hits the area and makes a

Lining extensions should involve realistic conditions including thick cover, timber, and marshlands.

circle search for the find. Move the bumper location to alternating sides between lessons.

Circle Memory Double Hub

The double hub is a modification of the single circle memory exercise described in Chapter Five. Pick two reference points and salt four bumpers at each. As an example, consider a large field surrounding the upper portion of a pond. Establish a tree as one reference point. The other will be about 40 yards away in a willow-choked inlet with water and grass. With four bumpers in place, begin circling around the entire area in an ever-widening pattern. Stop and line for retrieves as you advance. The retrieves should alternate between the two established points, one pick made with each stop. By the time you reach the far side of the circle, you're almost running unseens. If the cover is heavy, use feather-laced bumpers to encourage a bold hunt. The pattern will become more challenging as distance expands and the dog is required to run past the shorter point for bumpers that are farther out. Also, it is a great memory-enhancement exercise for the dog.

MULTIPLE FALLS

Initial Drills

The initial skill set in establishing multiple falls is the short bird/long bird concept. Your objective is to condition the dog to ignore the short bird and line correctly for the long memories. Later, you may apply the same concept to marking and unseens.

The pattern is set up as a circle memory by placing two feather-laced bumpers or cold game birds into cover. As the circle nears completion, throw a short diversion to the center of the configuration. With the circle completed, line for the first placement past the short diversion. Direct the dog away from the diversion by saying "no" as a redirect. Take a couple of steps forward

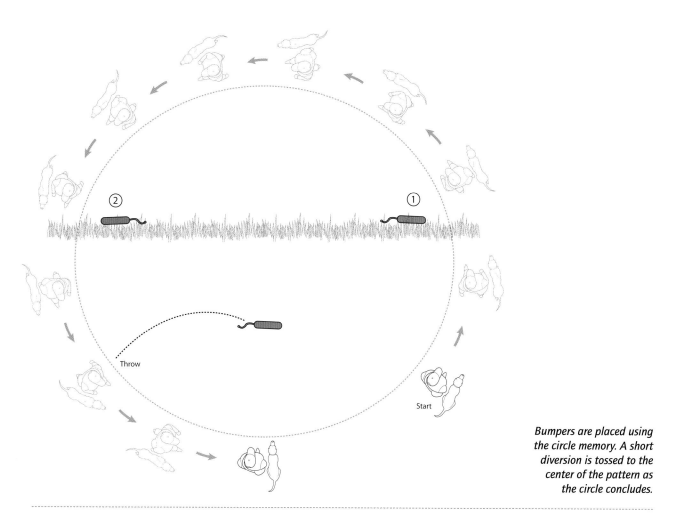

Start

Throw

② ①

Bumpers are placed using the circle memory. A short diversion is tossed to the center of the pattern as the circle concludes.

Retrieves are made in order of placement, oldest (bumper 1) followed by newest (bumper 2). If the dog pulls to the short bumper, use a primary reset. The short bumper becomes a denial.

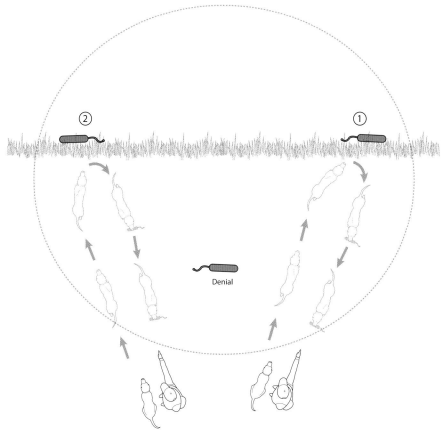

② ①

Denial

along the desired line, and then send for the memory. Follow up by retrieving the second memory. Conclude the exercise by placing the dog at sit and picking up the short bird yourself as a denial.

Multiple Pattern Drills

There are three basic Wildrose patterns to use to develop a dog's memory for multiple falls. You may use the concepts in a variety of ways—varying distance, terrain, cover, or how tight to establish the lines in relation to each other to create suction.

STEP 2: *Line for the first bumper placed and continue the retrieves in order of placement.*

Mercedes Drill
STEP 1: *Place bumpers using a circle memory and return to the center of the pattern.*

✦ **MERCEDES DRILL:** The name implies how the pattern is established; it is in the shape of a Mercedes-Benz three-point star logo. Using a circle memory, set two bumpers at fixed reference points relatively close together in a V pattern and set the third one quite long to the rear. This is a great way to start dogs on triples or quads without confusion. Pick the bumpers in the order of placement—first placed, first picked.

✦ **PECAN TRIPLE:** This drill is named after the location where we begin to teach this scenario at Wildrose—a pecan grove. Establish three trees or points of cover as reference points. Two should be relatively close to each other and farther out. The third should be closer and either to the right or left of the first two. Pick the two longer birds in order of placement, ignoring the short bird, which is picked last.

Pecan Triple

STEP 1: *Bumpers are placed at reference points in a circle memory. Bumpers 1 and 2 are in closer proximity to each other and at a longer distance from bumper 3.*

STEP 2: *Pick bumpers in order of placement.*

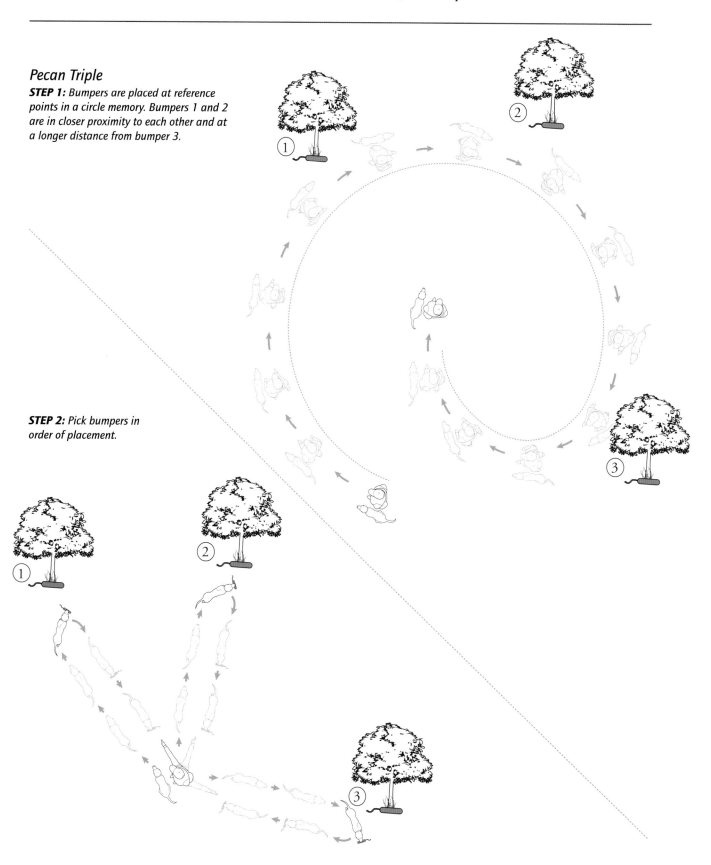

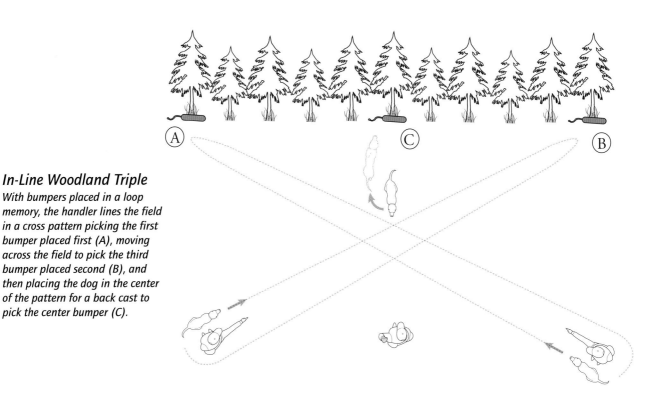

In-Line Woodland Triple
With bumpers placed in a loop memory, the handler lines the field in a cross pattern picking the first bumper placed first (A), moving across the field to pick the third bumper placed second (B), and then placing the dog in the center of the pattern for a back cast to pick the center bumper (C).

◆ **IN-LINE WOODLAND TRIPLE:** Place bumpers along a wood's edge as a loop memory about 30 yards apart at reference points using large trees or bushes. With the last bumper placed, the handler moves out in the field parallel to that reference point. The retrieving order is to pick the first bumper placed (A), followed by the handler then moving across the field to a position parallel to the first reference point. The retrieve is made for the last bumper placed (B). The second bumper placed (C) at the center of the pattern served as a distraction as your dog ran past. It now becomes retrieve number three as a back cast. Do not directly line for it. Place the dog in the center of the pattern with bumper three directly behind his position. Walk away and give a back cast.

Once established, you can easily modify these patterns by adding short bird diversions; reversing the order of placement or order of picking; moving your position to create different angles; or moving the patterns to different terrain. Modification is the key to keeping the dog's interest keen.

When the dog is totally familiar with the patterns at the same location, modify the scenario by preplacing feather-laced bumpers at each known reference point. Then, go get your dog. This time he hasn't seen the placement. Line exactly as you have been practicing. Your dog will likely get the picture immediately and line for each unseen. You have now established permanent unseens.

The next step is running cold unseens, which will be discussed in detail later in this chapter. Plus, you have accomplished these successes without the use of force or compromising the confidence of your dog.

HANDLING EXTENSIONS

Handling extensions involve two disciplines: the dog's ability to understand handling commands at greater distances, including whistles and hand signals, and the dog's ability to extend his range on casts left, right, and back.

To begin, return to the pull-casting method (which was described in Chapter Six), but now use it at greater distances. To avoid the possibility of your dog thinking that you lack control at these longer ranges, slowly increase the distances. Again, do this first on land where you can master the skills to provide direction that may not be possible on water. Once proficient, move the concept to as many different water sources as possible: flooded timber, deep water, creeks, and marshes. Practice

A gundog attempts to take a line from the confines of a layout blind.

opposite bank. Pull your dog into the water and stop, casting to either A or C. Next, line your dog across for bumper B. When he is halfway across, stop the dog and cast for the remaining bumper—either A or C. Upon completion, line for B straight across the water.

Unseen Casting

Set up a pull-cast pattern and repeat the lessons for several days at the same location on land or water. Preset the bumpers and then bring your dog and run the familiar pattern in the exact same place. This becomes a permanent unseen. Occasionally increase the significance of the find with cold game, which motivates the dog and keeps interest high.

You may also use the pull cast to teach the dog how to hold longer lines on a cast. For example, place three feather-laced bumpers as a ladder

handling while sitting at a ground position, such as a layout blind or from inside a blind. The dog needs to see as many potential scenarios as possible.

Set up pull-cast lessons in this fashion: Walk around the edge of a small water source and toss out a bumper at some distance into the water. Continue forward with the dog another 40 yards. Turn and leave the dog at sit as you walk past the bumper yet another 40 yards. Call the dog forward with a pull recall. Just as you stop the dog, throw a long bumper or fire a launcher as a diversion opposite the memory on the water. Cast your dog for the floating memory. Upon completion, merely reverse the exercise for another pull cast.

Another option is to establish a circle memory using three bumpers placed around the edge of a small pond. Place bumpers A and C at the water's edge as you circle with the dog. Return the dog back to the center, which will be in proximity to bumper B. With the dog at sit, walk around to the

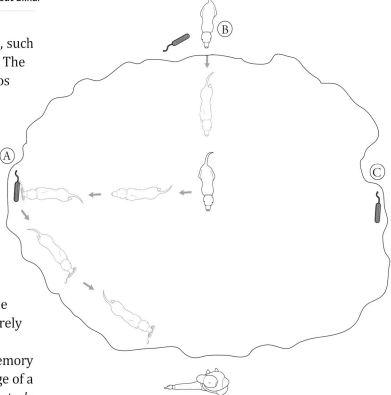

Casting on Water
With three bumpers placed, call the dog forward, stop, and cast to A; line the dog for B, stop midway, and cast for C; and finally, line for B.

beginning at 20 yards inside cover. Set the dog up for a pull cast some distance away from your position. Pull the dog forward, stop with the whistle, and follow with a cast into the cover. Next, reverse the pull cast and pick another bumper. Finally, pick the remaining bumper as a back cast by placing the dog with the last bumper directly behind him. Call the dog forward, whistle stop, toss a diversion directly in front of the dog, and follow with a back cast deep into cover (pull/push). If the dog does not hold a correct line on these retrieves, he will not be successful.

You may use the same methods to teach handling across moving water or casting into woodlands. Use the pull-cast approach combined with the occasional whistle stop when the dog is going out for the retrieve, but remember to avoid overhandling on the outbound to prevent dysfunctional popping, spinning, anticipation, or lack of confidence.

UNSEENS OR BLINDS

Unseens are retrieves to recover game that the dog didn't see fall. The skill is necessary for both finished upland and waterfowl retrievers. Examples include a duck that sails long into timber that the retriever couldn't see from his position in the duck blind or an upland flusher who did not see a bird fall behind the walk-up line. The same will be true on a covey flush where several quail drop in different directions, which cannot be marked by the dog simultaneously.

With the consistent use of memory patterns and handling exercises combined with the occasional permanent unseen, you have already laid the groundwork for lining for an unseen. There are four parts to running an unseen:

- ✦ **LINING:** The ability of the dog to take and carry the correct line or direct route to a bird despite influences.
- ✦ **HANDLING:** The control to direct the dog back to the correct line or to a fall area.
- ✦ **HUNTING:** Once in the area of the bird, the dog hunts aggressively and will hold to the area.

- ✦ **CONFIDENCE:** The dog's confidence in himself and his confidence in the handler's ability to direct him to the bird.

Unseens Made Easy

The progression to running an unseen includes four elements: memories, permanent unseens, time-delay memories, and cold unseens.

MEMORIES—including sight, trailing, circle, and loop—make the transition to unseens much easier than training programs that involve a great deal of marked retrieves, because in memories, like unseens, the dog does not see anything fall. The dog is more interdependent with the handler and does not rely as much on what he sees. Now you may understand the rationale behind

This dog exhibits the intense focus of a finished waterfowl retriever.

Wildrose Law No. 10: Memories before hand signals, hand signals before marks.

PERMANENT UNSEENS are just an extension of frequently run memories that the dog has experienced multiple times. Preplace the bumper, collect your dog, and then run the unseen. The dog goes out with the confidence of familiarity even though he has not seen anything fall or be placed.

TIME-DELAY MEMORIES (TDMs) may be used frequently in training to build the dog's ability to remember old falls. As the name implies, TDMs are extended delays in which the bird or bumper is placed as the dog watches early in the cyclical training model, perhaps during the energy burn power walk. Complete all lessons, then return to make the TDM pick as a counter skill. Sometimes as the dog advances, you may run the retrieve from different positions than where they were established. In group work, the time delay before the actual retrieve is made could be more than one hour. You can use TDMs on water as long as you place the bumper where it will not be blown around by the wind. The longer the delay, the closer you are to running a cold unseen.

COLD UNSEENS are retrieves to make picks the dog has never experienced and did not mark. Begin cold unseens quite early in combination with memory patterns. For instance, as you complete the pecan drill, when the dog goes out for the final and last retrieve, toss out a feathered bumper directly behind your position in the opposite direction of the three previous memories. When your dog returns, turn and line for the short unseen. You are beginning to establish a solid initial line for cold unseens. The dog has confidence that when you line and point there is something out there to pick. It is a good practice to make cold unseens high-value targets like tennis balls (my dogs love them), birds, or feathered bumpers. Begin with short retrieves and gradually extend the distance of each cold unseen.

Preset an unseen at the base of a reference point. Bring the dog and set up a training exercise. Upon completion of the exercise, turn and line for the reference point. Gradually extend your line or even include a double unseen, but make sure the routine you are establishing becomes familiar to the dog. Each exercise ends with an unseen to the rear running toward an unfamiliar location that you identify and point out. As your advanced training continues to evolve, it is advisable to run cold unseens at a ratio of one unseen to five memories. While memories, TDMs, and permanent unseens build the dog's confidence, drive, and style, as well as enhancing his ability to line, cold unseens may result in confusion, resets, handling, and redirects. Progress slowly and use unseens judiciously as the value of balance in training cannot be overstated.

ADVANCED WATER WORK

Advanced training on water involves quite a shopping list of skills:

✦ Multiple retrieves.
✦ Handling on the water.
✦ Across-water exit extension on land.
✦ River work and retrieves involving moving water.

Across-Water Retrieves

Your dog must be experienced in crossing bodies of water to make picks along the far bank; hunting cover in shallow water just as proficiently as he would on land; and, finally, being able to exit water on a far bank, line out at a distance on land to make a long pick, and then return directly across the water to the original location.

Using the sight or circle memory, place a large white bumper along the bank of a water source. Walk around the water's edge to the opposite bank. From the far bank you can see the bumper as you line and so can the dog. As soon as the dog makes contact with the bumper, begin an aggressive recall whistle to encourage him to return and not fully exit the bank. If you use several bumpers, keep the bumper placement wide enough to discourage switching. Also, do not

Powerful water entries are stylish, but particularly dangerous due to underwater hazards. Sweep the area before the hunt.

place the bumper too close to a bank parallel to the retrieve line, which would encourage the dog to come out and run back along that bank.

Once proficient, begin to gradually place a single bumper retrieve farther away from the water's edge. Now, the dog must exit the water and run straight up the bank to make the pick and then return through the water on the same line. Ladders work great for these types of drills. To progress even further, you will want to minimize the visual and use feathered bumpers or tennis balls in a bit of cover to encourage the hunt.

Hunting Cover on Water

Hunting cover on water is a step that is often overlooked in waterdog training. Dogs are normally taught to hunt cover on land, but the skill should be taught on water as well. Locate some fresh-cut limbs or timber. Fresh-cut brush puts out lots of scent to disguise the bird. Now, make a large pile of brush out on the water, tangling the limbs and the foliage. Your dog will find it necessary to work his way under and through the tangle to locate a bird while on the water; this is quite different than hunting on ground or grass. At first, you want to keep the water about chest-deep for the dog so he can bound around. Lace a firehose bumper with duck feathers and place it under the pile using a trailing memory. The dog watches you place the bumper under the brush

and you heel him away to line back to the pile.

Later, run the exercise as a permanent or cold unseen. What you want to see in your dog is an aggressive hunt deep in the core of the pile, weaving in and out of the limbs for the scented bumper. Now, you can move it to deeper water, in which the dog has to swim to accomplish the task.

Train for hunting cover on water to make tough picks of hidden waterfowl.

Water-Land Extensions

Using the linked-in method, you will be able to teach your dog to run longer lines to a water's edge, then swim across the water and exit on the far bank to carry that line farther to pick the memory. On the hunt, this is the retrieve that will bring back a bird that is pricked high and sails long over the water before falling into cover on the far bank.

First, train the dog to pick a single bumper on the bank across the water (point B to C). At the same time, train the dog to run a long memory to a natural reference point 40 yards beyond the water's edge (point C to D).

With the two links established, salt the reference point D with three bumpers. Back away

to point C and, while standing in the water, line to point D.

With the retrieve complete, drop a bumper at point C, circle around the lake to point B, and line from B to C for the first retrieve. Upon the dog's return, line to D.

The dog will likely stop briefly at point C, but with a whistle stop and back cast, the dog's memory should prevail. Once across the water and a long land exit retrieve has been completed, back away to point A and run straight through from A to D.

If any problems develop in the sequence, return and practice each individual link to the point of success before progressively returning to the entire exercise.

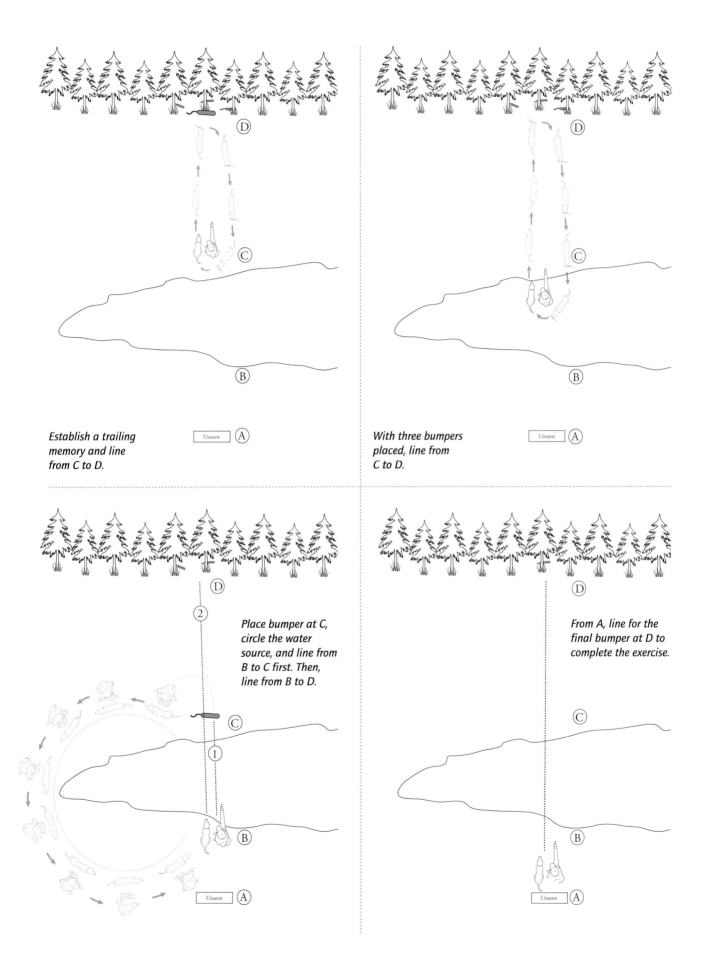

Establish a trailing memory and line from C to D.

With three bumpers placed, line from C to D.

Place bumper at C, circle the water source, and line from B to C first. Then, line from B to D.

From A, line for the final bumper at D to complete the exercise.

Handling on Water

Water handling modifies the patterns previously established to include different types of retrieves in realistic conditions. But there is one special technique that you need to consider: handling away from a known bird for one that is an unseen. Now you will really experience the power of suction. You will need a dog that responds well to direction and has a high level of trust in you as the handler.

Scenario 1: You will need a helper for this. Place a memory at the edge of a pond in thick cover. Make it small and well-scented or use cold game. As you circle the pond to make your pick from the far bank, the helper picks up the bumper or bird. Send your dog across for the memory and attempt to hold him in the area of the memory, hunting cover aggressively. Next, fire a shot as your assistant tosses out a large rock that will splash into the water as a diversion about 30 yards away from where the dog is hunting. The shot and splash will likely capture the dog's attention. Your job is to keep the dog on the search of the cover,

Advanced waterfowl retrievers respond well to hand signals and whistle commands on water as well as land.

ignoring the splash. If he switches, he will find nothing and receive no reward. Handle back to the correct area. Once the dog proves that he can hold the hunt area, the helper tosses the bumper or bird back in the cover when the dog is not looking. When the dog makes the find, you are again proven correct in his eyes.

Scenario 2: Hide an unseen on the bank of a water source or in cover on the water. Bring your dog and shotgun. Your assistant will toss a big rock away from the area of the hidden bird, making a splash across the pond as you shoot. After a brief delay, send your dog. When the dog is about halfway to the splash zone, stop and handle him to the unseen. If he ignores the handle, he will find no reward at the fall. A variation of this setup is to line the dog away from the splash directly to the unseen.

Bank Running

Cheating or bank running is a practice normally frowned upon among retriever enthusiasts, yet in some instances a run of the bank to make a retrieve on a hunt is advisable. This will be discussed more in the next section on river work, but basically, if you have a downed bird in fast-moving water, the dog that takes a direct line to the place of the fall will find nothing and then must swim to catch the bird or may lose that bird altogether in a hard current.

The better approach may be for the dog to stay on the bank while running to overtake the floater, then enter the water when close to the bird. In most situations, I prefer the retriever to line directly for the bird, taking the most direct route possible. Bank running can get the cheater into trouble should he encounter an obstruction or an abrupt change in terrain at the water's edge. In such cases, the dog will lose the bird's location.

Cheating on a return has pros and cons as well. If the bird is picked close to the water's edge at a point parallel to the bank in proximity to the hunter, the dog may choose the land route back. This approach often offers the dog the chance to build body heat with the run rather

Bank running—the practice has both advantages and disadvantages.

than lose energy on a cold water swim. Plus, the dog will get back quicker.

If the bird falls farther away from the bank and the dog elects to pick the bird and swim to the closest point of land in an attempt to run the bank rather than taking the most direct route back by water, that is a dysfunction. The dog may become disoriented, run into obstructions, or otherwise waste time on the return. There is also the possibility that he will drop the bird in an unknown location.

To discourage this possibility, do not walk your dog *around* any obstructions or walk around the water's edge too close to the bank. Your dog will pattern your behavior. Instead, walk *across* any obstruction, whether it is a log or creek, and when you circle a water source, circle very wide away from the contour of the water's edge.

Train for the situation in two ways. First, place a single bumper in the center of a long bank at the water's edge, circle wide around the water, and make the pick directly across from the memory. Drop a bumper at your present location, then return back around to the far bank and make your second pick.

Next, use a trailing memory triple. Place three bumpers clearly visible at the water's edge along the water line. Circle wide to a position

Across-Water Retrieves

Place multiple bumpers as circle memories at a great distance from the edge of the water source.

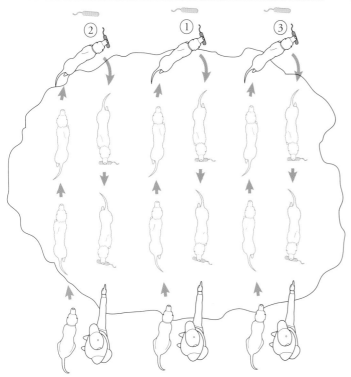

From the opposite bank, line for the center bumper first and gradually work toward the outer edges of the bank as the dog's skill progresses.

across the water from the memories. Pick the center bumper first, where it's most difficult for the dog to cheat. If you see the dog starting to run the bank on the return, aggressively recall him with your whistle and a hand signal while walking in the opposite direction. Often your body language will pull your dog to you and away from the influence of the bank. If the dog fails, widen the distance of the bumper on the opposite bank from the edge around the water.

Use ladders to encourage straight exits and reentries across water. Use large bumpers in short cover to give your dog a visible target. Run each retrieve across the center of the lake. One repetition of this exercise each day is adequate. Progressively use the aforementioned exercises to include islands, land protrusions, and retrieves closer to parallel banks.

River Work

Training waterfowl gundogs for moving water is highly recommended. Rivers and fast water present unique conditions; mainly, the water is moving and the fallen bird or bumper won't remain where it was marked. Also, as the dog crosses the water he will encounter current and will drift off the correct direction of travel—unless he is trained to overcome the current's influences.

First, teach the dog to cross moving water and negotiate the current. At the water's edge, toss a large white bumper to the opposite bank. Turn and walk away, creating a trailing memory. Line the dog straight across the stream for the visible bumper. With repetition, the dog will learn how to swim against the

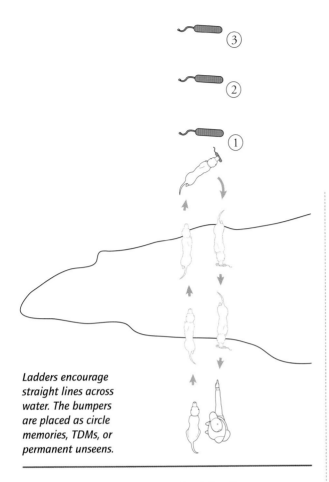

Ladders encourage straight lines across water. The bumpers are placed as circle memories, TDMs, or permanent unseens.

current and hold a line to the fall. If he arrives on the far bank out of the area, you'll need to use hand signals to put him back on target.

Falls that are across the bank upstream or downstream will require angle entries into the water. Angle entries are challenging enough, but now the water's movement complicates them even further. There are two options to avoid this:

OPTION ONE: Line the dog straight to a point across the river from your position. As the dog exits on the far bank, handle up or down the bank to the target area.

OPTION TWO: Line straight up or down the riverbank on your side and then stop the dog directly across from the bird and cast across.

Floaters in the river offer confusing challenges for the retriever. The object does not remain in the fall area. Toss out a bumper into moving water and wait a few seconds before sending the dog up or down the bank. Once he is

parallel to the floater, cast in the direction of the floating bumper.

Use large white bumpers as floaters, which the dog can easily see once he is on the water. To teach the floater concept, toss the bumper in as the dog sits on the bank and observes. The dog should focus on the float as the bumper drifts by or as it moves away downstream. Hold the dog's attention on the bumper for longer periods of time before the release. Keep the dog steady as long as he will stay focused on the target.

Retrieves Across Moving Water

For Option 1, angle lines directly across moving water.
For Option 2, line parallel to the water and down the bank, stop, and cast directly across the moving water for the retrieve.

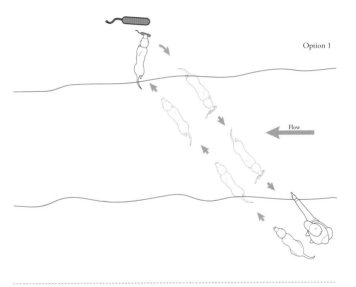

Option 1

Flow

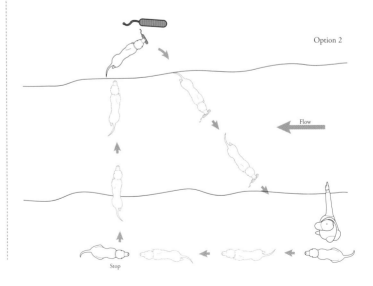

Option 2

Flow

Stop

Dressing Your Dog for the Water

Thermal neoprene vests offer cold water protection for your dog and are an important consideration. First, the thermal vest is an excellent accessory that provides body warmth for your dog just like a wetsuit does for a diver. It greatly enhances the dog's ability to maintain body heat and avoid hypothermia. It also provides body protection against hidden obstructions underwater. The vest should fit securely so that nothing can become lodged between the vest and the dog's body, yet it should not constrict movement.

A: Place the vest on the ground in front of your dog.

B: Stand over the dog and lift his legs, placing them into the leg holes.

C: With the legs in place, lift the whole suit and secure it around the dog's body.

D: Notice the secure fit and that the dog is not wearing a collar. Never hunt a dog with a collar. It may get tangled when your dog is out on a retrieve.

E: In cold water conditions, keep your dog high and dry between retrieves to conserve energy. The dog burns maximum energy by attempting to stay warm—energy and endurance that would be better used for retrieves. Whenever possible, keep your dog out of cold water.

Marking may become difficult on the hunt when dogs have limited visibility and are working from hides.

MARKING ENHANCEMENT

Waterfowlers want a dog that continually scans the sky for birds, marks the location of a downed bird, drives out enthusiastically straight to the fall area on command, and hunts the area closely. As the trainer, you can greatly enhance a retriever's marking by addressing each individual component skill necessary for effective marking. Pinpoint marking skills include concentration and focus, steadiness, memory, distance estimation, negotiating obstacles, lining, hunting cover, and ignoring diversions, among others.

A quick word of caution before you begin: Excessive marking drills can promote unsteadiness and often result in a self-employed dog—that is, a dog confident in getting the job done on his own. Handling and memory exercises, on the other hand, promote interdependence between the handler and the dog. Balance in training is important.

Concentration

If a dog is to be an excellent marker, he must concentrate and remain alert to the activities in the field. Concentration requires steadiness. Dogs that run in on the shot or fall of a bird will not see multiple falls. Patience and concentration are key components of effective marking.

Marking requires concentration along with distance estimation and lining ability.

The "watch" cue reestablishes a hunting dog's concentration on the sky after a short period of idleness. Begin quietly instructing the dog to watch as the thrower prepares to provide a mark in training, and also repeat the command as you make a toss of the bumper to place sight memories. This will condition the dog to understand that he should watch toward the sky or field in anticipation of an action that is about to occur. If done consistently, the dog will learn to focus his attention on the sky looking for birds in flight, ready for action when he hears the word "watch."

Distance Estimation

It is common to see a dog that breaks down at a certain distance on a drive out to a mark as though he hit an invisible barrier. A dog that does this has become accustomed to training sessions in which he always finds marks and memories within a certain range from the handler. The trainer has unintentionally conditioned the dog to drive out only to a certain distance. If a dog is never exposed to marks, memories, or unseens beyond a specific range—say 50 yards— that will become the dog's maximum search range. The handler will find it difficult to push the dog farther.

Developing a dog's ability to run long distances to pick a mark takes practice, but also remember that repetitious marks compromise patience and steadiness. Train marking extensions through the use of memories. Select an area that will support long trailing memories. Ensure proficiency first on land before transferring the exercise to water. Select an obvious reference point and salt with four bumpers. Begin your first retrieve from at least 50 yards away. Between each retrieve, back away from the target an additional 20 yards in length to extend the line. After the dog picks four successful memories, do not move from your position. Have a helper throw a mark back to the reference point and pick the mark. Your dog will likely be marking a bird at more than 100 yards and you have accomplished this skill without compromising steadiness.

Influences

The same factors that negatively influence a dog's line to a memory can disrupt a line to a mark. Once you establish a basic marking pattern,

Influences are any factors that can disrupt a dog's line to a mark or an unseen.

Walking singles, established at varied distances, involve honing the dog's marking ability while moving.

involve as many different variables in training as possible—from terrain to distance to multiple marks.

Walking Singles

This is a simple marking drill that uses a stationary thrower with the dog and the handler moving in an ever-widening circle around the thrower. Usually, the bumpers fall into a fixed reference point that involves cover on land, marsh, or water. Confidence is promoted when the thrower ensures that the bumpers fall in the same exact area for each retrieve, yet the dog's distance to the mark and visual perspective will change with each retrieve. This is a great drill that includes multitasking. The dog must stay at heel, remain steady, and mark. It is a great exercise for the versatile game dog because it is totally applicable for waterfowl and upland gundogs alike.

Do not disrupt your dog's concentration on a single mark by attempting to line him. If he has sighted the location, gradually extend the duration between the bumper fall and the release—which is a delay to enhance focus—then release the dog with his name without setting him up to line. When your retriever has locked on the bird, stand perfectly still and release the dog verbally. If multiple retrieves are involved, you may wish to pick a different bumper than the one the dog has focused on. Then, you should line the dog with a redirect "no" for the mark and line for the preferred bird.

Visibility

The dog's ability to "sight" a mark in an actual hunting situation is usually limited. It is one of the problems of overemphasizing multiple marking drills in hunting retrievers. Just how many opportunities will the dog have to see multiple birds fall while he is tucked inside a duck blind, dog hide, or with you inside a layout blind? Here is when your dog's handling abilities—for an unseen and marking by sound—become invaluable. Revisit these skills frequently to balance the training experience with visual marks.

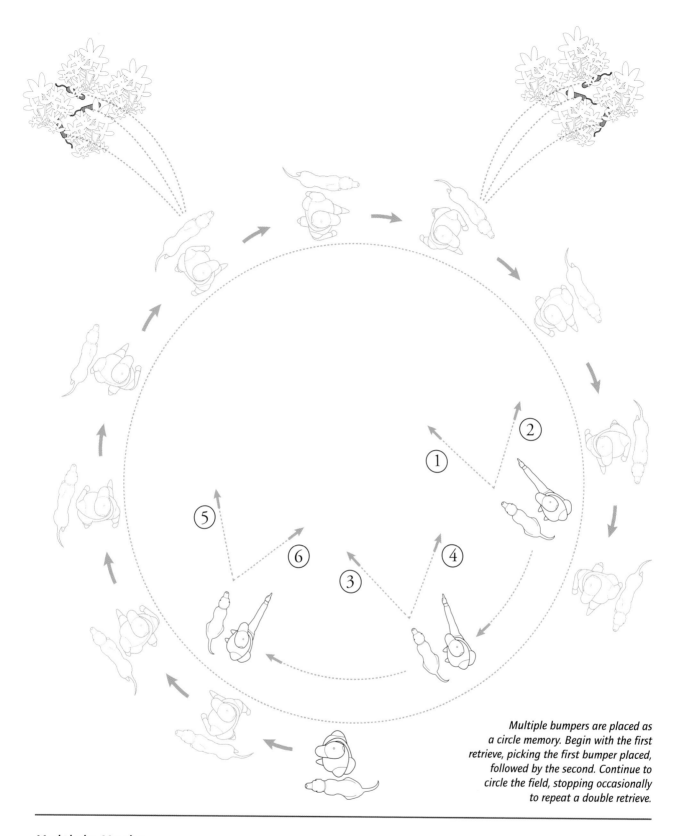

Multiple bumpers are placed as a circle memory. Begin with the first retrieve, picking the first bumper placed, followed by the second. Continue to circle the field, stopping occasionally to repeat a double retrieve.

Multiple Marks

The best way to teach long multiple falls is with a memory loop exercise. Select a large open area that offers two distinct reference points. Set up the exercise by first placing three scatters at the longest point, then looping around to the second point to place three more. Continue the loop to

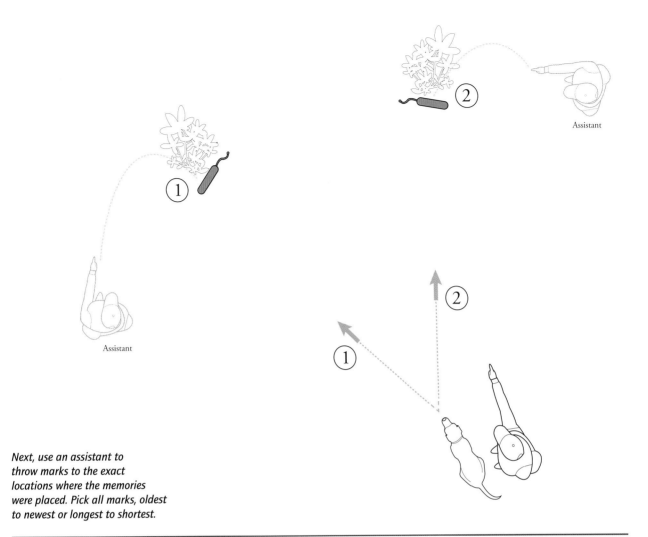

Next, use an assistant to throw marks to the exact locations where the memories were placed. Pick all marks, oldest to newest or longest to shortest.

set up a long bird/short bird pattern with the last birds placed closest to your position.

Position yourself at an angle between the two points that will create a short bird/long bird pattern. From each position, as you circle the area, pick the long bird first, followed by the shorter bird, until all bumpers have been picked. Now, with two helpers, prepare to mark the doubles. Have your helper throw the long bird first to the same reference point, followed by the shorter. Pick the retrieves in that order. If the dog pulls to the shorter of the two marks, use a primary reset, recall the dog, and widen the angle. Have the helpers pick the bumpers up and repeat the exercise.

Try not to let a marking exercise degenerate into a handling experience. You want the dog to be successful with a correct visual and a straight line to the correct area. Once again, reinforce the exercise by implementing the stimulus package (refer to Chapter Six). Variables will include water and different terrain, but you can also modify to include different distances as well as additional memories that can develop into triple marks or cold unseens.

Scattered Marks

Duck hunting involves a great deal of confusion and fast action. Several guns may be firing when a group of birds passes. The dog may not have the luxury of marking one single bird at a time as presented in a training scenario. Set up a simulated duck blind or just tuck into thick brush along the water's edge. With two helpers, one on each side, blow a few duck calls and wait patiently. Without warning, have the first helper throw multiple bumpers in the air at the same time as you shoot

Hunting dogs must become accustomed to other working dogs in close proximity and must remain focused on their own retrieves.

with bumpers falling all around from different directions. Then, from the opposite side, have the second helper fire a launcher or throw additional bumpers into the water. (Don't forget the occasional fall behind your position.) Now, there are birds scattered all over the water at different distances and you can have some real fun combining marks with lining challenges for memories. This is a great opportunity to have more than one dog working at the same time to make the retrieves.

Double dogs at work: Deke makes a pick of a mallard first, while Rebel backs him with a second retrieve simultaneously.

■ Parting Thoughts

Hunting retrievers must become accustomed to ignoring another dog making a retrieve or a bird that a dog may have picked while making a simultaneous retrieve. Quite often more than one dog may be afield completing a retrieve as another is doing the same. Train for this situation. Your dog must remain focused on his bird while ignoring the confusion and excitement that may be occurring all around him. Successful hunting dogs for both upland and waterfowl are competent at working simultaneously.

CHAPTER 8

The Upland Dog

■ The Upland Experience

The flush of a pheasant by an enthusiastic gundog yielding a spectacular rooster in flight; a perfect point of a quail in thick cover with a setter locked motionless except for the flicker of an eye; a hot peg on a dove field where the fast, migratory birds approach from abrupt angles like bats exploding from a cave; your steady retriever at your side with a breathless focus on the sky just waiting for his chance—nothing could be better.

Upland hunting without a dog is tantamount to skipping ahead to read the last page of a great book. The result is the same, but there is no pleasure in it. From the moment a puppy appears and the flood of possibilities fills a hunter's heart, every bird brought to hand from the dog is a story in itself. As hunters, we travel a long road with our dogs. They become part of us and we praise and cajole and scold our way to an understanding that plays itself out in hundreds of fields over the years. Every bird is an additional chapter, every point, flush, and retrieve a new paragraph to add to the manuscript, which ultimately becomes the story of the dog's life. A great book is disappointing only when it ends. The same can be said for a great upland dog.

These are the reasons to train a versatile gundog to locate, flush, or point, then retrieve game birds at a variety of destinations. Game-finders trained to flush grouse or retrieve dove and quail; a retriever that could work as a strike dog with pointers; pointers conditioned to quarter close

Spaniels are excellent retrievers of dove.

to the hunter; or a rough-shooting dog that will flush pheasant or chukar close to the gun—these are all examples of an upland Gentleman's Gundog, a sporting dog of quality that would leave a wingshooting enthusiast standing in the field contemplating that nothing could be better.

Many of the exercises outlined in Chapter Seven designed for waterfowling are, with modification, perfectly applicable to the upland gundog. Review the material carefully. The primary difference between the training of a waterfowl retriever and an upland game dog can be summarized in two ways:

RANGE: The uplander must stay very close to the guns to be effective. The waterfowler is conditioned to pick the long ones.

PATTERNING: The waterfowl retriever needs to run long, straight lines to pick a mark or unseen, while the uplander is a more independent gamefinder and needs to quarter (that is, to hunt cover in a zigzag pattern to locate game close to the hunter).

Both types of bird dogs will require:

✦ Brilliant scenting ability.
✦ Exceptional handling skills.
✦ Controllability and focus on the handler.
✦ Supreme steadiness to birds in flight, a flush, shot, or fall.

QUARTERING

Quartering is when the gundog—whether a pointer, flusher, or retriever—works in a zigzag pattern across the field close to the hunter to locate game. The trick is to keep the dog in close to the guns. For flushers, the dog should work in a tight pattern about 15 to 20 yards out front and no farther than that to the left or right, otherwise flushed game will be out of gun range.

Many foot hunters also prefer their pointers to range closer as well and work a quartering pattern. Before beginning quartering training, be sure your dog responds well to the whistle signals—especially the stop blast—and is proficient on recall despite distractions in the field. Even if a bird flushes, you can call your dog back in closer. He doesn't chase game. He responds quickly to left, right, and back hand signals. He understands hunting patterns like pull casts and switching on doubles. The hunt-in whistle command and hand signal are also very important should a dog overrun a bird. To review, the hunt-in whistle is a slow repetitious blast of the whistle and the hand signal points toward the ground as if bouncing a basketball to direct the dog to hunt back closer while using lots of nose.

Bending or changing directions is a new whistle command. Bending is two quick blasts of the whistle to signal your dog to change directions on the quartering pattern. When the dog reaches the outside of the desired distance from your position, give a quick stop whistle. (Note: Once proficient at the quartering pattern, eliminate the stop and only use the bend whistle signal to indicate a turn.) When the dog looks back, you change directions and give a cast hand signal combined with two blasts of the whistle to turn the dog in the desired direction. As the dog moves

A walk-up begins with dogs quartering close to the guns.

back across, if he moves too far out, simply use the recall whistle to keep him in range. Continue to walk in a zigzag pattern. When the dog gets to the opposite side of the desired quartering range, change directions again, repeat the bend whistle signal, cast the student, and continue the quartering pattern.

Basically, you are holding the dog in the pattern with the whistle stop, recall, the new bending whistle command, your body language, and hand signals. Once the dog is handling well and knows the whistle signals, the transition to quartering a field should be quite easy. Over time, the upland dog should learn to work this way naturally, but in the beginning you should use these tools to reinforce the pattern and keep the dog in the desired area. It is also advisable to practice casting while carrying a shotgun. It requires a bit of extra coordination on your part, but your dog needs to be accustomed to its presence.

The Five-Option Drill

One of the first exercises to teach quartering is a drill designed to train the dog to be responsive to the handler while at a distance in the field. Place the dog, facing you, at the approximate distance as if he was quartering, about 15 yards out from your position and within gun range. Practice every option with the dog in the same location. With the dog at sit, back away to the desired distance and practice the options:

OPTION ONE: Toss a feathered bumper to the right or left of the dog. Hold the dog in place for 15 to 20 seconds, and then cast the dog for the mark.

OPTION TWO: This time the bumper flies, but it is a denial and you walk out and pick it up yourself.

OPTION THREE: Toss another bumper, recall the dog to you with the whistle, and then turn and line the dog back for the retrieve.

OPTION FOUR: Toss a bumper, hold the dog steady

The honor dog remains motionless as the retrieve is made, then reacts to the next command.

in the field, and allow another dog to make the retrieve.

OPTION FIVE: Toss the bumper to the right or left and hold the dog's focus for 15 to 20 seconds, walk to the dog, reward him enthusiastically, and line him for the bumper.

This exercise prepares the dog to remain steady for a flush and a shot, and then await further instruction from the handler. It keeps the dog under control, with his attention redirected on you, waiting to respond to a variety of commands depending on the situation rather than making a self-initiated decision to make a chase

> ⚜ WILDROSE TIP ⚜
> *Be sure to reward the dog for the denial and honor just as enthusiastically as you would for the retrieve.*

or the pick. Your dog should be steady and understand that every bird is not his, a concept that you have been working on since the very beginning.

Hunting Cover Diversions

You will need an assistant to set up this exercise. Toss a scented tennis ball into cover and turn and walk your dog away about the same distance you did in the five-option drill. Your partner picks up the tennis ball as you are walking away. Turn, wait for a few moments, and then send the dog back to the memory area. As the dog begins to hunt, blow the whistle to get the dog's attention, throw a bumper, cold game, or even a live bird to the right or left of the dog's position, and fire a shot. The dog should mark the flyer and turn his attention back to you just as he would in the five-option drill. Practice any of the five options you choose. As your dog responds to your command, your partner throws the tennis ball back into the original cover without the dog's knowledge. Handle the dog back to the area to continue the hunt and find the original memory.

Switching On Doubles

This exercise combines stop, handling, and lining in preparation for quartering.

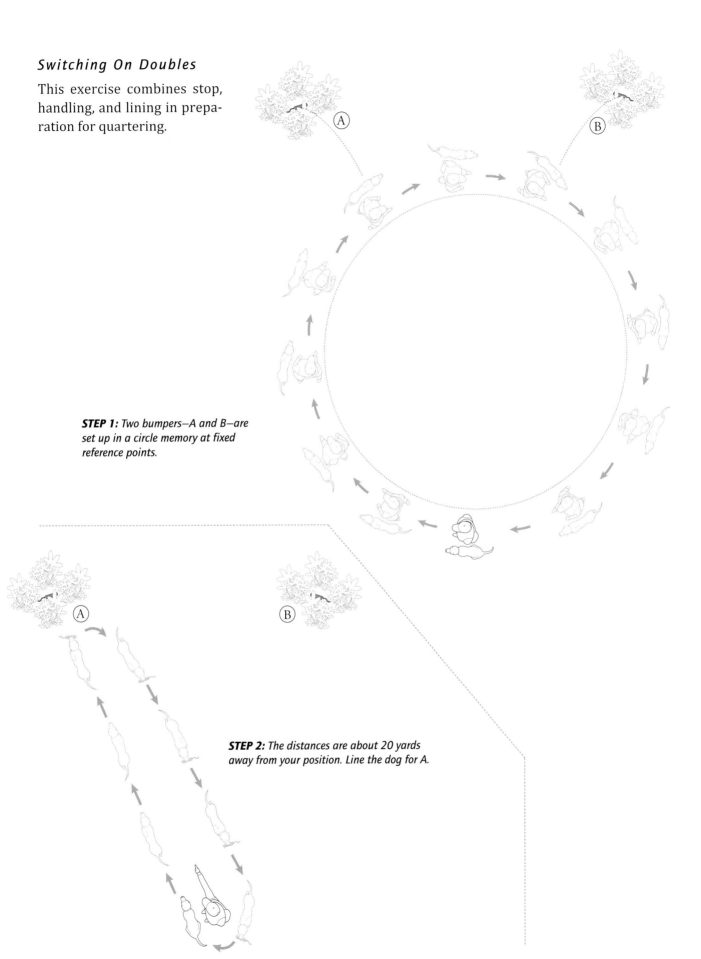

STEP 1: Two bumpers—A and B—are set up in a circle memory at fixed reference points.

STEP 2: The distances are about 20 yards away from your position. Line the dog for A.

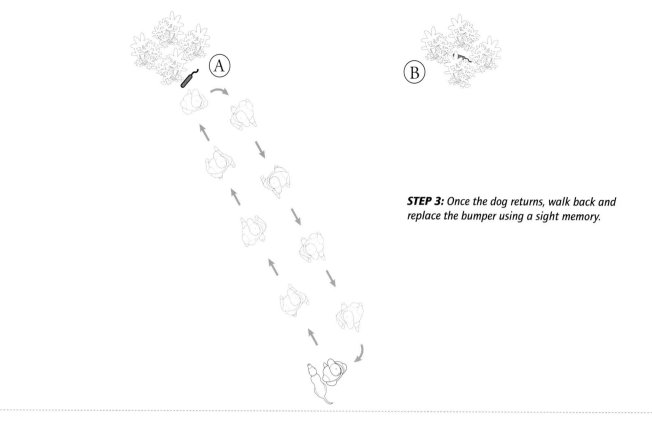

STEP 3: Once the dog returns, walk back and replace the bumper using a sight memory.

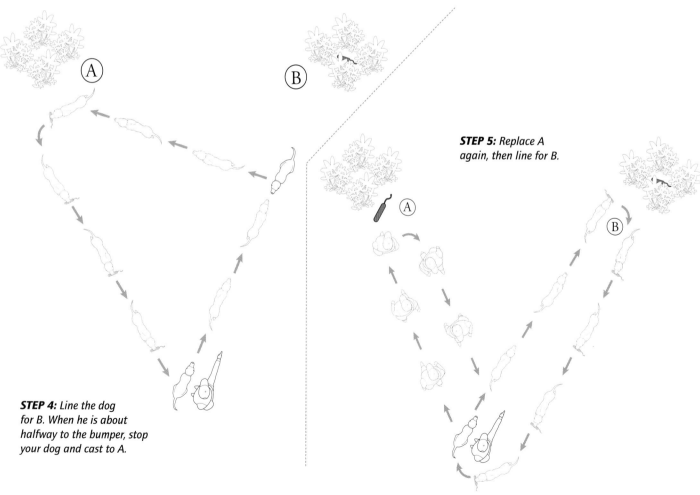

STEP 4: Line the dog for B. When he is about halfway to the bumper, stop your dog and cast to A.

STEP 5: Replace A again, then line for B.

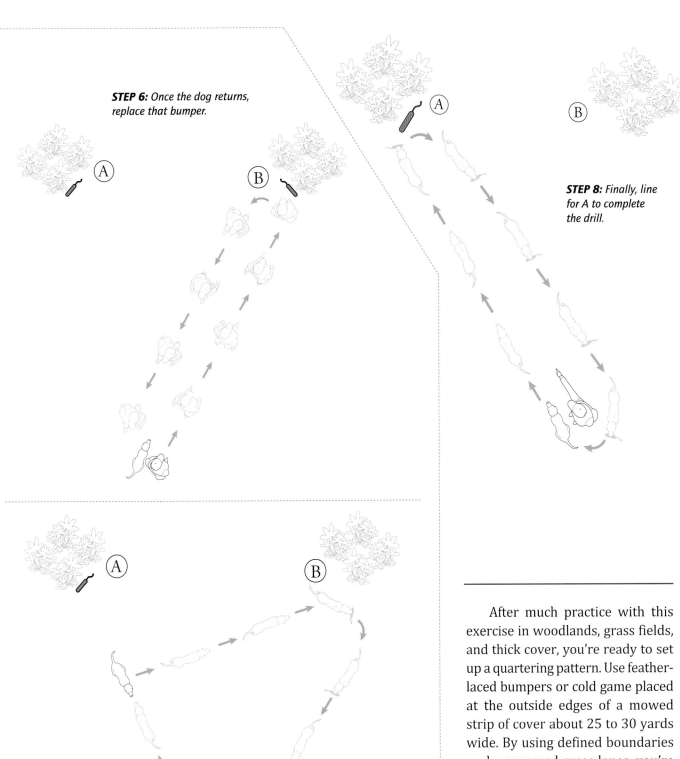

STEP 6: Once the dog returns, replace that bumper.

STEP 8: Finally, line for A to complete the drill.

STEP 7: Line the dog for A, stop halfway, and then cast for B.

After much practice with this exercise in woodlands, grass fields, and thick cover, you're ready to set up a quartering pattern. Use feather-laced bumpers or cold game placed at the outside edges of a mowed strip of cover about 25 to 30 yards wide. By using defined boundaries such as mowed grass lanes, you're giving the dog a psychological barrier that will encourage the quartering pattern. If you try to teach quartering in a large open field or cover, the dog has no defining boundaries to assist in developing a pattern. The lane allows you to keep the dog in appropriate range while building the habit of proper turns. There are two approaches to placing the bumpers:

APPROACH ONE: The *throw down* is when the dog is quartering and you toss out bumpers into the desired location where you want the dog to find them. The advantage here is that the dog only locates the reward when he's in the correct range. If the dog charges ahead and the bumpers are preplaced, he may find his reward 30 to 40 yards ahead and well out of range of your gun. You control the find. The disadvantage of the throw down is that the dog starts watching you when he catches on that you have the bumpers and are likely to make the toss.

APPROACH TWO: *Preplaced* bumpers or cold game birds are set out four to six at a time along the edges of the mowed strip in an alternating pattern side-to-side.

Mowed lanes in cover can encourage the quartering pattern.

Always place bumpers on the outside edges of the cover and at the point where the dog should make his turn. This practice encourages the dog to hunt from side-to-side to achieve success versus finding his reward in the middle of the lane. As you set up the pattern, consider the wind direction. Which way is the wind pushing the scent? If you're running into the wind, you have an advantage in getting the dog to quarter, as dogs don't like to run directly into the wind. The disadvantage is that the dog will smell the birds ahead if they're preplaced. A tailwind will push the dog along, which may require more handling and recall, but the benefit is that your dog won't run into the scent out of range. Crosswinds can push the scent completely out of the cover and the pattern itself.

You will now need to select a command to use for quartering. I use "hunt 'em up" and don't line the dog. With the dog at heel, I snap my fingers with my hands close to my body, give the command, and begin to walk in a zigzag pattern. Over a period of time, the dog learns the difference between lining for an unseen and quartering.

As you give the quartering command, walk in a zigzag pattern. Your pace matters. Often hunters walk a field far too fast, passing completely over a cock pheasant or a hidden quail. Go slow and zigzag.

Encourage the dog to move across the full width of the cover or the mowed strip. When the dog reaches the outside edge, stop him with the whistle, hold his attention, and then give him the two-blast whistle to indicate the bend or turn. Give the hand signal and walk in the opposite direction until the dog reaches the edge once again, then turn to repeat by going back in the other direction. Keep the dog within gun range by using the recall whistle. Gradually, your dog will learn to turn and maintain the proper distances on the bend and recall whistle signals only with no whistle stops necessary.

If the dog misses a bumper, don't let him find one behind your position. Always keep the dog out front. Dogs should only find birds in front of the gun line. Also, do not re-hunt a field that the dog just quartered. If your dog did not locate a bumper, return to the field and find it later.

Applications

Quartering has many applications, including pushing a field for pheasants, locating downed game after a drive (which is referred to as sweeping), pursuing chukar on a mountainside, or trying to put up grouse along a roadside. Early training for quartering is just combining previously perfected skills—including hunting cover, handling, and steadiness—into a systematic pattern. After practicing the basic zigzag pattern in various types of cover, the quartering pattern should become predictable and the whistle commands eagerly respected.

When teaching your dog how to quarter a field, it is important to keep the gundog's interest keen. He may need to locate exciting finds, such as feather-laced tennis balls, cold game birds, or the occasional live flush of a planted bird. The diversity will keep the dog from becoming bored. With live bird flushes in training, the student not only learns not to chase a flyer, he learns that not all birds are his. Do not always shoot the flushed birds. Some birds will escape on the hunt and you do not want chasers of game. This will be the ultimate test of control, so train for this type of situation. Begin by keeping the flush distance very close to you and be ready with the whistle. Once your dog pushes the bird up, immediately use the recall whistle to bring your dog all the way back to your position. Then, lavish him with praise—"Good dog!"

Specialized Terrain

Quartering a dog on a side pattern parallel to your position—sweeping a ditch bank, steep hillside, or the side of the road rather than directly moving from side-to-side in front of the handler—takes special training. The best way to teach this concept is to find a very defined area of cover—for instance, a narrow ditch bordered by two clear fields. Preplace birds at varying distances at the outer edges of the cover in a zigzag format.

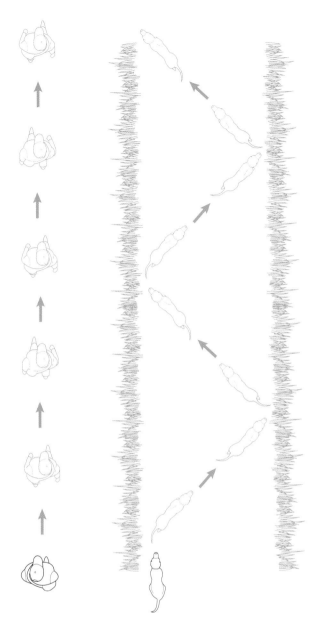

Cast the dog side-to-side in the cover as you slowly progress to the outside.

Send the dog into the cover to quarter and keep the dog moving to your side using hand signals and whistle stops. If at first you need to simplify, you can enter the ditch or cover and walk down the center quartering your dog side-to-side. Once the dog understands the concept of staying in the cover, move out of the ditch, cover, or wind row and continue the exercise with the dog working to your side. The most common parallel quartering situations are ditches, pond levees, cattail marshes, roadsides, shelter belts, and steep hillsides.

Cover variables are another consideration. Do not assume that the training you have successfully completed in mowed grasslands will transfer readily to row crops, cattail slashes, or timberland. Remember that dogs do not generalize well; you must train for each specific type of terrain. Once the dog is familiar with the close pattern required for effective quartering, remove the crutch of the defined boundaries. Take on large grass fields and thick woodlands where you might find quail, pheasants, or grouse. Your expectation should remain that the dog stays within the gun range pattern.

WALK-UPS

Walk-up training prepares your dog for group hunting situations when birds will be flushed or pointed as the line of hunters pushes a field. Walk-ups are commonly used for pheasant hunting in row crops or grass fields, but you can also use the tactic to hunt sharptail grouse, quail, or chukar.

All walk-up situations require a dog that heels extremely well off lead, remains steady to the flush and shot, honors other working dogs—whether they are retrievers or dogs that are hunting cover to locate game—and lines and marks well while ignoring diversions, secondary flushes, and distractions. Also, obviously you need a dog that hunts cover aggressively.

The walk-up training session requires a group, so you will need other people with dogs to make retrieves, to shoot, and to throw bumpers or fire launchers.

The field you select for the exercise should involve contours and cover just as you might expect on the hunt. A dog learns to negotiate through the cover, remaining at heel with one eye on you and one eye on the birds that could flush or fall.

Begin by placing one trailing memory for each dog at a reference point you can remember. Turn the line and walk forward together, keeping the line straight, and walking slowly in a zigzag pattern just as you would when pushing a field.

As the line moves forward, create a bit of wingshooting chaos. From each end of the line, feather-laced bumpers fly all around, creating multiple falls as a shooter fires several shots, and a few bumpers should fall behind the walk-up line as well. Begin from each end of the line to retrieve the falls. Select the birds that fell across the line rather than the easy birds that fell just in front of your position. Each handler and shooter should pick up

Walk-ups are designed to push birds forward to be flushed or pointed in front of the gun line.

Field Position on Walk-ups

Generally, the upland gundog has three possible functions: pointer, flusher, or picker. You may often see a combination of these roles at work in one hunt, but each different type of hunt may present opportunities that demand different requirements for preparation. Let's take a look at the popular group pheasant hunt scenario that one might experience in the Dakotas. Specifically, there are four positions on a pheasant walk-up hunt:

FLUSHERS: Rough-shooting dogs that quarter the field just ahead of the line to point or flush game.

PUSHERS: The dogs and hunters that are assembled in a long line to push birds as they walk through the field. Hunters may take shots at birds flushed within range as they progress. The walk-up gundogs must be conditioned to remain very steady off lead and are responsible for retrieving and locating lost game. Also, selected hunting dogs may be directed to quarter the field to point or flush game in front of the walk-up line as the field is pushed.

PINCHERS: The shooters positioned just ahead of a walk-up line moving parallel and wide in order to keep the birds from moving out of the field ahead of the guns. Dogs of the pinchers are also walk-up dogs that are steady and quiet at heel.

BLOCKERS: The hunters positioned at the end of the field that is being pushed. They are present to prevent the escape of the birds ahead of the line. Here, the dogs become driven retrievers (see Chapter Nine for more information). Basically, they must ignore birds that fly out or fall close to their position while concentrating on picking long marks or unseens that could be lost. Again, steady, quiet behaviors are of high value.

I mention these positions to accentuate the need for a highly controlled dog on a hot pheasant field or quail preserve. When working a dog in such situations, normally you do not send the dog for a retrieve too far forward of the walk-up line into the area to be pushed or an area that has not been hunted. The dog entering the area could flush game. Just mark the location of the fall and pick the bird up as a memory as the line advances through the area.

Runners are another matter. Wounded birds must be picked quickly, but when you send a dog into cover that has not been hunted, the opportunity for secondary flushes of birds is highly likely. Make sure you have a controllable dog before making such a daring retrieve. If your dog runs amok, switching from the downed bird to pursuing live flushes, your popularity among other hunters is likely to diminish. Retrieves to the side or behind the walk-up line can be picked as needed during the shoot. Just be cautious about sending your dog for a retrieve too far ahead into new ground that is about to be pushed.

Walk-up lines should remain straight for safety and to push all birds forward.

a couple of the diversion bumpers as denials. Then, have one or two of the dogs retrieve the trailing memories. With all the bumpers collected, the line is ready to move forward in unison for another round. Don't forget factors like crossing ditches, woodlands, and negotiating fences. Involve as much realism in training as possible.

Blockers

Training for blocking positions is similar to training for continental tower shoots or the British-style driven shoot, which Chapter Nine will cover. Blockers are stationary positions with the purpose of retaining (holding) birds in the area to be hunted or taking birds that are flushed as dogs and hunters approach the end of a drive. The blocker dog is a picker that must be exceptionally steady and quiet while marking multiple falls, handling off diversions to pick an unseen, and tracking runners to prevent a wounded bird's escape.

To prepare gundogs for blocking, line several dogs with handlers at the end of a field. Establish a second line of walk-up dogs and handlers across the field. As the walk-up line approaches, the handlers begin to shoot and throw bumpers, firing repeated dummy launchers overhead to land

A blocking retriever makes a powerful pick from a cornfield.

Walk-up Tips:

✦ Make sure your dog experiences across-the-line retrieves, not just marks in front.

✦ Rotate the dogs so that each can work from the outside or last position in the group's line.

✦ All bumpers should not fall to the front of the line. Many must fall behind the walk-up line and to the side.

✦ Multiple tosses should land at varying distances from the handlers.

✦ Occasionally, before the picking begins, handlers may walk out from the line for a denial, which reinforces remote steadiness.

✦ Freely use diversions thrown and shot as dogs return from retrieves. Other dogs may pick the diversions or turn them into denials.

✦ A great way to add stimulus to the walk-up experience is handheld dummy launchers shot across the line, or a handheld clay thrower. Both add shots and exciting visuals to be tracked airborne. The clay thrower gives a target to shoot, adding realism with the added benefit of not providing an object to retrieve should the unsteady dog run in.

✦ Walk-up dogs should be steady at heel despite dogs hunting and quartering out in front of the pushers.

✦ You can easily implement preplaced birds or bumpers to be found by the pointers or rough-shooting flushing dogs as the walk-up line moves forward, or you may find the throw-down method just as effective.

A walk-up gun line prepares retrievers for angle retrieves through a wind row of trees.

behind and to the sides of the blockers' positions. Keep up the throwing and shooting for several minutes before the pushers' approach stops. Now, with many targets all around, both blockers and walk-up dogs can begin their retrieves.

The required skills will touch on marking, picking unseens, steadiness, and honoring other dogs working the field. It adds stimulus, preparing your hunting pal for the real thing.

Walking Guns and Barriers

A variation of the walk-up is when hunters must push the edge of a field, thicket, or thick cover, which is divided by a ditch, a tree line, or an overgrown fence row. A dog often finds retrieving through a barrier of this kind a bit challenging, particularly when the line to a mark or unseen is run through a barrier at an angle.

Place two handlers with their dogs on each side of a barrier such as a tree line. The two outside handlers and dogs A and D make the picks first, while B and C are the honor dogs. The line walks forward together. A bumper is thrown very high on one side of the tree line by Handler D and a shot is made by Handler C. Line dog A through the barrier to make the pick. Now, reverse the scenario with a shot being made at the other end of the line by Handler B to a bumper thrown by Handler A. Dog D makes the pick. Once completed, let the

inside honor dogs B and C exchange places and repeat the drill. Freely add unseens, memories, and diversions as you wish.

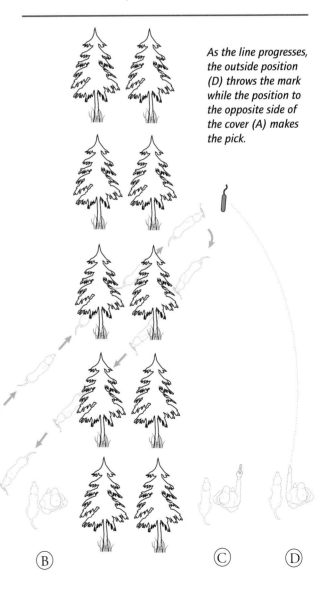

As the line progresses, the outside position (D) throws the mark while the position to the opposite side of the cover (A) makes the pick.

Ⓐ   Ⓑ   Ⓒ   Ⓓ

Placing a pigeon in cover, ready to flush, requires only a few simple steps.

BIRD WORK

You simply cannot train a game dog without frequent exposure to birds, both live and cold game. Pigeon and quail work great for this purpose. For both pointers and flushers, planted birds are a must. You can easily plant birds once they are dizzy. Just stick their heads under their wings, shake lightly a couple of times, tuck the birds into cover with their heads remaining under their wings, and they will stay put. For a covey flush, place a few quail in a pillowcase, give them a few spins, and just shake them into thick cover. Lightly dizzied birds should stay put until located or flushed by your game dog.

Mature pigeon and quail can be kept short-term in proper cages, which are protected from the elements and predators. The other option for bird exposure is a local game preserve. Most services will gladly plant game birds to your specifications to meet your training needs when they are not heavily booked with hunters. Also, volunteering to pick up (retrieve birds) at local shooting clubs that offer continental tower shoots or guided hunts is great bird exposure for your dog.

Electronic bird launchers are effective tools for training pointers and flushers and for providing diversions. Electronic launchers allow the handler to put the bird in the air, or to not do so, just at the right moment, which is obviously a big benefit.

What about steadying a dog to the flush when a bird flies away? A missed shot, a hen pheasant, or a bird flushed out of gun range must not become an opportunity to chase. Using a pigeon, attach a short section of a water hose directly to the bird's legs with string. The hose serves as a weight, but you will experience a nice flush. The bird can fly freely for a short distance, then will drop, usually in sight, without harm. Add gunfire if you would like. This tool provides excellent training opportunities to reinforce steadiness to the flush and for recall. Of course, the "hosed" bird will become a denial that your dog will watch (likely with much disappointment) as you pick up.

With these simple approaches to bird exposure, all you need is a talented dog, a shotgun, and the countryside for realistic hunting conditions.

HANDLING OFF OLD FALLS

An old fall is a bird that has been previously picked but its scent and feathers remain in the area. If the dog made a successful retrieve at that location or saw another dog do so, he may be drawn to the old fall area rather than lining for a new unseen. This type of suction often occurs if the direction of travel is in close proximity to the old fall.

You need a dog that is willing to trust the handler more than what his nose and memory indicate. This is a skill that will be most beneficial on dove hunts, blocking for pheasants, duck hunts as discussed in Chapter Seven, and picking up on tower shoots as discussed in Chapter Nine.

Steady to Flush or Not?

There are two schools of thought concerning a dog being steady to flush, shot, and fall. Actually, these are two different parts to one singular behavior: steady to flush and steady to shot and fall. Steadiness as the birds flush may be desirable, as it gives the handler controlled options—recall, continue to hunt if the bird escapes, or retrieve if the bird is shot. Do you want your dog to remain in position after the flush?

Steadiness to the shot and fall involves the five-option drill previously discussed. Some hunters want their dogs to remain steady to the mark and wait until released on command, while other hunters want the dog to break immediately to secure the bird and prevent a wounded bird's escape.

There are advantages to the steady dog at flush, shot, and fall. He will be better at multiple marking. He will be safer, as he is not as likely to fall victim to a random low shot at a covey flush. A steady dog will also avoid running into fresh ground and inadvertently flushing other birds. An unsteady dog will ultimately lose less wounded birds that could become runners. He will be at the point of fall faster. He is also totally focused on that single mark and will

make a more accurate and quicker pick of a single. Both approaches have advantages and disadvantages. The choice is yours.

These gundogs are steady to point, but will they remain steady to flush and shot?

To prepare to handle off an old fall, use a helper and begin by hiding an unseen in cover. Use a cold game bird as a high-value reward. About 20 yards away, take another cold game bird, rub it on the ground, pluck a few feathers, and scatter them in the area.

Collect your dog and set up a trailing memory using the point where you spread the scent, which is in line with the unseen. Toss the bumper in the scented area and then walk away. While you are walking away, the helper picks up the bumper. Turn and line your dog for the memory.

When the dog strikes the scent area, a hunt will begin. Allow the dog to thoroughly hunt the area. With a whistle stop, give a back cast off the old fall to the hidden unseen directly behind.

If the dog takes the correct cast, he will find a high-value prize, the cold game bird. Conduct this exercise infrequently, as the practice of handling off an area of scent must be balanced with holding the area on a hunt to locate a difficult bird. As in all training, one lesson or skill may be counterintuitive to another. Never overemphasize one skill at the expense of another.

Marking off the gun is important for the rough-shooting gundog or pointer.

PINPOINT MARKING

As the game dog is hunting or quartering the field, practice marks. Marking development was discussed in Chapter Seven, but now it is necessary to implement a bit of variation for the upland gundog. First, the marks will be shorter and more numerous in a "scatter" of locations. Second, you will use small scented items, like feather-laced puppy bumpers, scented tennis balls, or even a couple of small game-bird wings taped to a tennis ball tossed out as marks with a Chuck-It. Your goal is to develop the dog into a pinpoint marker in cover while at a remote position away from the handler. Effective marking while busy with hunting pursuits is quite different than when a dog is sitting still beside you or walking at heel.

In thick cover, you want your gundog to use the point of your shotgun and the direction of the shot as an indication of where the bird is in the air. An astute student will quickly catch on to marking off the gun.

As your dog quarters or is hunting cover, first there's the shot in the direction that the bumper or bird will be thrown. As the dog looks, continue to point the shotgun in the direction of the toss. When the dog's attention diverts first to the shot, then to the flyer, and finally marks the fall, wait until the dog's eyes redirect to you for instruction. Then, send the dog—or perhaps not. To provide the appropriate balance in training, use the five-option drill previously mentioned. The sequence is shot, continue the point of the gun, and then toss. Experienced upland dogs will also learn to:

✦ Keep an eye on other dogs that are working the fields and watching for a flush.

✦ Watch pointing dogs that might lock up on a point.

✦ Respond with heads in the air to verbal shouts from other hunters: "Birds up!" or "Rooster!"

Marking by Sound

Marking, which is largely a skill of eyesight and lining ability, should be practiced in realistic conditions just as you may find on the hunt. But, as previously mentioned in other chapters, there is another important training aspect to marking—marking by sound. Upland hunting dogs commonly find themselves in tough hunting conditions that limit their ability to see a bird fall, but dogs have acute hearing, so be sure to develop this gift to your advantage.

Begin with a dummy shot from a retriever launcher into thick woodlands. The shot captures the dog's attention and is followed by a large canvas bumper falling through the branches that provides just the noise you need for this exercise. With the dog walking at heel, practice a quartering pattern or hunting cover. The dog is attracted to the shot, sees the fall, hears the location of the mark, and then is sent for the retrieve.

Dogs have acute hearing; make sure to develop their ability to mark by sound.

Next, repeat the lesson, but this time limit the dog's ability to see the fall by working in tall cover or covering the dog's eyes. Now he must rely on his hearing. You will see your dog's immediate reaction to the shot, then to the sound of the fall. Just add the point of your shotgun. At the time of the launcher shot, point your gun in the direction of the fall and hold it there. You will be combining marking off the gun and marking by sound. Occasionally, to add stimulus along with complexity, shoot your shotgun in the direction of the thrown bumper, but ensure that the falling bumper drops through tree branches or tall row crops to provide enough sound to be marked by the dog.

As with all upland retriever training, marks should fall in all directions of your position just like you will experience in the field. A good balance would be one-third to the front, one-third behind you to the rear, and one-third to your extreme right and left.

QUARTERING AND UNSEENS

Well, it's time to put a few things together for your upland finished gundog. Your dog must learn to distinguish between when you want him to quarter to flush birds very close to the guns and when it's time to line out straight for an unseen retrieve.

First, you need to have thoroughly taught both skills separately, both quartering and lining for an unseen. You have learned a distinctive command and body language for each skill:

✦ For quartering, use "hunt 'em up." With a snap of your fingers, remaining upright with a hand signal to the side of the body, give an indication as to the direction by walking in that direction at an angle toward the side of the field.

✦ For lining, use "dead bird." Indicate a long, straight path to the target using the standard lining posture and hand point, whether you've chosen Continental-style or American-style as discussed earlier. With practice, the dog learns the distinction between the two very different skills.

On day one, once the dog understands the signals, pick a grass field bordered by trees or brush and set up a circle memory or a loop. Your reference points for each bumper will be in a row along the edge of the field at locations you can remember and that are distinctive for the dog. With your dog at heel, drop the scented bumpers or birds at distances apart.

Circle back around to the start of the grass field. In the first lesson, just walk along and push through the cover with your dog *at heel* in a zigzag pattern, occasionally stopping to line for each memory from different angles.

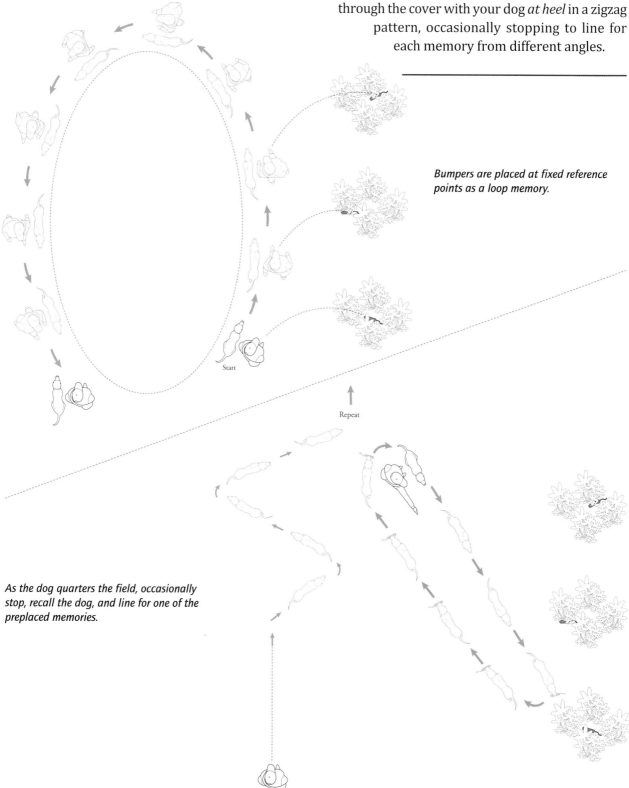

Bumpers are placed at fixed reference points as a loop memory.

As the dog quarters the field, occasionally stop, recall the dog, and line for one of the preplaced memories.

On day two, as the dog watches, set up the same exercise with bumpers in exactly the same locations. After memories are set, have the dog *quarter* the grass field that borders the planted memories, occasionally stopping and calling the dog in to line for a memory. After a pick, send the dog back out to quarter. Allow the dog to make some finds as it quarters. Occasionally stop your progression and pick the next memory from a different angle. Work this exercise for several days, quartering and lining for memories as you add different skills to the scenario:

✦ Gunshot and a diversion.

✦ Hidden feather-laced bumpers in the field.

✦ As the dog quarters, another dog walking in line with the handlers picks a mark.

✦ The dog continues to quarter and is occasionally stopped, recalled to the handler, and lined to pick a memory, TDM, or unseen.

Just as you did in your progression to unseens, set up other areas as time-delay memories (TDMs) and permanent unseens for more quartering and lining exercises. Be sure to include a diversity of cover and terrain, including ditches and creeks. Then, it's on to cold unseen retrieves combined with quartering. Begin with the shorter, uncomplicated unseens and gradually extend the distance and complexity of the terrain. Remember, run more memories than cold unseens to ensure confidence in your gundog.

TRACKING

The ability to track down a wounded bird is an important quality for a finished upland dog. This section explores how to prepare your dog to track the trickiest of game birds. Tracking is really an extension of the previously perfected skills of hunting cover on command. You're simply adding movement to these skills.

You want to ensure that your dog will hold the area on a hunt very well before you encourage him to leave to begin a track. Perfect the art of hunting birds under the thickest of cover, like

Prepare dogs to locate scent well above ground level.

a bird hidden deep under a brush pile or on top of a brush pile. Make sure the dog can locate off-the-ground finds with bumpers placed in vines, bushes, and row crops. Not all birds afield will be located on the ground. Also, the upland dog must learn to search out birds that may go to the ground—for instance, in a hole or under a log. The dog must be proficient in hunting fall areas before you teach him how to locate and pick a runner.

It is not advisable to provide too many tracking opportunities for young dogs until they are proficient in pointing or quartering a field. I normally teach tracking after a dog's first hunting season. Early on, just use a few scented tennis balls rolled along the ground to awaken the youngster's instinct of picking up on an unseen scent line and following the trail.

You do not want to confuse your student while he is learning to quarter. In the field, youngsters will experience bird scent ahead of them on a hunt. Live birds, especially pheasants, will be running ahead of the hunters. If encouraged to follow scent trails too early, the dog may well abandon the quarter pattern and run the scent, ultimately flushing the birds out of range.

Your dog must distinguish between when to hold the quartering pattern—despite the scent trails or the headwind blowing fresh bird scent directly into his face—and when you want him to track. This will require maturity and take time in training as well as actual field experience.

Tracking is a very independent behavior for the hunting dog, so make haste slowly. After developing solid hunting and quartering skills, move to extending scent lines using scented tennis balls. You can easily put down a longer scent line using freshly scented tennis balls rolled along the ground with a Chuck-It, which will often put in a little bounce to prepare dogs for the occasional break in the scent line. A long hillside of shorter grass or woodlands will allow the ball to roll and bounce quite a distance.

Single Drag

To prepare for the track of a runner, begin with a simple single drag. Use a check cord of 20 to 30 feet in length. Working into the wind, pull a cold game bird along the surface of thick grasses. After 15 yards, create a slight bend (angle) in the line, then walk another 10 yards before disconnecting the bird. Return in a wide circle to collect your dog. Do not walk over the freshly scented area. If possible, have another person lay out this line so the dog won't be running your familiar scent.

To show your tracking rookie where to start, toss out a clump of dirt—something that will break apart on impact—and give your hunt command. Slowly walk forward. Encourage your dog toward the direction of the line, but allow him time to work the scent out on his own if he can. Avoid the temptation to overhandle. Only direct your dog back to the area if he is totally removed from the correct location. As you move forward, the scent should become more pronounced for the dog. Once completed, move to a new area for fresh ground and begin to extend trails.

Double Drag

The next step is to introduce the double drag. With the single, you are laying down human scent along with the bird scent all in the same line. The double drag gives the bird its own scent trail.

Use two cords or very small ropes with two helpers. Attach the cold game bird between the two cords so it may be pulled along between the helpers, who remain at a distance from the scent line so that the bird remains on the ground during the drag. As the drag continues, you can coordinate bends in the line, as well as the occasional break or skip in the scent trail. Just lift the bird off the ground briefly. Be sure to also incorporate various cover that could influence the track, such as dry grasses, dusty plowed ground, or lush green cover—all excellent for disguising scent.

The track begins with a "hunt dead" command close to the start of the trail. Encourage your dog to thoroughly hunt the area and pick up the line on his own. Remember that scent will move and drift, so do not be concerned if your dog does not work on the exact trail put down as he works the line. Let the dog work out the problem. On the hunt, you will likely have no idea where your runner went. Trust your dog and only put him back in the area if he goes too far afield. At this point, you are developing an independent, self-confident hunter.

Establishing a double drag requires two people. The bird is pulled between the two to establish the line to be tracked.

With each lesson, add distance, more bends, and different terrain. If there is a break in the scent, your hunter must not abandon the area on a frolic. You want a close-hunting pattern at gradually increasing distances until the dog picks up the scent again. Practice tracking in all types of weather and wind conditions. A headwind makes the job easier, unless there is an abrupt bend in the trail where the bird changes direction. Then, the dog is likely to overrun and must be talented enough to return and locate the line. A tailwind will push the scent ahead of the dog, making the trail less distinctive. Crosswinds push the scent off the actual line. Some days afield I think winds exist merely to interfere with my tracking fun. It is best to prepare your dog to overcome the negative influences of all three types of barriers: environmental, psychological, and physical.

Once your tracker is proficient in cold-game drags, move to the release of live birds, if the opportunity exists. Using a wing-secured duck or pheasant—birds that will run—you can establish a realistic track. Release the bird as an unseen in fresh cover, giving it a brief head start before sending the tracker in pursuit. Make sure your dog has a soft mouth and a good delivery so no damage is done to the bird when it is located and caught. You do not want to create a delivery or hard mouth problem. Remember Wildrose Law No. 4: Don't condition in a problem that must be trained out later.

Wagon dogs wait patiently to be called forward when needed.

WAGON DOG

A wagon dog is a game dog trained to multitask while working from a wagon or vehicle. A wagon dog is expected to:

✦ Retrieve downed birds.

✦ Walk with hunters at heel and back dogs on point.

✦ Act as a strike dog, trained to flush birds in thick cover or put running birds in the air.

✦ Locate and flush singles.

✦ Ride peacefully on a wagon or vehicle while on the hunt, always ready to assist when called.

The wagon dog must be comfortable riding on a wagon or in open, motorized vehicles such as ATVs, jeeps, or platforms on trucks. The dog may need to work around horses and mules, and should respect moving vehicles like the wagon itself or other vehicles involved in the hunt.

During basic gundog introductions, you indoctrinated your future wagon dog to riding on vehicles. You taught your dog to load and exit the vehicle on command. The command I prefer is "load" or "out." If this behavior is not ingrained, now is the time for reinforcement—before expecting your hunter to sit patiently on a horse-drawn wagon, a towed trailer, the front of a dog truck, or an ATV. The most basic skill is mastered first—stay safely and quietly on that wagon.

For the first rides, usually on an ATV or a towed trailer for training purposes, the dog should be secured by a short lead tied with a slipknot for quick release. Or, you can ride with the dog. The spooked dog may try to jump from the vehicle on his first trip. To promote steadiness on a wagon in training, with the dog at sit on a trailer, ATV, or vehicle, walk out and toss out a few denials, fire a couple of shots for excitement, and then return to the vehicle.

If the dog needs to make a retrieve in training or the field, do not get into the habit of calling him off the vehicle. This should occur infrequently and only in situations that demand the immediate response of the dog. Otherwise, return to the wagon to collect the dog. Your dog must learn to stay steady while awaiting your return. Your wagon dog training exercises will usually involve riding around the property on whatever vehicle is available that will duplicate the wagon concept. As you ride, stop occasionally to pick a few time-delay memories or preplaced unseens, combined with steady-denial exposures.

A very beneficial skill to teach a wagon dog is how to return to the wagon or vehicle on command from any location. Begin close to the wagon and use your load command. Slowly increase the distance and angles. For a touch of class, teach your dog to hold and carry a bird back to the wagon master from your field position. The experienced wagon dog accepts the bird from the shooter and finds the wagon on his own for a nice delivery to hand. Very stylish.

Later, on a hunt with dogs on point or birds down after a flush, you may need to call your dog forward off the wagon by name and whistle. The wagon dog should come directly to heel, ready for action, either to stay steady while backing the pointer to make a flush or perhaps to retrieve.

CANINES AND HORSES

If it is ever likely that your dog will experience a traditional plantation-style quail hunt with horses, it's time to introduce the horse. Given the unpredictable nature of a horse and the fact that most readers of this book likely do not have a horse of the temperament necessary to put up with an

Heel work with horses requires specialized training and a calm, focused dog once afield.

energetic dog readily available in their backyard, let's discuss how to approach this training.

Begin with the bicycle that is collecting dust in your garage. Teach your dog to heel with the bike, but be careful with this lesson. Handlers have been known to incur scrapes and bruises with this technique! If you can ride around the dog and he remains still, take a ride with your companion at heel, including turns in both directions. Keep going until you feel confident that your dog understands how to keep a watchful eye on your movements and that suspicious bike. Now, you may progress to heel work with an ATV. Fol-

low the same concept here—acclimate your dog to run, walk, and turn with the movement of the ATV. Once he is proficient, find a horse.

With your dog on lead, take a calm horse for a walk. Always make introductions while you are safely in control on the ground. The dog should be at the heel position at your side and the horse should be on your other side.

With practice, your dog will learn to watch the horse's turns while at heel, just as he did with the bike and ATV. Dogs must stay clear of the horse's legs and hooves. Involve numerous turns in your practice sessions before mounting. Next, place the dog at sit, mount, and ride your steed around your suspicious hunter as he remains patient at sit. Finally, take a brief ride with the dog at heel. Initially, keep your path straight while talking to your dog so he remains focused on your elevated position and that of the horse. Obviously, do not use a check cord on the dog! Slowly incorporate turns, the hardest of which is the turn away from the dog, which requires him to turn wide to the outside of the horse. When you encounter rough terrain, it may be preferable for your dog to move forward as you ride rather than staying close at heel. Just make sure he has learned to stay clear of the horses.

THE STRIKE DOG

The strike dog works in tandem with pointers most commonly on quail hunts. These able game-finders are trained to flush birds that may be running in front of pointers or those holding tight in cover too thick to navigate. In both situations, the strike dog charges the birds, putting them in flight. The striker also works as a flusher of singles missed by the pointers and as a retriever of downed game. Normally, most strike dogs are spaniels or perhaps

retriever breeds that love to work close and have a passionate prey drive. Really, this is a simple concept. The strike is just a short unseen into thick cover or a brush pile followed by the dog remaining steady on the flush. But one thing is for sure— you will need to prepare your strike dog flusher to get into the thick cover despite briars or tangles.

Steady to the flush is an imperative skill for the strike flusher. Chasing will be particularly dangerous after the flush. Your dog must remain still until told to do otherwise, despite the action. To prepare for the flush, salt a brush pile with several scented bumpers or birds, all set as unseens deep under the brush. Collect your dog and circle the pile, lining for the unseens deep under the brush. Once the dog understands the concept, plant a few live birds, give your dog a cue like "put 'em up," and then line for the unseen. With some birds down and others allowed to fly away, there should be no chasing. After a covey flush, strike dogs are often used to quarter the area to locate downed birds, flush singles, or pick running wounded birds. Add this dimension to your training after the flush and shots.

Working when teamed with pointers will take a bit of additional training, such as backing

An aggressive spaniel strikes quail from cover.

Drake backs pointers just before striking a covey in thick cover.

the point. The process is much the same as teaching a pointer to back. Stack the pointers on a tethered bird. Bring in your strike dog to back. With your student at sit or standing steady, walk around throwing out a few feathered bumpers as denials as you fire a shot and flush the bird. Your dog must remain steady despite the flush or the reaction of the pointing dog to the flush.

With the tethered bird picked up, reward your dog's steadiness with praise and the retrieve. If the dog runs in, snatch up the bird so there is no reward to pick. You are always in control.

It is important to condition your dog to ignore the actions of other dogs on a bird hunt. He must remain focused on his job and you, not the antics of other hunters or the pointers. You may prepare for such situations earlier in training by using scattered marks. With several dogs in a walk-up line, have helpers throw bumpers in all directions almost simultaneously, much like a covey flush. Each dog is allowed to make retrieves as fast as possible. The retrievers are

expected to ignore the others to get their own job done. Then, just add the pointer. If you don't have a close-working pointer that will stay in the training area as you practice, place an active pointer on a lunge line to keep him close. As you walk the field, helpers toss bumpers ahead of the group as marks, simulating a covey flush as the pointer runs back and forth. Your retriever should stay focused to make his picks and pay no attention to the pointers.

This type of action is likely what will happen after a flush. It can be chaos—pointers running around; retrievers all in action at once. You will need a dog with exceptional focus. Start with simple singles, then progress to more realistic cover and intensify the action with multiple flushes, live birds, gunfire, and more dogs in the mix.

A great strike dog provides a whole new dimension to the upland hunting experience— a retriever, flusher, and tracker that will make the most effective combination when teamed with pointers.

10 Rules of Etiquette When Hunting in a Group

This guide to etiquette comes from Wildrose client and avid wingshooter Grayson Schaffer, senior editor at Outside Magazine *and a young man of passion for game dogs, shooting sports, and the pageantry of the upland experience.*

Some people have Burning Man. For the last two years, I've cleared my schedule and made the 17-hour drive north to vacation at a certain repurposed mine-foreman's house in North Dakota. On the agenda for the week: pheasants. My editor at *Outside* recently asked me if I was really taking a vacation and driving cross-country just to kill things—again. To be fair, chasing ditch parrots, as the Nodakkers call them, makes at least as much sense as driving to a place that's good for riding bicycles or kayaking down a freezing rocky river where you could drown, or any of the other things people do for fun.

The simple explanation, for the uninitiated, is that bird hunting is actually more about the hunting dogs than anything else. Here's an animal endowed by nature to run faster, jump higher, and smell more acutely than any human. And through years of selective breeding, patience, reinforcement, and— who are we kidding—the occasional profane outburst, a good Lab will put those inhuman abilities to work for his handler. Occasionally, when everything aligns perfectly—

bird and gun and scent and dog—it can seem like the connection between retriever and handler is plain English.

It's that connection that brings this same crew—most of them from Alaska—together every year. We all have dogs from Wildrose, and we all do our best to train using the low-force, positive-reinforcement ethic that Mike Stewart promotes. Getting together means getting a lot of good dogs together. When you turn 15 dogs loose in the same pheasant field, there's either chaos or there isn't. Mostly, for us, there isn't.

Grayson and Cooper await approaching ducks at a prairie pothole in North Dakota.

A Gentleman's Gundog hunts ducks in the morning, pheasants in the afternoon, and relaxes at fireside in the evening.

Here, then, are my 10 rules of etiquette for people who take their gundogs seriously—but not too seriously:

1- Your dog might be the best dog in the field back home, but that likelihood decreases with each mile driven.

2- Always undersell your dog. He can speak for himself.

3- Every time you're about to brag about your dog, stop yourself and compliment another dog's fine retrieve instead.

4- Complimenting another man's dog is never a selfless act because only the underdog can over-achieve. The best the overdog can do is meet expectations.

5- If your dog breaks and steals a retrieve from another dog, you must berate your dog loudly. This is for the benefit of the other hunter and will have no effect on your dog's behavior whatsoever.

6- OK, now put a leash on him.

7- Never give another guy a hard time about his dog. Believe me, he knows.

8- Instead, refer to Rule No. 3. An acceptable response: "That dog sure has a lot of drive."

9- When your dog honors, then makes a long retrieve through heavy cover, and returns with a lightly wounded bird, you'd better sound at least as happy as an eight-year-old girl who's been given a pony for Christmas.

10- When your dog leans against you, it either means that he's trying to dominate you or that he has an itch he'd like you to scratch. Your call.

CHAPTER 9

Picking Up

▮ Driven Shoots

n the early 1800s, British and European wingshooting sports began to flourish along with the rise of empires, industrial wealth, new firearm technology, and the popularity of sporting dog breeds, such as the spaniel, flat coat, curly coat, and the newly arrived ancestor of what is today known as the Labrador.

Driven game shooting was the prince of sports for the late Victorian gentry; it involved beautiful estates, elaborate feasts, splendidly attired gentlemen and ladies, and of course, fine guns hand-built to a hunter's specifications and sporting dogs that embellished the splendor of a day in the countryside. As society evolved, social barriers blurred and shooting opportunities that were once reserved for the elite became more accessible to the public. Travel became easier, enabling shooters and gundog enthusiasts the accessibility to participate in the pageantry of an estate driven shoot.

Today, authentic drivens in the United Kingdom, the Republic of Ireland, and Central Europe still embrace the "classics" when it comes to wing-shooting. Participants dress in proper attire and display a high degree of etiquette, gentlemanly behavior, and sportsmanship. There is a wonderful respect for the game, a decent shot, and fine game dogs.

A true driven shoot complete with beaters, loaders, and game birds pushed in droves from row crops is difficult to find in North America. Driven shoots take an enormous amount of manpower, resources, birds, and property, not to mention skill. It is costly and labor-intensive. It is my personal opinion that to pick up with a retriever or spaniel on an authentic driven wing-shoot is a "bucket list" experience for most sporting dog enthusiasts.

More common in the United States are released bird shoots in which retrievers and spaniels are used to collect game and locate escaped birds after the flight is complete. These shooting events are usually referred to as British or continental shoots, duck flights, tower shoots, or pigeon flights. To handle a working game dog on one of these types of shoots is a fantastically entertaining experience and a splendid opportunity for your hunting companion to gain bird experience. Don't miss the opportunity to pick up on a tower shoot or a duck flight. Just understand at the outset of this discussion on "picking up" that it would be incorrect to refer to any type of released bird shoot as a driven. That is the first point of order to becoming a proper picker.

Authentic Driven Shooting

Lars Magnusson of Blixt and Co. in Jackson Hole, Wyoming, offers authentic driven shooting opportunities in the United States. His past experience on driven shoots in both England and Sweden—as well as his time spent as a shooting instructor for the West London Shooting School in England and Griffin and Howe in the United States—affords him splendid insight into the culture and operation of authentic driven shooting.

What truly separates driven shooting from other types of game-bird shooting is the finest quality and presentation of pheasants and partridge and the highest standards of sportsmanship and etiquette. This includes the quality of environment for the birds, as well as their flying qualities on the day.

Birds are released many weeks before the beginning of the shooting season. This enables them to acclimate to their surroundings. A professional gamekeeper's job is to ensure the health and welfare of the birds and to encourage them to remain in the shooting area. This is not accomplished by pens or fences, but by good animal husbandry, habitat, and environmental enhancement on the ranch or estate.

Birds are "driven" over a waiting gun line. Tradition has always called for eight guns (shooters), often accompanied by a loader. These guns wait patiently in a predetermined place, usually spaced between 30 and 40 yards apart. The gamekeeper and his team of beaters drive the birds by tapping sticks and using flags to encourage the now "wild" birds toward a flushing point—somewhere short of the guns. This space enables the birds to gain height and speed before they fly over the facing gun line. The guns now have the birds flying over their heads in front of them. This presents a very different target than the traditional American walk-up.

With numerous birds in the air at once, a member is expected to shoot only the birds best suited to his or her personal ability. With this combination of beating and shooting, a shooter gets an unparalleled shooting experience.

Etiquette remains a critical part of the driven shooting tradition. This includes the use of traditional break-barrel guns, traditional English dress, and the highest level of sportsmanship toward the game and fellow shooters.

Lars Magnusson is properly attired for an authentic driven shoot.

A picker training retrievers to work as a team on peg.

Picking Up

So, just what constitutes picking up? The term "picker" originated on the fine estate shoots of the United Kingdom and is a description for the handlers and their dogs that retrieve birds that are shot by guest shooters or guns. Drivens also involve dogs—both retrievers and spaniel breeds—to locate game missed by the retrievers after the completion of each drive. Handlers may also use close-working spaniels with the beaters' line to push birds from thick cover. The different roles of picking up sporting dogs include:

PEG DOG: A dog that is handled by the gun while occupying a peg. A peg is a position identified for the placement of each shooter during the drive, normally marked with a number. The peg dog stays with the gun, is handled by the shooter, and picks up birds in the immediate area after the drive.

SWEEPER: A dog that is trained to quarter the area around the gun line after a drive in an effort to locate game missed by the retrievers during and just after the drive.

PICKER: A retriever team assigned to either one or two gun positions during each drive. A single gun has a picker located out of sight at a short distance behind his peg to retrieve any bird that falls within the picker's area. When covering double pegs, the picker's position is between two pegs and covers a larger area.

BACKSTOP: Dogs with their handlers positioned well behind the picker's line, normally out of

The value of a well-trained working dog on any shoot is to bring back the birds that otherwise would be lost, but the picker also adds a great deal of prestige and pageantry to the wing-shooter's experience. A well-trained dog and a knowledgeable handler should complement the guests' experience rather than interfering, interrupting, or detracting from it. Whether it is an authentic driven shoot or a local club tower shoot, good dog work and proper handling etiquette matters.

QUALITIES OF AN EFFECTIVE PICKING UP TEAM FOR A CLASSIC SHOOTING EXPERIENCE

The Dog: Performance Expectations

There are a number of expectations set by a shoot's staff, guests, and other handlers for the conduct and ability of a proper driven shooting dog. These include:

OFF-LEAD OBEDIENCE AND STEADINESS: This must be impeccable. The dog in no way may interfere with the drive, birds in flight, or the attention of the guns. No whining, barking, running in, or out-of-control behavior will be tolerated. With birds flying in great numbers overhead and falling all around, the dog's steadiness will be tested. Dogs must maintain patience and focus, ignore shots

A back stop is in position for a drive.

sight of the gun line or the other pickers. The backstop marks the fall of birds that cannot be picked by the regular retrievers due to the distance and range of the fall.

The primary function of a picker is to locate all game that is hit. Keepers of both driven and tower shoots pride themselves on two things: how high the birds fly and the bird count on the game cart at the end of the day. Lost birds reduce that count. It's also humane and shows respect for the bird. Wounded birds should be located.

A picking dog must be totally under control and quiet.

and falls, and line as instructed for longer birds that could be lost.

HONORING: Dogs should never interfere with another dog's retrieve. A great retriever stays true to his bird and does not create problems by scuffling with another dog over a bird.

DIVERSIONS: There will be many high-stimulus factors on a shoot. Guests will not be amused by a dog that is running around, mindlessly switching from bird to bird as they fall. The dog must be able to ignore diversions of secondary falls and distractions. The dog that picks up a bird but drops it on the return to switch to another will lose game. The first bird, if wounded, could escape. The handler might not notice the placement of the drop and thus the bird could be lost. The dog is expected to ignore close birds that fall around the peg, opting instead to pick the long falls and runners deep in the cover, and he will surely encounter an unseen and must ignore the obvious birds lying close. Lining for the unseen through the thickest of cover will now become necessary, despite the influence of the seen birds.

DELIVERY: The delivery of an undamaged bird is important. No mouthing, plucking, or chewing is acceptable. The dog should not repeatedly drop the bird on the return, as a wounded bird will escape a sloppy-mouthed dog. That said, hard-mouthed dogs that crush birds destined for the table are also unwelcome on any shoot.

CONTROL: This is the primary responsibility of a handler. A driven dog must easily stop and recall without requiring excessive noise, and they must handle well, whether retrieving or sweeping. Shooters respect quiet handlers. Noise distracts the guns and frightens birds.

TEMPERAMENT: Socially acceptable behavior is expected of all dogs. No aggression, inappropriate behavior, excessive noise, or out-of-control frolics will be tolerated. Dogs that require numerous

Game-finding ability is of supreme importance.

A peg dog waits patiently during a drive.

This is a typical tower shoot configuration.

corrections to maintain performance or proper behavior should not be on a shoot of this type.

GAME-FINDING ABILITY: This is of supreme importance. The overriding obligation to collect game and dispatch it humanely is the primary function of a picking team. Shoot managers and gamekeepers value dogs that know birds and have a discriminating scent capability; dogs that track runners and possess the willingness to punch into the thickest of cover will be high-value assets to any event.

The Handler: Traditions and Etiquette

In addition to the clear expectations for dogs, there is also a culture for a proper driven or continental tower shoot that is well established. All participants and staff—including dogs and handlers— are expected to adhere to this gentlemanly code.

Imperative is courtesy to others, proper firearm safety, respect for game birds and dogs,

and a realization that more value is put on the skill of the shot than the number of birds taken. Those that respect the traditions of a classic shooting experience will shun excessive, inappropriate celebration or loss of temper. Shooting is a social experience with estate or club managers, gamekeepers, and staff taking great pride in the presentation of their birds. It is inappropriate for a guest on a shoot to ask the property owner or manager how many acres they manage or how many birds they will release. This principle applies to the pickers as well. Criticism of a shoot should be a quiet affair between paying guests and the management. The picker or handler "does not have a dog in that race," to use an old Southern metaphor, so keep your opinions to yourself. Respect the culture of the shoot, and always keep these guidelines in mind:

✦ Do not interfere with the shoot. Be a quiet handler and keep your dog under control.

- Do not make picks in front of the guns or pegs during the flight.
- This is not a time for dog training. There should be no inappropriate corrections or loud handling on a shoot.
- Research attire expectations before you arrive. Some shoots expect a more traditional sporting appearance, which would not include camouflage clothing. Others may require the wearing of orange for visibility.
- As with all staff members, pickers should arrive at the destination early and should be prepared. Thoroughly air your dog before reporting to your post and do not be late for a flight.
- Never criticize a guest's shooting ability or lack thereof, or engage in an argument with anyone, including other handlers.
- Project a voluntary spirit by offering assistance to guests when appropriate and be approachable if someone inquires about your dog.
- Clean up after your dog immediately.
- Do not allow your dog to go into ground that has not yet been pushed or near the tower where the birds are retained.
- Respect game by picking and dispatching wounded birds quickly and in a humane, discreet manner.
- Have an appropriate place to keep birds, like a game carrier or game bag.
- Count birds downed in your area. Rest assured that the shooters are doing the same. Guns take great pride in their hits, keep score, and expect you to find every bird picked.

Training for Driven Shoots

All of the previous chapters in this book are relevant to the discipline of picking up on a driven or tower shoot—handling, steadiness, lining past diversions for an unseen, tracking runners, and

A picking retriever must drive deep into woodlands.

quartering to sweep after a flight. These are all applicable skills for waterfowl retrievers, upland flushers, and certainly pickers. The Wildrose Way takes training for driven shoots one step further by developing a few specific exercises to define skills that will benefit the picker.

CIRCLE MEMORY HUB AND COVER PENETRATION

This concept is similar to the circle memory single and double hubs outlined in previous chapters, but you'll modify the lesson to acclimate the dog to

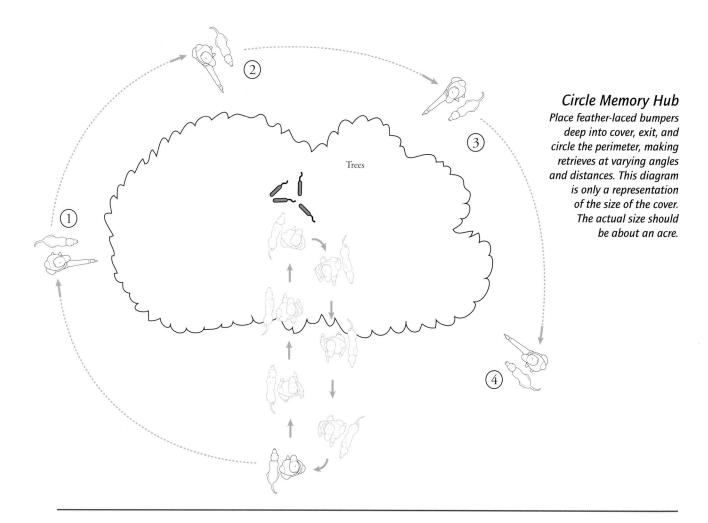

Trees

Circle Memory Hub
Place feather-laced bumpers deep into cover, exit, and circle the perimeter, making retrieves at varying angles and distances. This diagram is only a representation of the size of the cover. The actual size should be about an acre.

picking birds—both marks and memories—that fall deep into cover, whether it's woodlands, grass fields, or row crops. A dog that is not accustomed to lining well beyond the borders of heavy cover may stop short of the target to begin his search, especially if the dog is no longer in sight of the handler. A picker or backstop will need a dog that will hold a straight line into cover 40 yards or more.

To develop this skill, begin with a circle memory hub. Select an island of woodlands or heavy cover in a field that you can walk fully or partially around to create a wagon wheel effect. With your dog at heel, enter the cover to its core and place three to four scented bumpers. There should be more than 20 yards between the bumpers and any edge of the cover.

Exit the woodlands and begin to circle around the perimeter. Stop and line the dog into the cover with the "dead bird" command to indicate an unseen. If the dog stops short, walk in to

assist. You may find it beneficial to set the first bumper as a trailing memory. Continue to circle around the cover, stopping at different points and making the next pick with deeper penetrating lines with each retrieve.

LINING THROUGH HEAVY COVER

Select an area of heavy cover like a grass field and mow lanes to create a pattern designed specifically to line through thick cover at angles and not be influenced by the contours and lanes that may interrupt the line to a bird. These exercises are limited only by your imagination, locations that provide tall cover, and an available mower. Cut lanes at different angles, with the outer edges of the pattern around the area mowed short.

OPPOSITE: Many birds fall into thick cover, which requires exceptional lining skills.

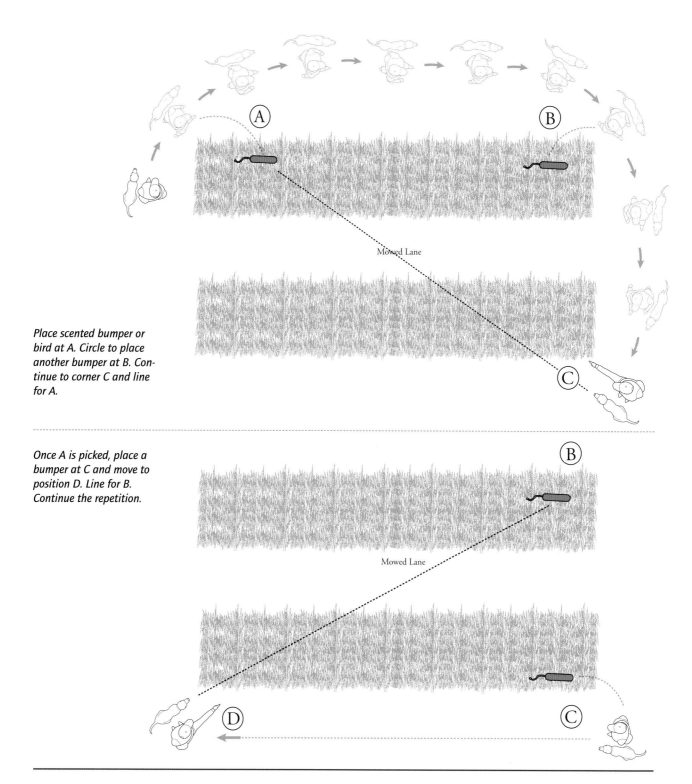

Place scented bumper or bird at A. Circle to place another bumper at B. Continue to corner C and line for A.

Once A is picked, place a bumper at C and move to position D. Line for B. Continue the repetition.

Railroad Track Pattern

The Railroad Track pattern is a single strip mowed down the center of a rectangular or square area of tall grasses. With the dog at heel, begin a circle memory by placing a single scented bumper at one corner of the pattern (A).

Walk around and place another bumper at the next corner (B). Continue to the next corner (C) and line diagonally across for A. If your dog experiences problems with the effect of the mowed lane down the center of the pattern, shorten the distances until your dog overcomes

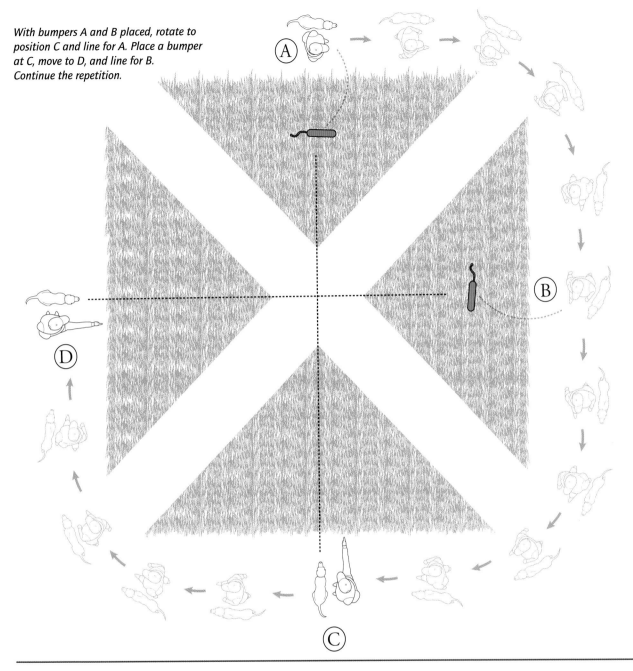

With bumpers A and B placed, rotate to position C and line for A. Place a bumper at C, move to D, and line for B. Continue the repetition.

the influence. Once the dog picks A, place the bumper at your present position (C), walk to the next corner (D), and line diagonally for the bumper at B. You are lining your dog through the cover from corner to corner in an X pattern. If you choose, you can continue to place another bumper and move to the next corner for another retrieve. This is an excellent exercise for all retrievers of game, but it is especially useful for pickers, who will encounter so many distracting variables in cover on a shoot.

Stars and Bars Pattern

The Stars and Bars pattern is cut in cover duplicating the lines of a Confederate flag or an X with the outer edges mowed. Set bumpers using the circle memory as described above, but this time place the bumpers at the center of the design's outer edges. The dogs run in a T pattern through the cover, avoiding the influences of the cross-cut lanes. Place bumper A and B, then move to the C position to pick A. Replant the bumper at C and move to D to pick B. The circle pattern continues to make all four picks.

Training for picking up requires extensive group work exposure.

Group Activities and 180s

To prepare adequately for the stimulus and confusion of an active shoot, you will need to incorporate group work sessions. One exercise that is particularly effective is set up as a 180 with the following elements:

✦ Trailing memory scatters in cover to the rear of the dog line.

✦ Multiple marks fired by a remote launcher or assistant into cover in front of the dog line.

✦ Short bumpers tossed all around the line as short diversions.

✦ Multiple gunshots by assistants.

The group begins by setting up trailing memories for each dog in cover as scatters. Use an equal number of bumpers for each dog. Return across the field and line up the dogs facing the woodlands in the opposite direction of the memories. The dogs should be off lead. Two or more throwers and shooters should be forward, mimicking the guns. The action begins as fast as possible, launching bumpers deep into the woods at different angles. Other bumpers, accompanied by shots, fall all around the dog line between the memories and the marks in the woods. If a dog runs in, stop long enough to recover the dog and then continue the action. The more exciting chaos, the better.

Excellent pickers in this exercise must focus on two things: paying attention to their dog—as a dog knows when you're distracted and may seize the opportunity to bolt—and concentrating on marking downed birds. Effective pickers must disregard other working dogs, handlers, or activities outside of their area.

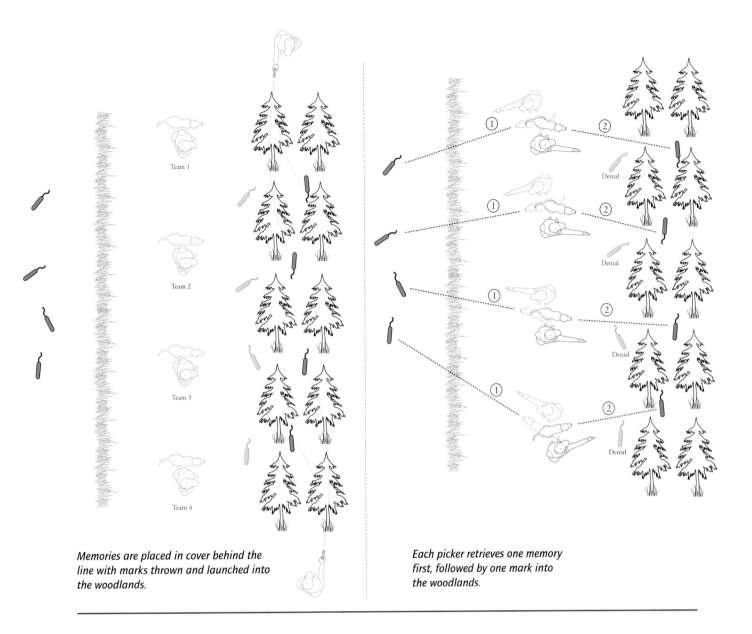

Memories are placed in cover behind the line with marks thrown and launched into the woodlands.

Each picker retrieves one memory first, followed by one mark into the woodlands.

Once the shoot concludes, handlers walk out and pick up the short bumpers as denials. Then, randomly and as quickly as possible, each dog picks a memory and then a mark into the woods. Remember, you will have little time on an actual shoot to make picks before another flight begins. You may make retrieves during a shoot as long as your dog does not interfere with the guns or the birds in flight. But after the flight concludes, you will be expected to locate the birds quickly and accurately, and then sweep your area to ensure that no birds have been left behind. Practice quick pickups with this exercise.

Send the least experienced dogs first, as long as they've been steady and quiet, as there will be more opportunities for a successful pick. Do not reward a disruptive dog with a retrieve.

CANYON PICKERS

In a variation of the exercise described above, use a steep hillside to duplicate high flyers coming down toward the guns and falling well behind both the guns and the pickers at the bottom of the hillside. Place the launchers high above the gun line and pickers. Pickers are

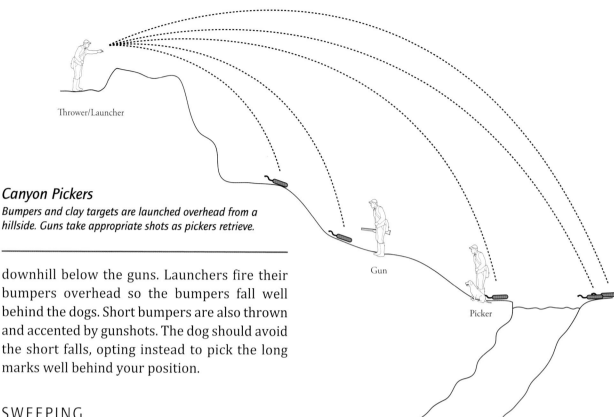

Canyon Pickers
Bumpers and clay targets are launched overhead from a hillside. Guns take appropriate shots as pickers retrieve.

Labels in figure: Thrower/Launcher · Gun · Picker

downhill below the guns. Launchers fire their bumpers overhead so the bumpers fall well behind the dogs. Short bumpers are also thrown and accented by gunshots. The dog should avoid the short falls, opting instead to pick the long marks well behind your position.

SWEEPING

This activity is nothing more than quartering an area after a drive to locate birds that retrievers missed or that escaped during the flight. To prepare, see the exercises on quartering in Chapter Eight. A great tracker or sweeper is of high value to any shoot. Sweepers may also be called upon during some shoots to do cleanup rough-shooting. This is when birds that have escaped are pursued as a separate hunt. Guns walk with pointers or upland flushers to find birds that remain around the area of a shoot. Some shoots even have separate walk-up days just for this purpose. This is yet another opportunity for the well-trained and versatile shooting dog.

TRANSITIONAL FIELD EXERCISES

An excellent way to condition a dog for a bird flight shoot is to involve sporting clays. Use one or more clay throwers high on a hillside like the canyon picker exercise described above. Several guns located below are invited to hit as many clays as they possibly can as they sail overhead.

The setup has the pickers behind the guns with two or three assistants to serve as throwers using scented bumpers, released birds, cold game, or numerous handheld bumper launchers. To have a meaningful effect, you'll want at least two guns and four dogs, but more is even better.

With everyone in position, the action begins with clays flying overhead and shots being fired. Simultaneously, throwers go to work firing, tossing, and releasing marks, unseens, and diversions. The goal is to duplicate the confusion and stimulus of an actual shoot. Once the drive is concluded with the sound of a whistle or a horn, the dogs go to work—many times simultaneously—to make their picks.

A word of caution to the throwers: Make sure to count the bumpers beforehand or some may be lost. After all the retrieves are made, sweep the area to ensure that all the bumpers were found. This is an exercise that is great fun for everyone and is excellent conditioning for your dog.

Parting Thoughts

Great dog work on a commercial bird flight experience involves more than just the necessity to locate game. The competent dog handler is a huge part of the total wingshooting experience. It is imperative for you to ensure that your dog is up to the expected standards. There is no pleasure in being accompanied by an animal that runs in, squeaks, is uncontrollable during a flight, or runs wild at the end of a drive. As a picker, the guns, staff, and other handlers will look upon your dog's inappropriate or poor performance not with amusement, but rather with annoyance and displeasure. To be sure, picking up is a superb way for the finished dog to gain bird experience, but keep in mind that only the best picker teams will be welcome on a credible commercial wingshooting operation. Make sure you and your dog are among them.

Superb game dogs complement the entire shooting experience.

CHAPTER 10

The Destination Wingshooter

T he ultimate sporting dog companion developed the Wildrose Way is a versatile game-finder prepared to go anywhere, anytime. The perfect description of the lifestyle of a traveling wingshooter and his or her canine companion comes from Richard Boone's classic western television show of the early 1960s: *Have Gun—Will Travel*. With a fully trained gundog at your side, you are now ready to live that experience, but before departing, there are a few things a destination wingshooter should consider. Put away the road map for a moment and let's get properly prepared.

■ Preseason Preparation

This subject is as valuable to a local hunter as it is to a traveling wingshooter. Often a fully trained gundog spends the off-season months lounging about on soft beds in air-conditioned environments, eating well, and experiencing a general lack of exercise during the hot summer months. If this is the case, your hunting pal will need some preseason conditioning. Athletes need training camp. Dogs are no different.

Training camp includes physical conditioning and a refocus on proper nutrition. The reconditioning of your dog must occur gradually. Problems can occur when rushing or pushing the dog in an attempt to get him ready for the season. It's no different than an athlete in training camp; there is a risk of heat exhaustion, muscle strain, joint stress, or (for the dog) sore pads.

Destination wingshooting gundogs pose with the morning's take.

EXERCISE

First, consider your dog's overall body weight. An overweight dog will require a diet and exercise in moderation. If your dog is underweight (which is less likely), you may find him lacking in endurance and the ability to withstand cold weather conditions. Exercise should begin with walks or short retrieves followed by jogging or road conditioning with a bike or an ATV. Never expose a young dog—less than two years old—to exercise involving high impact for long dura-

tions, as his joints may be damaged. Build endurance through short but frequent exercise. Nothing beats swimming. The dog stays cool and burns calories, but the joints of an overweight or underage dog are protected.

NUTRITION

Provide a reasonable diet of highly digestible dog food with a correct balance of protein and fats to meet your dog's needs. Dogs of high energy, like

pointers and bird dog breeds, can burn higher levels of protein and fat than the less active breeds, like the companion Labrador. Fat ensures that the dog has the energy to meet the physical demands of the hunt and it is fat that the dog's body uses to provide warmth. That said, a dog food that is too "hot" (high levels of protein and fat) can be detrimental to a less active hunting dog. Consult your veterinarian or a canine nutritionist for recommendations specific to your hunting companion. Also, ensure that your

feed contains appropriate levels of balanced omega fatty acids for coat conditioning. Oily, healthy coats shed water.

During hunting season, game dogs burn more calories due to the strenuous and continuous activity and to maintain their body temperature on cold icy days. Your dog will likely need up to 30 percent more calories than usual just to maintain his body condition if you hunt him hard. Cold weather and water deplete a dog's endurance quickly, which will diminish his hunting ability. It is advisable to get your dog acclimated to cold weather before exposing him to foul weather or cold waters, especially if the gundog has grown accustomed to parlor life. Outside exposure to cold weather for extended periods is recommended.

PRESEASON PHYSICAL

Make sure all inoculations are in order, including parvo, rabies, and kennel cough. Make sure your pal is up-to-date on heartworm prevention; it is advisable to complete a heartworm screening every two years to ensure that your dog is clear. Clean teeth are extremely important to the health of a dog. Poor dental care can cause serious infections that can migrate and negatively affect your dog's scenting ability. Make sure the dog's weight is in the proper range and his respiratory and heart condition are sound. Finally, trim nails to minimize the chance of breakage.

If you are planning to fly your dog commercially to a destination, a health certificate from your vet may be required by the airlines. Check with the carrier in advance of your vet visit. With your dog in good physical condition and a clean bill of health, you are ready to hit the road for that wingshooting adventure.

◾ On the Road Again

Most hunters will at some point travel overnight with their dogs. There are some special items for wingshooters to consider before hitting the road. Two of the important "early start" lessons, which should be mastered by now, will complement extended travel: crate training and acclimating to riding in a vehicle.

Kennel training is a necessity on the road. A dog must remain quiet in the kennel at all times while traveling and especially in a hotel. Your dog has come to recognize his kennel as a "home away from home" and should feel quite secure in it, which reduces the stress of travel either by vehicle or by aircraft. It is advisable to keep your dog in a kennel when traveling in a motor vehi-

cle in case of an accident. Many people like to have their dog inside the vehicle with them while on the road. If you choose to do so, the dog definitely needs to ride in the backseat of the vehicle, preferably restrained. You do not want to consider the ramifications of a dog becoming a flying object if an accident were to occur.

Dogs should be totally housebroken before entering any motel, lodge, or public place. They should be conditioned to relieve themselves on command so you can better select the preferred location, which should be away from public areas and landscaping. Always have plastic disposable bags and cleanup materials ready to address any accidents.

Adjust your dog's feeding schedule so that he eats at the end of the day and get him used to it before beginning the trip. This will be the time of feeding on the road. To avoid an upset stomach, don't feed a dog in the morning before traveling. Take ample food along for the entire trip. In fact, take more than necessary just in case your trip lasts longer than expected. This tip holds true even for a weekend excursion. Switching foods can make for bad business when combined with the stress of travel. You can store water in containers or coolers. A very nice addition to any trip is a no-spill water bowl that you can place in the kennel with the dog as you travel. The bowl helps to prevent spillage in the motel room as well.

When on the road, pick places to stop that will protect your dog from the elements of extreme heat or cold while the vehicle is parked. Don't leave a dog confined in a hot car or park in a lot that provides no shade in hot weather. In winter, cover the travel crate to insulate it from the cold, or—if it's in the back of a truck—from the wind and rain.

Make frequent stops along the route to allow your dog exercise and relief, but watch out for traffic. Roadside rest stops are good, but be mindful of other vehicles. Keep your dog on lead in high traffic areas. It is a good idea for your dog to wear an orange collar that includes your name and telephone number just in case of separation. Microchip implantation offers the value of perma-

Dogs must remain under control while loading and unloading vehicles.

nent identification, increasing the chance of recovery should your dog become lost on the journey or in the field. Offer your dog plenty of water during stops, but hold off on the food until evening.

Preplan your trip. Call ahead to ensure that your hunting pal will be welcome at the lodging that you may choose. Today, overnight facilities are becoming more pet-friendly, but many designate a limited number of rooms for canine companions. Call ahead for reservations. Make sure that your dog is on his best behavior at the hotel or other lodging. Dogs must be "good citizens" if they are to remain welcomed guests. No chewing, barking, soiling floors, lounging on furniture, or tracking in mud. Your hunter should be brushed daily before he enters the lodging. To reduce any undesirable dog-related odors, spray your hunting companion with a solution made of one-third

Listerine and two-thirds water. Inside the room, the dog should never be left unattended unless he's in the crate and he must remain quiet at all times. Even for a well-behaved canine, dog beds or mats are a must. Always keep your dog under control on a lead when around the hotel, which shows courtesy to others. Good citizenship counts! You want your hunter to be welcomed in the future at any location.

If your journey will take you to unknown places, take the initiative and locate a vet in the area should an emergency arise. Time-sensitive emergencies that require immediate care, not rectifiable by field first aid—such as snake bites, fractures, severe punctures, heat exhaustion, or lacerations—do not offer the luxury of a search for local health care. You need numbers and locations before your arrival.

Insulated crate covers are a necessity during cold weather travel.

To review, the essentials for successful over-land travel with your gundog include: a comfortable crate, weather-resistant crate cover, a lead, no-spill bowls, a dry storage dog food bag (avoid the misery of taking food in the manufacturer's sack), portable dog mat, collar with name plate attached, paper towels, disinfectant spray, and plastic pickup bags for cleanup. Finally, you should always have a first aid kit regardless of the duration of the trip. Always be a good scout and be prepared.

Field First Aid

It's bound to happen, so get ready. He's the unwelcome intruder that occasionally shows up on one of your hunting trips. Everyone dreads his inevitable appearance. It's Murphy and his law—"Whatever can go wrong, will go wrong." So your rule for the road and the field must become, "Be prepared." Your athletic hunter, enthusiastic in his quest for game, becomes a likely candidate for injury. It's imperative that handlers keep a first aid kit on hand—no matter the destination, purpose of the outing, or duration—and possess the basic knowledge to address field emergencies when a veterinarian is not readily available.

LACERATIONS

Cuts are common with hunting dogs. Your response should be to clean the wound with clean water or peroxide, apply a disinfectant, cover the cut with a thick layer of gauze or a clean towel, and apply direct pressure with your hand for three to five minutes to stop the bleeding. Dress the wound by re-washing it with hydrogen peroxide, and then apply an antiseptic, like an iodine solution, and a topical antibiotic ointment. Secure a clean gauze pad in place with a self-adhesive vet wrap bandage. Minor lacerations may be closed with a staple gun designed specifically for that purpose after the wound is cleaned and antiseptic is applied. Transport the dog to the vet if necessary.

If sutures are required, do not use the "superglue" adhesive products designed for cuts. Take the time to do it right. My dog, Kane, was running in the Grand National Bird Hunt in Oklahoma when I dropped a quail over a very tightly strung barbed-wire fence. While making the retrieve, he unwisely elected to jump the fence instead of simply going under it. He hit his back leg, leaving a gash from his knee to his ankle. A quick inspection revealed that the cut only tore the skin and was not deep in the muscle. Upon returning to the truck, I washed and treated the 12-inch cut with peroxide, followed with an iodine solution to disinfect the wound, and applied a heavy gauze layer between the wound and the vet wrap. Once completed, we were off to the vet. The veterinarian we located only worked with large animals and stitched poor Kane with huge cattle sutures. Kane's back leg looked like a young Frankenstein. The vet did, however, compliment the field dressing. I had prepared the area so that sutures could be applied properly and prevented infection. Without an appropriately stocked first aid kit, Kane would have suffered for hours.

PUNCTURE WOUNDS

Puncture wounds to the body cavity can be serious. For other parts of the body, they are treated similar to lacerations, with the exception of the wound being left open to facilitate drainage and reduce infection. In both cases, stop the bleeding with direct pressure and dress the wound. To bandage the wound, disinfect the area thor-

A well-stocked first aid kit is a necessity on the road.

oughly and secure the gauze in place by wrapping the bandage completely around the body part. Take care not to restrict circulation. If the puncture is deep in the dog's body cavity, there could be internal injury. If the object remains in the body cavity, leave it and bandage the area. Seek medical attention immediately.

TOENAILS

Damaged toenails and cuts to the dog's pads are common and may bleed profusely. Trim toenails before the hunt. If an injury occurs, control the bleeding with direct pressure. You may find it necessary to remove a severely damaged nail. Disinfect the wound as described above and dress with an extra gauze pad over, under, and between the injured toes. Secure with an outer wrap. Use a towel or T-shirt, something to offer extra padding, for serious foot wounds. Hold the padding in place with a second wrap around the leg and foot.

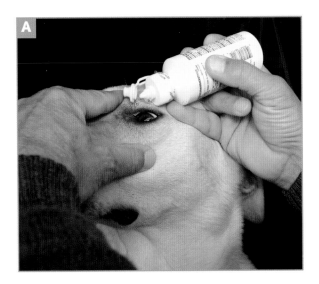

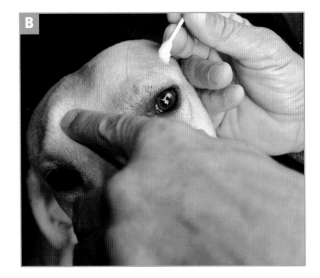

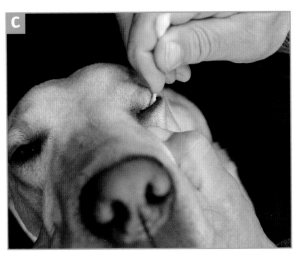

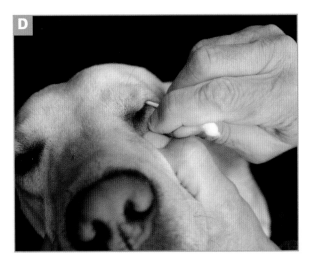

A: To remove debris, flush with saline solution. *B:* Insert swab tip under the eyelid at the tear duct. *C:* Rotate downward.
D: Continue the rotation 360 degrees under the eyelid to clear debris.

EYES AND EARS

Inspect the eyes of upland dogs twice a day and flush with a saline solution to ensure that no debris is trapped under the eyelids. Remove grass seeds and particles with a clean swab. You can easily remove an object following the eye wash by inserting the swab's tip under the dog's eyelid in the corner of the eye at the tear duct. Rotate the swab 360 degrees around the eye under the eyelid to clear any debris.

The ears of waterdogs require special attention to avoid infections. After the hunt, dry the ear canals and drip hydrogen peroxide into the ear canal to flush. Then, clean again with a soft towel.

SNAKE BITES

Hunters in many areas of the country must put up with snakes and the poisonous ones do occasionally strike a hunting dog. If your dog has been bitten and the snake is visible, kill it immediately to prevent a secondary bite of you or the dog and to identify the type of snake.

Keep the dog subdued and immobilized. Attempt to locate the fang punctures. If the bite is on the leg, immobilize the limb to restrict movement, but do not apply a tourniquet or ice. Swelling will likely occur. Rush the dog to a vet while keeping him still, cool, and quiet. You can administer Benadryl to minimize inflammation

First Aid Kit

All handlers should have a well-stocked first aid kit on hand in the field or blind. At some point, your sporting dog will need first-aid attention. The supplies should be contained in a waterproof bag or box and should include the following:

- Self-adhesive vet wrap bandage
- Gauze sponges and pads
- Hydrogen peroxide (to clean wounds or induce vomiting)
- Pepto-Bismol or Kaopectate (for upset stomachs)
- Buffered aspirin
- Antiseptic ointments
- Alcohol
- Swabs
- Syringe
- Iodine solution

- Saline solution (for flushing eyes)
- Nail clippers
- Clean hand towel

- Tweezers or hemostats
- Folding lock blade knife
- Staple gun
- First-aid book

and to relax the dog, but do not give the dog aspirin and do not cut the puncture wound in an attempt to drain out venom. If an antivenom medicine is to be effective, a vet must administer it as soon as possible.

Poisonous snake bites require immediate medical attention.

VOMITING

If it becomes necessary to induce vomiting because your dog has ingested something he shouldn't have, hydrogen peroxide will do the trick. Using a syringe, administer 20 cc (cubic centimeters) of hydrogen peroxide orally. After the dog swallows the substance, begin to walk him around. Usually one dose will be adequate to induce regurgitation.

STOMACH DISORDERS

An upset stomach and diarrhea are common occurrences on road trips. Disorders may result from stress, overeating, or drinking unclean water; the list of possible causes is quite long. The best treatment is a product like Pepto-Bismol or Kaopectate, along with a reduced amount of food. Liquid forms work the fastest, but are more difficult to administer than tablets.

BEE STINGS OR SPIDER BITES

Antihistamines (like Benadryl) administered orally or by injection will counteract the reaction to bee stings or spider bites.

HEAT EXHAUSTION

Heat exhaustion is the number one killer of sporting dogs in the field. Every year excellent hunting dogs are lost in training or hunting in warm weather. If you will be working a hunting dog in warmer climates, beware! Heat will sneak up on your dog faster than you may realize. Athletic gundogs overexert themselves with little regard for temperatures. Some dogs just don't know when to quit. When their body temperature rises to the point of danger, it is difficult to get it down quickly.

In a dove field or on an early season upland hunt, the hot weather can cause an active dog to build heat at a faster rate than the dog can expel given his limited rapid-cooling capabilities. Dogs reduce body temperature in three ways:

✦ Through their mouths by moisture and panting.
✦ Through their pads.
✦ Through water evaporation.

Swimming in cool water does reduce body heat, but in hot weather the water temperature can actually be quite warm above the water's thermal line and evaporation is all that benefits the dog. The dog's mouth is often occupied with carrying objects, which restricts air intake. As for the pads, this is a small area to cool a large body and the ground is usually hot and dry. The situation is even worse for an overweight dog.

Hydrate your hunter well before the field outing by offering as much water as he will drink. Do not offer food. Food digestion creates body heat, further complicating matters. When possible, keep the dog out of the direct sunlight. Always have water available in the field and don't house a dog that is hot in a travel box, especially in the direct sunlight. Allow time for pre-cooling before returning the hunter to his dog box or crate. It sounds obvious, but dogs are lost in these ways every single year.

Hunting in weather warmer than 75 degrees is dangerous. Rotate active dogs frequently. Provide lots of rest stops in cool areas with water. Get your dog wet occasionally if you can. In a dove field, stay out of the direct sunlight. Provide water between each retrieve and limit the number of retrieves. Some hunters even take ice bags to place in a crate with their dog, keeping him cool and wet.

Know the danger signs of heat exhaustion—rapid short or hard breathing; glazed eyes; staggered gait; tongue hanging out long, yet curling into a cup; and foaming at the mouth. Your reaction should be immediate. Get water into the dog and cool him down at once. Find shade and make an indention in the soil. Soak the dog with water, but not ice water. Use cool wet towels and provide continuous liquid to the mouth. Most dogs will not voluntarily drink water at this point, but force water down the dog's throat. Avoid using soda or sports drinks. Keep the dog inactive and very wet. Do not take a risk. Heat is a killer, so transport the dog to a vet immediately. It's your job to know the signs of heat exhaustion and to take action if those signs appear. Be careful out there.

HYPOTHERMIA

Hypothermia is the drastic reduction in a dog's body temperature below 96 degrees, resulting in a weak pulse, shivering staggered gait, and even unconsciousness. Prevention is the best approach for hypothermia. While hunting, use a thermal water vest and keep the dog elevated out of cold waters while inactive. In cold weather, duck dogs need a high-energy food source. Remember that highly digestible fat supplements in foods, which convert to energy, keep the dog warm on the hunt.

If a dog succumbs to cold weather conditions, get him indoors immediately or inside a

Many great hunting destinations require extensive travel.

warm vehicle if possible. Wrap the dog in a blanket and watch for signs of shock. Dogs subjected to extreme cold dehydrate just like they do when overheated. Provide adequate liquids.

HUNTING SITE INSPECTION

On the hunt, waterfowlers and dove hunters should closely inspect the surrounding area where the dog will be working to identify dangers. Check under the water around tree stands, blinds, or boats for underwater obstructions, including beaver snags, stumps, or posts. An unseen obstacle can seriously injure a dog jumping into the water for a retrieve.

In a dove field, before the hunt, check out the cover around your position for obstructions like wire, glass, sharp objects, and even snakes, yellow jackets, or fire ants. You don't want any surprises.

HEARING PROTECTION

A realistic concern for all wingshooters using a hunting dog in the field is protecting the dog's hearing from the damaging effect of the shotgun blast. This point rang clear to me on a duck hunt in a pit blind in a flooded Missouri cornfield. The concrete sunken blind was much like a military pillbox in a battlefield, with four hunters in the hide. Drake sat outside the blind to my left. During the hunt, I dropped inside the blind to fetch a handful of shells while my neighbor in the same blind took a shot at a bird overhead. His muzzle was directly over my position and Drake's, although well high and quite safe. Yet, the concussion and sound were extreme. The effect was reminiscent of being hit in the head with a plastic whiffle bat (surely, you remember those plastic bats?). My ears rang for hours. But what about

Hearing protection for hunting dogs requires awareness and precaution.

Drake? His head was actually much closer to the muzzle in that pit. No doubt he was affected and if such practices were to continue, negative effects to his hearing would occur.

As responsible hunters, you should take precautions to protect your hearing while shooting. There are many products on the market to accomplish this for us, but no products are available to protect a gundog from the effects of the muzzle blast. It becomes the handler's responsibility to protect the dog. Several dangerous situations come to mind:

+ Shooting directly over a dog on point.

+ Shooting over a flushing dog just he passes directly in front.

+ Shooting over the head of a dog in a duck blind, boat, or tree stand.

+ Shooting directly over the dog just as he approaches after returning from a retrieve.

Flushers, pointers, retrievers—there is no difference. If the dog is close in front of the shotgun when you pull the trigger, the noise level and damaging effect are significant. Combine this effect with a dog's acute sense of hearing. Dogs can distinguish sounds and pitches that humans cannot. Speaking from a non-medical, common sense position, it seems that the damage resulting from the muzzle blasts might be far more traumatic for a dog than for a human under the same circumstances. Awareness and precautions are necessary to protect your dog from hearing damage on the hunt. Keep these guidelines in mind:

1–Never shoot directly over a dog's head when he is in front of the gun muzzle or within a few yards. This also applies to dogs on point. Don't walk up directly beside them and fire overhead.

2– Don't shoot when the flusher passes close or directly in front of the gun muzzle.

3– In the blind or on the water stand, keep your dog beside you rather than in front to ensure that no one swings over his head for a shot. Dogs that "creep" often inch forward during the duck or dove hunt or bounce forward during a flush of upland birds. The creeper may find himself under the gun muzzle in the danger zone just as you fire. Train the anxious dog to stay steady without creeping.

4– Some duck blinds have dog positions enclosed on the sides and top by weatherproof plywood. The dog can enter from the front or rear, but he sits somewhat enclosed. The outer surfaces of the walls are further insulated with old pieces of weatherproof carpet. This construction drastically reduces the blast effects of the muzzle, which otherwise would be traumatic if the dog was sitting forward of multiple shooting positions. It is an inexpensive yet effective arrangement that affords the dog great visibility as he sits forward in the brushed, elevated blind while providing protection for his hearing.

5– An unsteady dog is as much a danger to himself as he is a nuisance on a hunt. A dog that breaks on the shot or flush may end up forward of the gun for repeated shots. The effect of continuously breaking should be obvious.

I'm sure you have seen many action shots in books and videos in which a dog takes to the air with his mouth open in pursuit of a flushed pheasant or an unsteady bird dog dashes after the flushed quarry. These make great photos, but are bad in practice. The dog will be forward of the gun and will absorb the maximum sound effects of the blast. The practice is also very dangerous to the dog's physical safety. An unsteady dog that leaps after the flushed birds in dense cover may not be seen by the hunters until it is too late, resulting in a tragedy.

Caring for a sporting dog in the field is a matter of preseason conditioning and the ability of the hunter to address field emergencies. Prevention, preparation, knowledge, and having the necessary resources available should an emergency occur—these are the best ways to make sure your next hunt is a smooth one.

The destination wingshooting gundog is prepared to go anywhere.

FINAL THOUGHTS

The discussion of the Wildrose Way started with the question of when to begin development of a personal shooting companion of distinction. At this point, I've come to realize the question of when to stop training has not been mentioned. It's a common concern among sporting enthusiasts: "How long does it take to train a finished dog?" I don't mean to be evasive, but the answer truly is: "It depends." It depends on your specific expectations—how much time you have available to invest, the amount of hunting exposure your dog receives, and how much diversity and field ability you expect from your dog.

The simple answer is it takes three years to finish a reliable gundog, including two full seasons on game, but in actuality, the journey never ends for most sporting enthusiasts; it encompasses the dog's entire life. There are so many experiences for the sporting dog to enjoy with his partner—the duck retriever becomes a walk-up gundog on a Northwest pheasant hunt; the upland spaniel learns to be an excellent companion on kayak float trips; the biddable pointer finds himself fireside camping with the family; the upland game dog cross-trains as a shed hunter; the retriever doubles as a blood tracker of deer on a game preserve. Gundogs may even cross-train for search and rescue or to become therapy dogs.

All of the aforementioned experiences hint at the excitement and the enrichment that a sporting dog trained the Wildrose Way may bring to one's life. I think little else complements one's sporting lifestyle more than a classic Gentleman's Gundog. At the end of the day, it's about the relationship. This book is dedicated to those hunters with a passion for sporting breeds, those who seriously care about their dog's welfare, the game they pursue, the splendor of the wild, and—most importantly—the bond of trust and mutual respect that can exist between themselves and their canine companions of the field. Truly, this is the meaning of the Wildrose Way.

GLOSSARY

BACK: A verbal command or hand signal to instruct a dog to turn around and go in the opposite direction, directly behind his position.

BACK CHAINING: Promotes progressive learning of a complex skill by connecting basic skills together, beginning with the last skill in the sequence and working backward to the first.

BACKING A POINT: A conditioned response by a dog to stop and hold steady when another dog goes on point.

BACKSTOP: A position for a handler and retriever on a driven shoot. The position is far behind the gun line and the pickers assigned to pegs. The position exists to locate birds that are hit by the guns but fall far behind the gun line, well out of sight of the pickers on peg.

BANK RUNNING: The action (either functional or dysfunctional) of a dog making a retrieve across the water and choosing to run the bank upon the return rather than through the water.

BEATER: A group of participants in a driven shoot assembled to drive or push birds forward in cover that ultimately will flush and fly over the waiting guns on peg. Often, beaters may use spaniels to push birds forward, as well as flags whipping cover as the line advances.

BEND OR BENDING: The dog's ability to change directions while quartering a field, either on his own initiative or on a whistle signal from the handler.

BLINDS: A term used to describe a hide or location to conceal hunters while wingshooting; or a term used to describe a dog's ability to retrieve a bird he did not see fall (also called an unseen).

BLOCKERS: Stationary hunters positioned at the end of the field that is being pushed (hunted by walk-up or quartering) to prevent the escape of birds ahead of the approaching hunters.

CASTING: Directing a dog to a specific area with the use of hand signals; casts include left and right direction, back, hunt toward the handler slowly, and recall or come.

CAUSAL RELATIONSHIP: A training approach that links one similar skill to another, which, when performed in sequence, will result in one action causing another to be remembered by the dog; a component to chaining and linked-in training.

CIRCLE MEMORY: Develops the dog's ability to run straight lines on doubles, triples, or even quads by establishing patterns in a cyclical manner.

COLD BLINDS: Retrieves at a location the dog has never experienced; a retrieve for a bird the dog did not see fall (an unseen).

COMBINATION LEAD: A three-piece, British-style slip lead designed by Wildrose Kennels that allows for variation in length when in use.

COUNTER SKILL: Revisiting a known, familiar skill, often one that the dog enjoys, usually applied at the end of the training session and unrelated to other training activities experienced on the day. The counter skill concludes a training session with a success while reaffirming the value of previously taught skills.

CREEPER: A dog that moves from position after the handler gives the command to sit, stay, or whoa and then moves away.

CUE: A verbal signal or body language that will elicit a response from the dog; a communicator; a signal for response.

CYCLICAL TRAINING: A Wildrose concept based on how canines think and learn as opposed to humans. The term universally applies to the model for the day's training plan or activity as it does to the application of establishing training lessons and patterns (e.g., circle memory).

DEAD BIRD OR HIGH LOSS: Command for the dog to hunt cover closely to locate lost game; to initiate a track.

DELAYS: The amount of time (duration) between the fall of the bird or placement of the bumper and the release of the dog for the retrieve.

DELIVERY: The dog's ability to bring a bird gently to hand without dropping or mouthing.

DENIALS: The action, used both in training and on the hunt, of not allowing the dog to make a retrieve.

DESENSITIZATION: Progressive and gradual exposure of a dog to new environments, people, places, and things in order to build confidence and to avoid possible problems of fear and distrust that can lead to dysfunctional behavior. Also called desent.

DIVERSIONS: Forms of steadiness that require no switching from one downed bird to another or ignoring one bird as directed to focus on another retrieve.

DOG'S NAME: The release command for a retrieve; should also precede any command to acquire the dog's attention if a bird is not present.

DOWN: The command for the dog to lie down and remain in position.

ENVIRONMENTAL BARRIERS: Perceived obstructions or interruptions to the dog's path or movement that are not physically restrictive, including abrupt changes in ground cover, shadows, snow, ice, shallow water, etc.

ENVIRONMENTAL FACTORS: Natural conditions that occur in nature—wind, snow, fog, cold, heat, and lighting—that are considerations for an effective retriever handler; conditions that can influence a dog's successful lining ability for marks and unseen retrieves.

FADE: The act of progressively eliminating a particular action or condition from a training sequence; the dog self-eliminating a behavior when it is not reinforced.

FALLS: A bird that is shot and drops to the ground, either dead or wounded.

FLUSHERS: Rough-shooting using dogs trained to quarter a field just ahead of the hunters to flush game in range of the shot of the hunters.

GENERALIZE: The ability to transfer a known skill or behavior correctly performed in one location to a different location.

GET ON: A verbal command used with a hand signal to cast left or right.

GET OVER: To jump an object (e.g., fence or log) or cross a barrier (e.g., ditch, stream, or river).

GIVE, DROP, OR DEAD: A release command for the dog to give up an object to hand; used with delivery to hand as a release.

GOOD: A positive, verbal marker; a reward; indicator of a correct decision; a verbal reinforcer.

GUN: A shooter on a driven or tower shoot.

HANDLING: Responding to whistle signals and taking directions by hand signals from a handler.

HEEL: Dog remains at the handler's side on loose lead or off lead whether sitting, walking, or running.

HERE OR COME: Dog is called to handler; the act of recall.

HOLDING THE LINE: The ability to stay on course, taking the most direct path to a bird or point of reference despite influences or conditions.

HONOR: Remaining steady and quiet as another dog works, not running in, not interfering with another dog's retrieve; backing a point.

HUNTING COVER: The dog's aggressive ability to search out game in grasses, woodlands, or any foliage; to locate game in cover.

INDISCRIMINATE PETTING: The misapplication or overuse of affection as a reinforcer.

INITIAL LINE: Running a straight direction of travel with confidence for the first 15 to 20 yards toward the location of the fall for either a mark or an unseen retrieve.

KENNEL: A command for the dog to enter or go inside something (e.g., a crate, trailer, or dog hide).

LADDERS: The practice of placing multiple bumpers 10 yards or more apart in a straight line to develop lining extensions, requiring the dog to run farther to find the next bumper.

LINE OR LINING: An indication by the handler for the dog to take the desired direction of travel to complete a retrieve.

LINING EXTENSIONS: Extension exercises that enhance the dog's memory capabilities and are designed to develop the dog's ability to run long straight lines to a fall despite influences; taking an initial direction of travel for an unseen or seen bird and carrying that line to the fall area without distraction.

LINKED-IN: Similar to back chaining in its progressive linking of individual skills and segments to complete an overall exercise, but it differs in that each required segment or link in the progression is taught separately and then linked together.

LOAD: A command for a dog to get onto something (e.g., a ramp, stand, or vehicle).

LOOP MEMORY: A variation of both the trailing memory and the circle memory that is used in difficult cover or terrain where a wide circle pattern is not possible; a method to establish a retrieve or pattern.

MARKING: A dog's ability to visually sight with accuracy a fallen bird, and the ability to go directly to the location when sent.

NO: A verbal de-select used to indicate a wrong decision; a command to indicate that the dog should not take action or the dog should leave an item alone; or a verbal correction.

OBEDIENCE: A category of basic skills and essential behaviors—sit, stay, come, down, place, etc.—associated with a proper and prompt response to a given command or signal; appropriate behavior and conduct.

Out: The command for a dog to exit or jump off of something.

Peg: A shooter's assigned position on a driven or tower shoot; the location of the gun (individual shooter).

Peg Dog: A dog trained to sit quietly during a driven shoot and make the necessary retrieves to locate birds taken by a specific shooter; a peg dog may be handled by the shooter or a picker.

Permanent Blinds: Unseens that are placed at familiar locations that have been frequently, successfully experienced as memories by the dog and are now placed without the observation of the dog.

Physical Barrier: Something that blocks the dog's path but remains negotiable (e.g., a mesh wire fence, fallen timber, deep ditch, or stone wall).

Picking Up: A term commonly used to describe the activity of retrieving birds at a driven shoot or continental tower shoot.

Pinchers: The upland shooters positioned just ahead of a walk-up line moving parallel and wide in order to keep the birds from flying or running out of the field ahead of the guns.

Place: Dog remains at a designated location; a command to remain at a specific spot.

Pointing: The dog's natural ability to locate game birds by scent or in some cases sight and hold steady in close proximity without flushing the birds.

Popping: A dysfunctional or functional behavior in which a gundog begins to stop on a retrieve on his own initiative to seek assistance from the handler.

Primary Reset: When a problem of significance occurs and the handler completely stops the retrieving effort, recalls the dog back to heel, and attempts another approach; a complete reboot and a fresh start of the exercise.

Pushers: A walk-up line of hunters with supporting gundogs that may include flushers, retrievers, or even a pointer; commonly used in pheasant hunting; the objective is to push birds forward to the point of flush within gun range.

Quartering: When the gundog works in a zigzag pattern across the field close to the hunter to locate and flush (or point) game.

Recall: The response or action to come when called.

Redirect: Defined as an action taken to divert a dog's attention away from one distraction or stimulus to focus on another; a voluntary response by the gundog seeking instruction from a handler.

Reinforcers: Actions (responses to behavior) timed properly by the handler in response to an action by the dog to capture or change behavior; there are positive, neutral, and negative reinforcers.

Remote Sit and Stay: Steady behavior by the dog when the handler is not positioned next to him, even with distractions.

Rough-shooting: A term commonly used for quartering; to flush game for the guns (shooters/hunters).

Runner: A wounded bird leaving the area by running or swimming.

Scatters: The practice of salting an area with bumpers to provide multiple retrieves in a common place that will offer the additional benefit of enhancing hunting skills by developing search patterns.

Secondary Fall: After a dog has been sent for a primary retrieve, another bird is shot and falls, either dead or wounded.

Secondary Reset: A corrective action that involves handling the dog by recall closer to the handler, shortening the distance, regaining focus, and attempting the signal or command again.

Shaping: Capturing and rewarding a small piece of an overall desirable behavior in order to form that behavior into a predictable habit.

Sight Memory: The dog sits at a fixed point watching as the handler or helper walks out to place the bumpers.

Sit or Whoa: Dog sits or stands in the same position without movement. Dog may be called from position during training.

Socialization: The ability to interact with people and other dogs at any place and under any conditions. Socialization involves continuous exposure to variables outside normal surroundings and leads to civil etiquette no matter what the situation.

Squeaking: A dog's noisiness by whining due to excitement.

Stay: A command for a permanent position; dog is never called from position; more permanent than sit; used when sit is not appropriate, e.g., in cold water.

Steadiness: The dog's ability to remain still and quiet during any type of activity—a shot, a falling bird, a flushed bird in flight, flush of game, or the distraction of another working dog or hunter.

Strike Dog: A retriever or flusher that works in tandem with pointers most commonly on quail hunts. These able game-finders are trained to flush birds that may be running in front of pointers or those holding tight in cover too thick to navigate by hunters.

SUCTION: Points of land protruding into the water, cover, scent from old falls, diversions, or distractions that may attract the attention of the dog or divert his progress.

SWEEPING: A term associated with quartering or hunting the area to locate downed game that was not retrieved after a flight on a driven shoot or continental tower shoot.

TDM (TIME DELAY MEMORY): Memories established as the dog watches, followed by a significant lapse of time between the placements of the memories and the retrieve.

TERRAIN: Slopes and contours of the land, ditches, abrupt changes in cover, water, and moving water.

THROW DOWN: The action of the handler or trainer; a technique used when the dog is quartering in training and bumpers or cold game are tossed out into desired locations for the dog to locate by scent.

TRAILING MEMORY: The dog walks at heel as a memory is placed. The handler retraces the route and follows up with a line to the placed bumpers.

TRANSITIONAL TRAINING: Training exercises designed to bridge the gap between field training activities and actual hunting conditions; the Wildrose Way is to train as you hunt, hunt as you train.

UNSEEN: A bird the dog did not see fall; a blind.

VARIABLE REINFORCER: The type and frequency of a reward for a behavior; varies in application or value based upon the dog's performance; used in behavioral modification.

WAGON DOG: A game dog trained to multitask while working from a wagon or vehicle.

WALK-UP: Handlers with their dogs and shooters move forward across a field to locate and flush game birds; commonly used in pheasant-hunting situations; walk-ups may involve retrievers, flushers, or pointing dogs.

WATCH: A verbal cue given by the handler that the dog should be aware of his surroundings—an action is about to occur; take notice.

WILDROSE STIMULUS PACKAGE: A series of exercises that introduce both complexity and distractions in order to produce a predictable response or behavior; a habit formation model.

LIST OF RESOURCES

✦ **VISIT WILDROSE TRADING COMPANY** for dog training supplies and accessories mentioned in this book. Wildrose Trading Company offers authentic equipment and apparel that is field-tested to meet our demanding standards. Call 662-234-8636 or visit www.wildrosetradingcompany.com for more information.

✦ **FOLLOW WILDROSE KENNELS ON FACEBOOK**, an excellent resource for obtaining more information about the Wildrose training methodology.

✦ **TO SIGN UP FOR OUR TRAINING E-NEWSLETTER**, "The Wildrose Journal," visit www.uklabs.com. This is the oldest continuously published, online sporting dog training monthly newsletter in existence. Join the journey.

✦ **EXPERIENCE THE WILDROSE WAY** firsthand at a Wildrose event or seminar, which are offered at various destinations across the country. A seminar schedule for "Training the Wildrose Way" can be found at www.uklabs.com.

✦ **WILDROSE PARTICIPATES IN THREE BLOGS** that embrace the Wildrose Way training methodology:

wildroseblog.wordpress.com

outsidek9.com

www.orvisnews.com/Dogs.aspx

✦ **TO SEE MORE OF CHIP LAUGHTON'S** beautiful images of sporting dogs in action, visit www.daysafieldphotography.com.

ACKNOWLEDGMENTS

I am confident that this book would have never been published without the hard work of my good friend, Paul Fersen, an Orvis executive, sporting dog enthusiast, and owner of Wildrose Murph, his splendid black Labrador retriever. It is because of his perseverance and hard work representing this project that a sporting tradition company such as Orvis and a publisher with the esteem of Rizzoli would consider publishing the book. Paul's tireless work was instrumental in refining the written format and artwork. I'd also like to thank his associate, designer and illustrator James Daley at Orvis, for all of the diagrams and illustrations in this book.

A special thanks to Candice Fehrman, who I suspect has never hunted a day in her life or ever owned a sporting dog, for her professional editing skills and patience. She performed an absolutely spectacular transformation of instructive written material into a beautiful, organized, concise training manual using her abilities of design and brilliant editorial skills.

Thanks to Chip Laughton of Days Afield Photography for his contributions to this work. Chip has been the photographer for Wildrose for more than a decade and it was only fitting that he should be the photographer for this book as well. Thanks for sharing the passion.

Special thanks to Lori S. Malkin, who designed the book. Her creative skills in layout greatly added to the beauty and user-friendliness of the book.

A very special recognition to the dedicated staff of Wildrose Kennels, including our associate trainers throughout the country, who make the Wildrose sporting lifestyle a reality for so many people. Over the years, two individuals in the United Kingdom have substantially contributed to the continuous development of Wildrose as well:

Nigel Carville, Portadown, North Ireland, winner of the 2010 Irish Championship; and Vic Barlow, Cheshire, England. I'm deeply appreciative of their friendship and support.

I must acknowledge my special friends—who contributed so much to the reality embedded in this book by providing unforgettable wingshooting experiences, who inspire me personally, and who support the experiential vision embraced at Wildrose and serve to expand our outreach— including Richard Adkerson at Clear Creek Ranch and San Tomas Hunting Club, Bill Behnke, Jeff Buckner, Steve Reynolds, Grayson Shaffer, Lars and Jen Magnusson, Brad Kennedy and Sunshine Mills, and the staff of fine organizations like Ducks Unlimited and Orvis that share our passion for the outdoors.

I knew when I undertook this project that it would be a difficult undertaking. The first person I solicited support from was my wife and partner, Cathy. Her assistance in the writing, eye for detail, and constant encouragement was so vital to making this project a reality.

There are so many people, writings, and field experiences that have influenced my beliefs in canine behavior, development, and training methodology over the decades, but no group more so than the wonderful dogs I have trained, hunted, and have been allowed to care for over the years. A final dedication to my best pals ever: Sam, Butch, Drummer, Angus, Opie, Drake, Deke, Indian, Penny, Whiskey, Kane, Trixie, and Pippi. There are so many more, but with each of these Gentleman's Gundogs and companions I could relate specific stories of how they made contributions to the Wildrose Way and enriched my life far more than I could have enriched theirs. Many are now gone, but none forgotten.